MICHAEL FREEMAN ON...

CREATIVE EXPOSURE

First published in the United Kingdom in 2024 by
Ilex, a division of Octopus Publishing Group Ltd
Carmelite House
50 Victoria Embankment
London, EC4Y 0DZ
www.octopusbooks.co.uk
www.octopusbooksusa.com

An Hachette UK Company
www.hachette.co.uk

ISBN 978-1-78157-942-8

A CIP catalogue record for this book
is available from the British Library

Printed and bound in China

10 9 8 7 6 5 4 3 2 1

Publisher: Alison Starling
Commissioning Editor: Richard Collins
Managing Editor: Rachel Silverlight
Editorial Assistant: Stephanie Selçuk-Frank
Art Director: Ben Gardiner
Designer: JC Lanaway
Picture Research Manager: Giulia Hetherington
Senior Production Manager: Peter Hunt

MICHAEL FREEMAN ON...

CREATIVE EXPOSURE

The Ultimate Photography Masterclass

ilex

CONTENTS

INTRODUCTION

I n the same way that the first book in this series, *...On Composition*, was a development from *The Photographer's Eye*, this title is intended to take off from where *Perfect Exposure*, which I wrote in 2008, ended. The basic reasons are the same: a lot has happened in photography in the intervening years, and I've had more time myself to think and adapt to these changes.

On the face of it, exposure might seem to be simpler, more technical and offer fewer possibilities for creative exploration than, say, composition. It certainly hinges on the camera's controls rather than the frame, and traditionally there's a very straightforward three-way choice as you operate any camera: the combination of shutter speed, aperture and the sensitivity of either the film or sensor. Often taught as the exposure triangle, there's a clean inevitability about it – just three controls to adjust to deliver a single dose of light – and it very quickly becomes second nature to any photographer who shoots regularly.

If you shot colour transparency film, which is what all the magazines wanted in the days of film and is what I used for the first half of my career, exposure was a once-and-forever decision. There was no revisiting the record that you'd just made, no second step of printing in the darkroom. You could bracket exposures if you were uncertain and had several seconds more to stay with the subject, but each frame would be a finished piece of film. Kodachrome, the preferred 35mm film choice for many professional photographers, was valued for its sharpness and richness, and was even less tolerant. Its contrast was quite high, overexposure was ugly and there wasn't even the possibility that other films offered of pushing or pulling in the lab (that is, less or more development to compensate for over- or underexposure).

Film is still around (although Kodachrome unfortunately not), so all of this still applies, but digital photography has taken things much further, both technically and – what interests me more – creatively. This is because modern sensors can now capture more information than film could, and computational photography can do a lot with this extra data. Don't get me wrong, I love film, because it has certain unique qualities, and these are a good part of the reason for its resurgence in popularity, which although niche is notable. The current state of digital, however, has expanded the exposure choices enormously. These include, incidentally, being able to mimic something of the look of film, which we will explore later.

THE LOOK

1

'll get straight to the point. Exposure is mainly responsible for the look of a photograph, and by 'creative exposure' I really mean how you can give a particular picture the appearance that you want it to have. You might want it to be luminous, rich, bright, airy, dark, flat, stark, punchy – or have one of many other appearances. These all have to do with light, tone, and a choice between colour and black and white, but the key control is exposure.

The way that digital photography now works – especially computationally – means that exposure choices are spread more widely than before. To start with, they're spread across time because of processing software. The choice may begin with capture, but it extends into the processing, which can be revisited at any time. Exposure choices are also spread across the frame because of differential exposure, which allows you to choose which areas and which subjects receive more or less exposure.

What I'd like to do with this book is to *not* let all this choice go to waste. Instead, I have some suggestions for creating looks based on exposure, and that means not just how, but why. It's good to have a reason for using the techniques, rather than just playing around with them. Every seriously taken photograph deserves to look its best and to make its point as effectively as possible.

It's also time to consider one of the really basic questions in photography: do I want to show this scene as I see it now, or do I want to turn it into something else? If it's the latter, you've entered the world of style, personality, expression and, if you like, creativity. That's why exposure can be both a pleasure and an experiment. It marks the point at which a photographer goes beyond the default idea of simply getting the brightness and contrast 'right' and starts to impose their personal taste on the image.

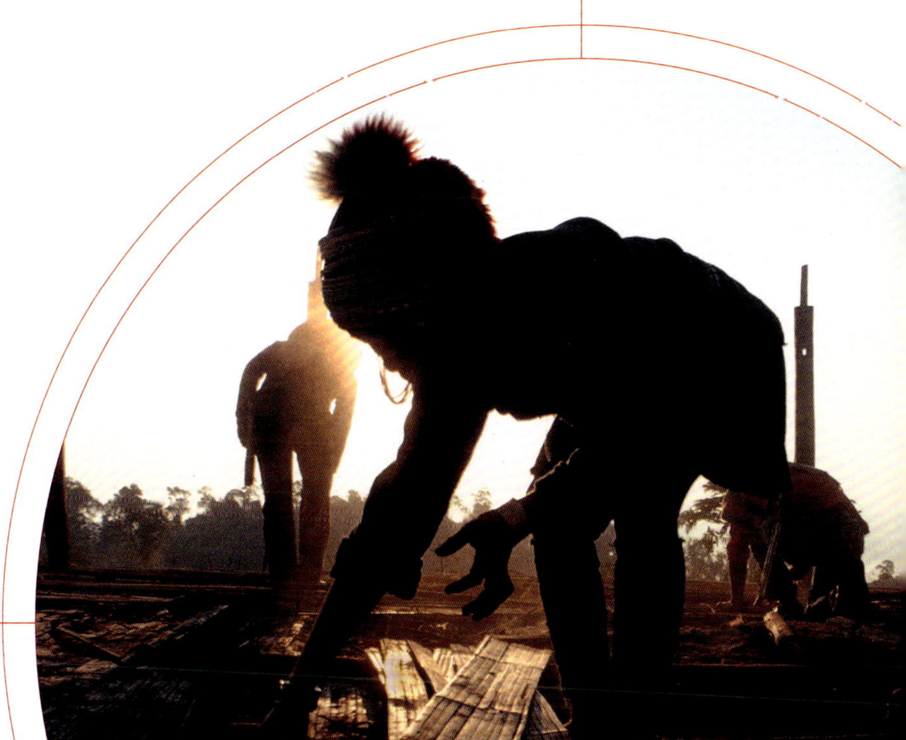

TWO VIEWS OF EXPOSURE

Exposure has two faces. One is the means of making it and controlling it, which is largely technique and skill, while the other is from the opposite side – how it looks in the final picture. No full exploration can do without both together, but what we can do is to make one the priority, the starting point. Throughout this book, the priority is the look, which is personal.

In this scene, the active subjects are in shade, but the sunlit surfaces in the background need to remain colourful, without any hint of overexposure. This requires a camera sensor with a high dynamic range, an exposure that just avoids clipping the bright flecks on the wall and careful processing.

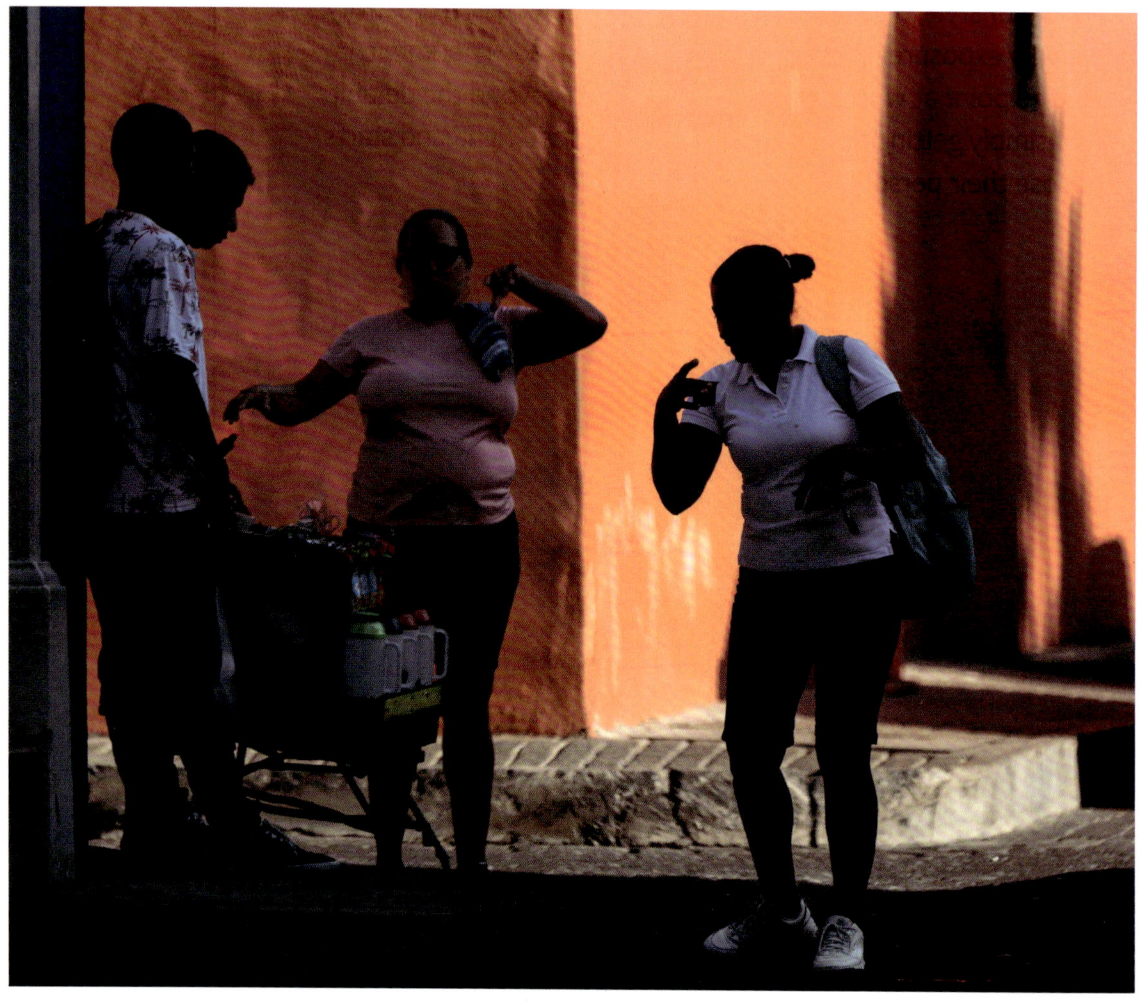

Choosing to shoot and process for a black-and-white image opens up more exposure possibilities. The absence of colour focuses attention on the final values, and areas of brightness and darkness can be enhanced or even reversed. In this rural landscape, the green fields where the sheep are grazing could just as easily have been made bright.

One of the large assumptions in my earlier book, *Perfect Exposure*, was the underlying task of 'getting it right'. The word 'perfect' in the title was, of course, provocative, as there is no universal perfection in anything to do with photography. There is the possibility of perfection for each photographer at each moment of shooting, though, and that's what the book set out to address. Here, however, let's look for creative expression in the way we set the exposure.

Two major movements in photography have changed the way many of us think about exposure; one technical, the other aesthetic. The technical one is the steady improvement in the range of tones that can be delivered in a photograph, and I say 'delivered' because it's due not only to better sensors, but also to processing, both in the camera and in software. There are several things at play. Sensor dynamic range is now above 14 stops in advanced cameras, and shooting Raw takes full advantage of this if you go on to use software such as Adobe Camera Raw.

Most of the time in this book I'll be using examples from Adobe's Photoshop and ACR simply because that's what I use. ACR's Highlights and Shadows algorithms do an excellent job of what looks like, to the user, recovery, while local adjustment is still the premier way to craft an image, as it always has been in wet darkrooms with negative film.

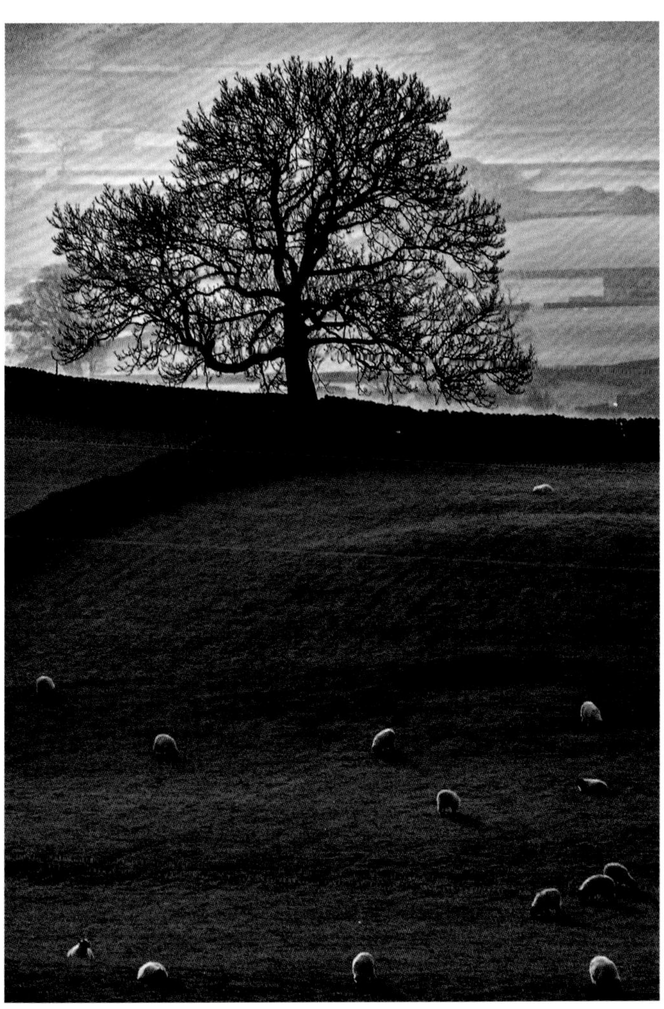

Modern sensors capture a significant exposure headroom – sometimes up to four stops more than the screen display can handle. From the point of view of exposure, this is more like shooting black-and-white negative film than colour transparency, which makes it a two-step process from the very start: you expose knowing what you can do with the image later, as black-and-white photographers have done for more than a century. In this way, exposure slides into processing, or another way of thinking about it is that processing becomes a part of exposure. That's the view I take, and done efficiently it's not about correcting mistakes. It's knowing what you want the image to look like and making the best exposure that will serve your purpose.

Polished metal surfaces – in this case, silver on a sideboard – are notoriously difficult to handle well because of their specular reflections, but here's an example of computational photography keeping everything in range: this is an 'as is' image from an iPhone.

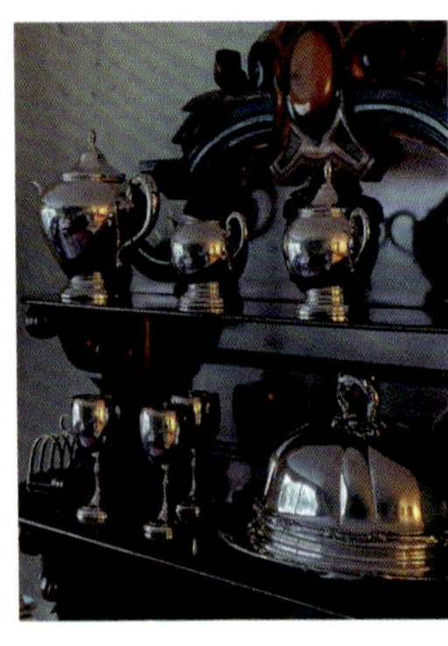

There is also computational exposure, which appeared first in smartphone cameras and is now extending rather slowly into dedicated cameras. This aims to do everything you could achieve with Raw files and skilled processing, but instantly, in-camera and automatically. Computational photography can handle large and difficult dynamic ranges in a scene by taking and combining a range of exposures. This approximates what you would do manually by shooting an HDR sequence, but the entire process becomes almost immediate.

Then there's semantic masking, which is an even more powerful technique. This involves recognizing and outlining subjects so they can be made brighter or darker (or almost anything). All of this continues to improve, and the new reality is that in principle you can shoot and expose to capture every tone in a scene. That's already an impressive achievement, but it raises a question that was rarely asked in the film-only era: do you actually *want* all that visual information?

In this scene in Saint Peter's Basilica, Rome, lowering the exposure during processing (right) makes the shafts of sunlight more prominent than in the original Raw file (below).

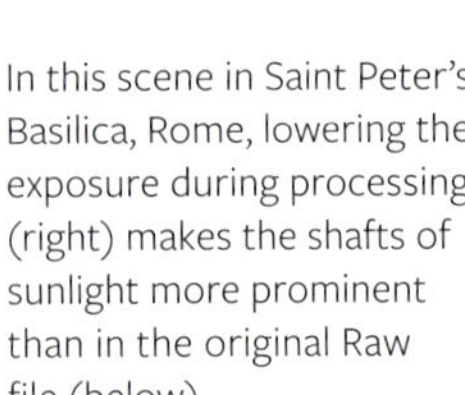

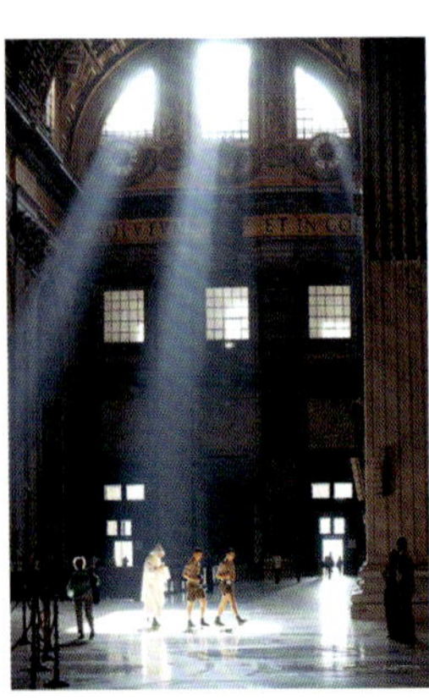

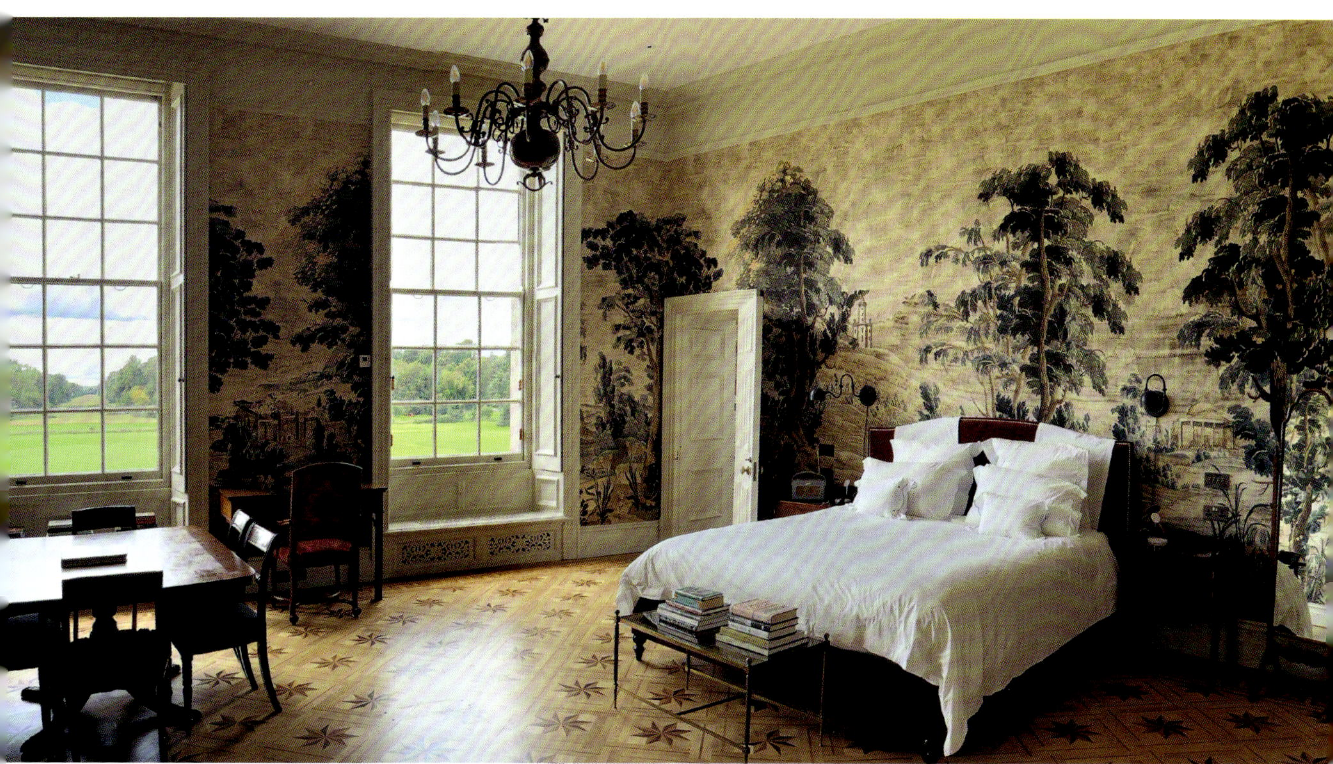

This interior in natural daylight was stitched from three overlapping frames shot on an iPhone. The view through the windows was several stops brighter than the bedroom, but the phone camera's computational algorithms have brought the two much closer in tone.

The bedroom interior shown above is a case in point. It's stitched together from overlapping frames that were shot handheld on an iPhone. I took the precaution to shoot Raw, so as to preserve more data in the DNG file, but apart from that, there is no other processing. Any interior or architectural photographer would be familiar with the problems of shooting an entirely day-lit room like this, looking directly towards the only sources of light – the windows. By calculating the distribution of light, and recognizing windows and their implications, the algorithms deliver an impressively balanced range of tones that tread the line between realistic and atmospheric. There's an important unspoken principle involved, which is delivering information; with the exception of a few shadows, there's detail visible everywhere. Compare this with the very different, more old-fashioned film treatment of the interior on page 119, where the windows glow and what lies beyond them is not a part of the image. That's a more distinctive look, while this one is more informational. That's a choice.

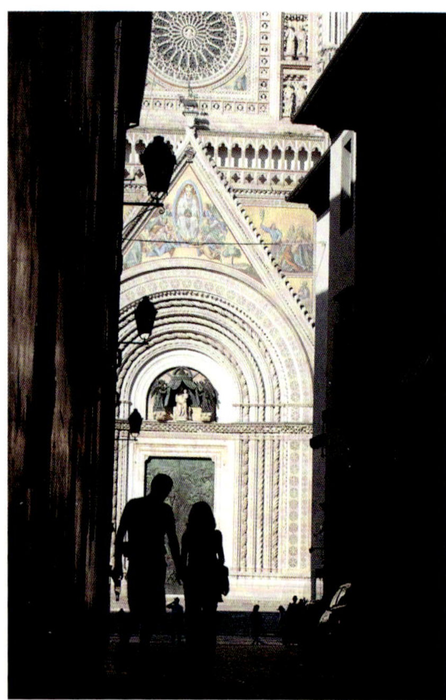

Original

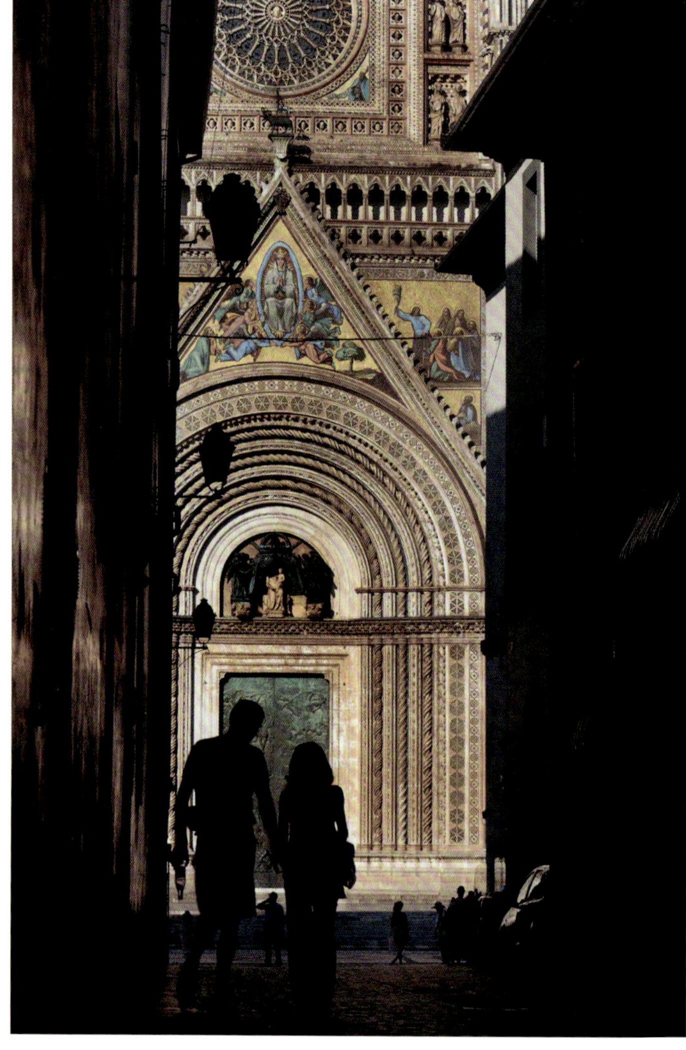

The dynamic range of this view towards a cathedral in an Italian town is certainly very high, but the bit-depth of a Raw file (here from a Nikon D850) allows the full richness of colour and tone to be recovered.

This is where the aesthetics of photography come in, and I'll make no excuses for using a word that many people react to as sounding precious, if not pretentious. Although it's often identified with beauty, it's more wide-ranging, and is about evaluating why and how we respond to certain image qualities. You can call it the 'look' if you like, but regardless of the name, it's now more important than ever. There's a general, basic way that photography is 'supposed' to look, and it won't come as any surprise that this has changed over the decades, and continues to evolve. It has a great deal to do with exposure, both for the overall brightness or darkness of the picture and for local areas inside the scene. For example, according to my reading, there's been a general drift towards darker and more contrasty imagery in recent years, to the point where the 'standard normal' of most photography has shifted.

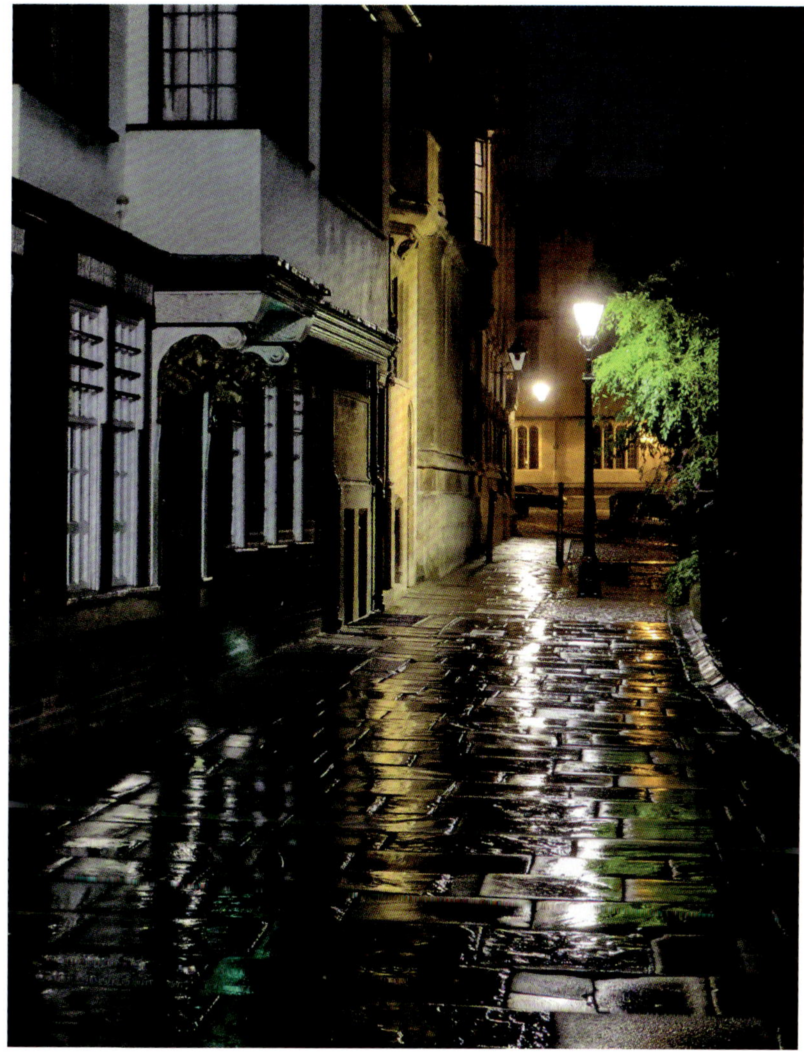

A night view of the lane leading to my old college in Oxford. Shot on an iPhone, and with no later adjustment, this computational shot would have been impossible on film.

That's very much a personal view, and I see it most in black-and-white shooting, but it shouldn't be a surprise that general public tastes change. Perhaps more significant is that there's now more variety of exposure than ever before, meaning more personal expression. The reason for this, I believe, lies in a shift away from traditional documentary shooting. Yes, that's a sweeping statement and needs defending, so let's start with that.

HOW LOOK TOOK OVER

For a long time, photography was driven primarily by people and media doing it professionally. What the various professional forms – magazine reportage, news coverage, advertising and fashion – have in common is a clear and recognizable view of things.

That, in turn, meant that clients, readers and viewers were for the most part accustomed to an expected exposure, along with sharp focus, appropriate depth of field and so on. Of course, there was always room for unexpected images, but the main thrust of shooting to show things to an audience included a normal, commonly accepted brightness and contrast. The subject and the way the photographer handled it through composition and lighting were more responsible for catching and holding attention. Longer-length assignments for mainstream magazines (of which I shot many from the 1970s onwards) were mainly about the story – the subject matter, the events, the physical presence of things and people – and a lot less about quirky treatments.

I need to qualify this a little, because I don't want it to sound as if picture editors wanted predictability. Far from it, they generally took great care to assign particular photographers to specific stories, recognizing that many professionals have that hard-to-define quality of a 'style'. Although many things can go into a style, with exposure there was almost always a demand for normality, or at least appropriateness. By way of an example, I once got pulled up for starting to deliver dark Kodachromes, because it made life more difficult for the repro house that did the scans and colour separations for printing. However, I was doing that because Kodachrome looked good on the lightbox when a little 'underexposed', and I knew that the repro house could pull up the darks, so it was my way of using the later stages of the image process to help my exposure choices. But my argument failed to persuade.

In other words, for a long time there was a kind of 'anchor' to the look of photography, so when Roy DeCarava decided to challenge convention and make overall dark images that stretched from black to a mid-grey at most, they really stood out. At the other end of the scale was Henry Wessel, whose roadscapes of the American West were so light that many would consider them overexposed – they *were* overexposed, but intentionally so, as his *Continental Divide* project used brightness and emptiness to try and convey the sheer vastness of the geography. Yet while these examples of creative exposure from the past show that it's not a new phenomenon, such experiments didn't fit the standard magazine needs of storytelling and documenting. That far from the mainstream, they were part of the slowly growing world of fine-art photography.

Shooting towards the light and deliberately underexposing is one of my preferred methods, as shown here. It was important to get the viewpoint and timing right so the silhouettes would read clearly against the background.

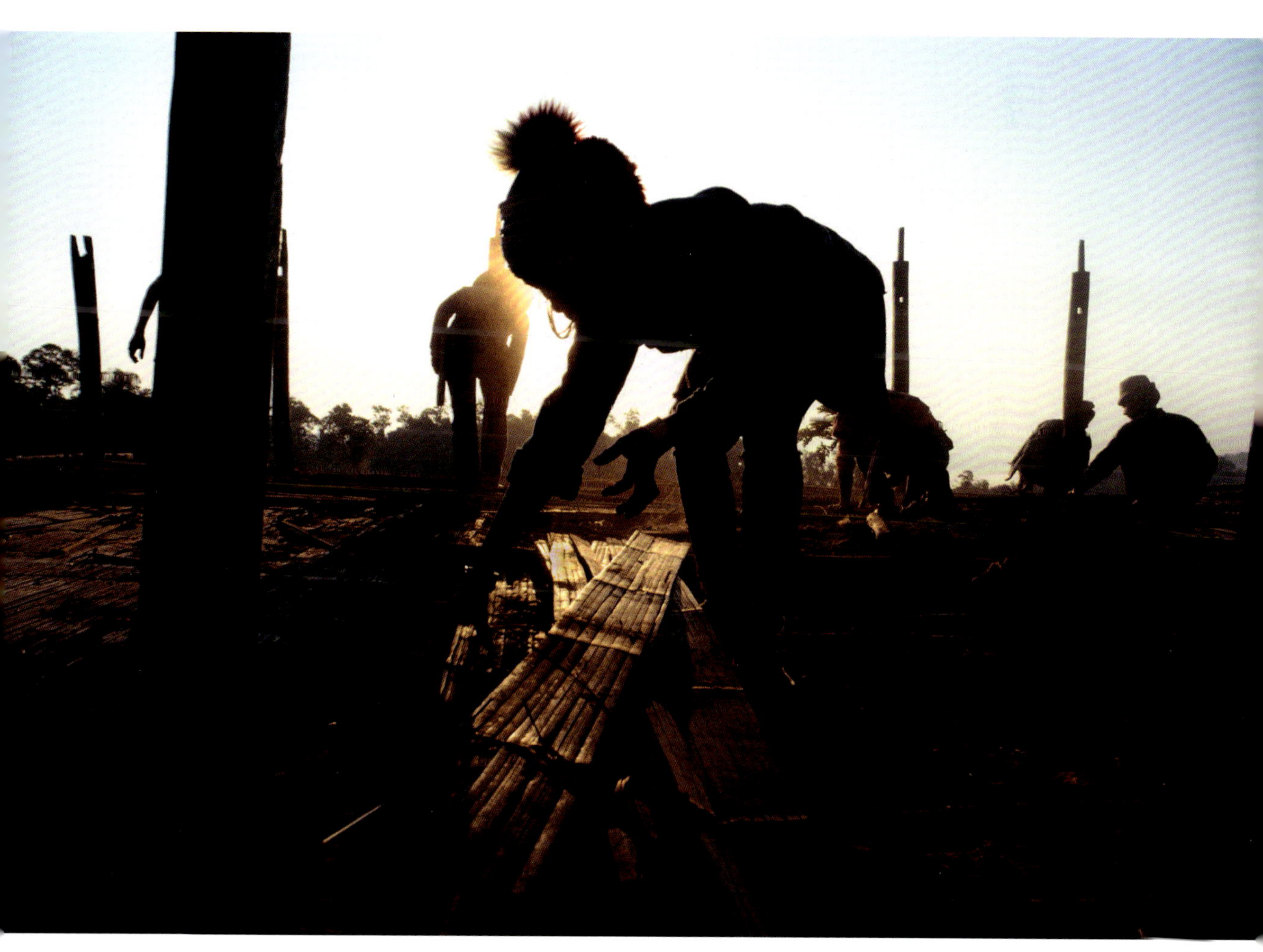

At the time, print magazines were the mainstay of photography. They carried advertising, fashion and feature stories – most of the photography of significance – and they supported professional photographers with assignments. It's hard to overstate how much photography depended on magazines around the world, and hard to overstate how they *controlled* photography, including setting the standards of how pictures should look. That assignment world has now all but disappeared, and with it the formal stories that were offered to photographers.

Instead, billions of us now take photographs, and maybe millions of people do it with proper attention and the aim to express something that's important to them individually. That's a lot of individuals for any media to handle and, like it or not, the vast output of personally motivated shooting that is shared on social media is redefining how photography in general looks. Successful professionals still command attention and have influence, but probably less so as time goes by. Today, story- and subject-driven shooting is on the decline, and that widens the choice of the 'look', be it bright, dark, contrasty, blurred, whatever. For a traditionalist, this sounds pretty bleak, but there are also many positives to it. Overall, success in photography now depends less and less on other professionals, such as picture editors, and I can already see an explosion of 'looks' that feature more exposure choices than ever before.

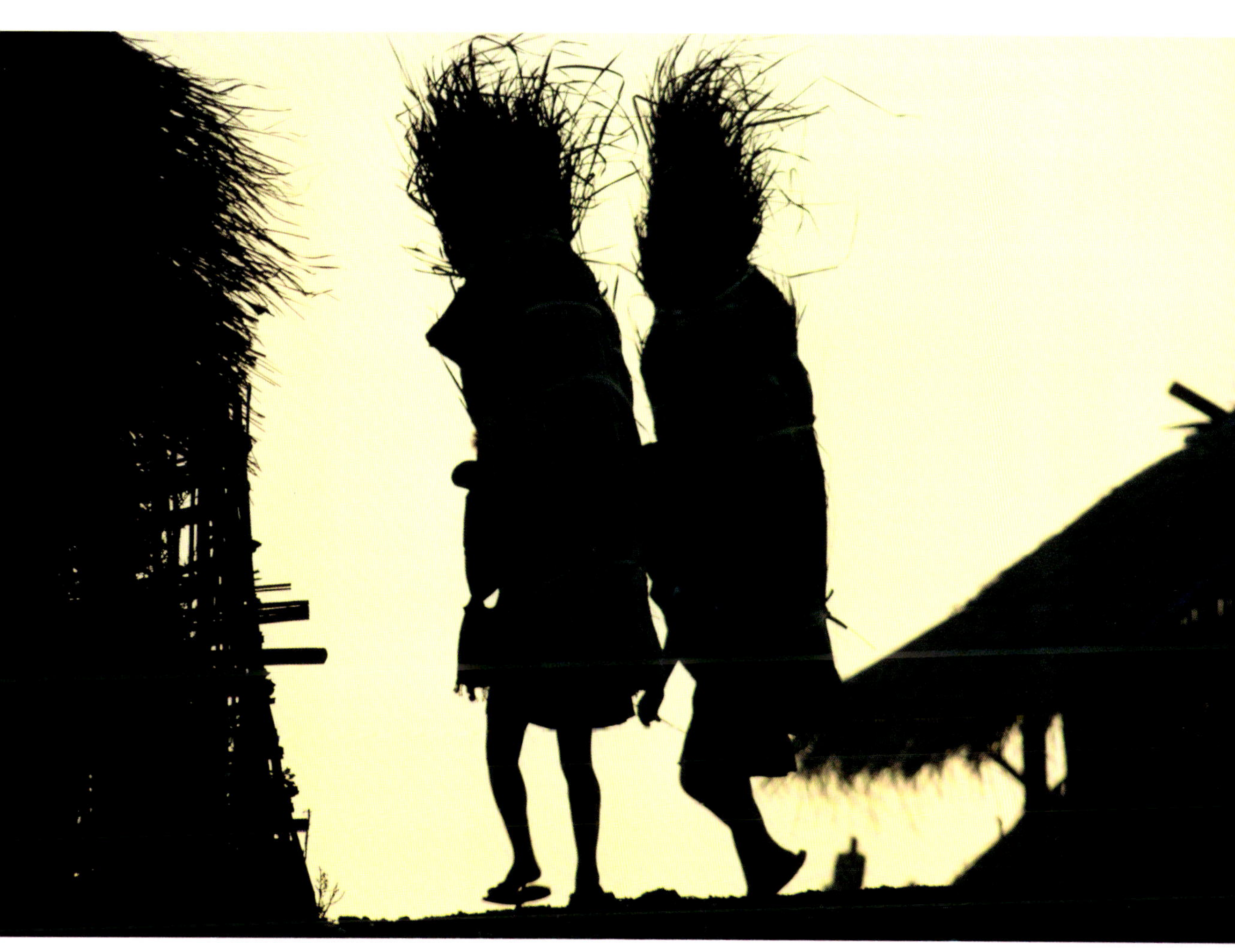

Here, just a few minutes later, the dark silhouettes of the same two figures conceal information, but have strangeness and mystery. This is my favourite image of the two, but the publisher, Time Life, preferred the other version because it explained more.

AWAY FROM AVERAGE

If the subject or the story comes first then it's usually more important to have it 'properly' exposed. That's a rather weak term, but a lot of people use it to mean the way in which most viewers would expect it to appear, and for it to be reasonably faithful to the scene as it looked.

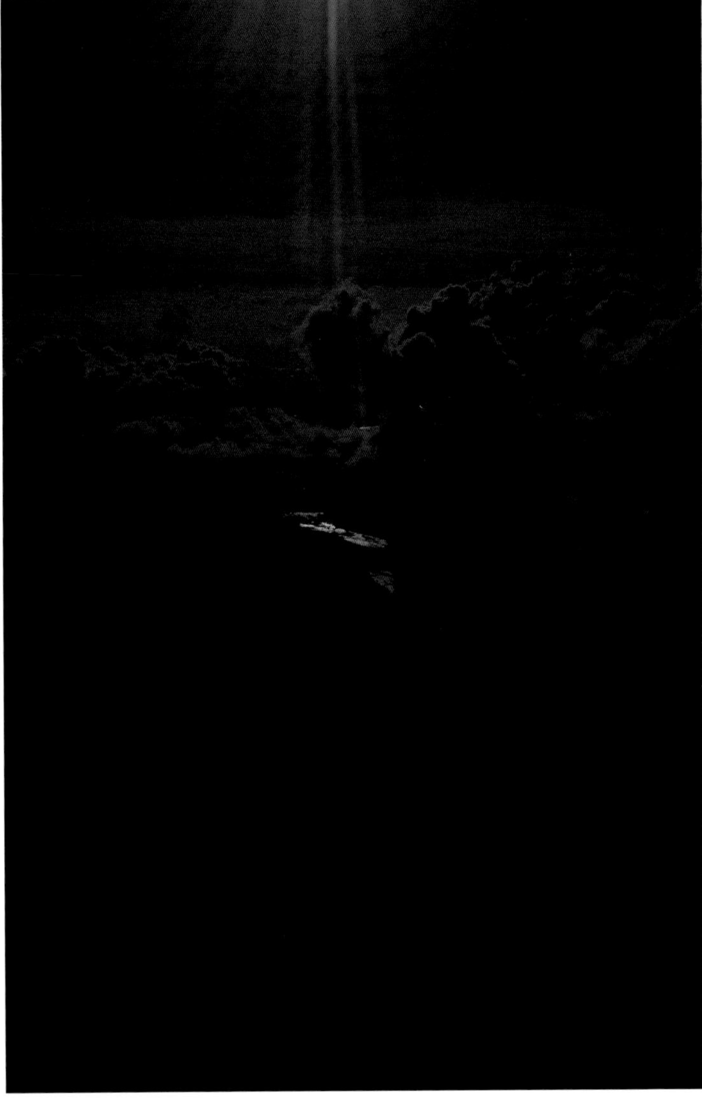

A deliberately extreme underexposure of an aerial view of the Orinoco River, Venezuela. Just a small stretch of the water glints golden in the sunlight, which also appears as a shaft of light reflecting from the window.

This has always been the default in photography, with everything centred on mid-tones, a full range from black to white, reasonable contrast that's neither too high nor flat, and colours that are believable, but rich where they need to be. The subject or scene also stays recognizable.

However, if that's not a top priority and we're just trying to make interesting imagery and experiment a little, then how dark or light, how contrasty and how colourful is up to us. Creative exposure is when we allow ourselves the freedom to be expressive rather than objective, and not always looking over our shoulder (metaphorically) to make sure we're pleasing the audience. If you're trained to be accurate, it takes some effort to break away from the average, but it can be worth it; average is, after all, expected.

While a workmanlike approach to exposure is certainly professional, moving away from this by even one stop, or adding more or less contrast or saturation can make certain pictures more striking and even more effective. With my background in assignment work, I still insist to myself on having a reason for doing this, as being different for its own sake doesn't cut much ice. But once you start to think about what the effect might be, it's interesting and even exciting to explore the possibilities of going darker or lighter, or more gentle with the tonal range (softer, flatter), or tougher, stronger (more contrast).

This may sound rather vague, but throughout this book I'll be looking at the specifics of individual scenes and subjects that might benefit from being different. Just that constant possibility hanging around in the background of being able to alter the effect that an image is going to have on the person looking at it is liberating. In its way, this is quite a radical idea when photographing and processing: instead of aiming to get it 'right' and as expected, it means doing more thinking and imagining to see how a picture might work better.

Sunrise in Monument Valley, over Bear and Rabbit rocks. Before sunrise, the colour of the sky was quite rich, but as the sun emerged from the rocks, it spread a glowing flare of light.

The white plumage of this parrot reflected the light very strongly. This suggested exposing down, not only to show the texture well, but also to reduce the attention that might otherwise be drawn to its owner's face

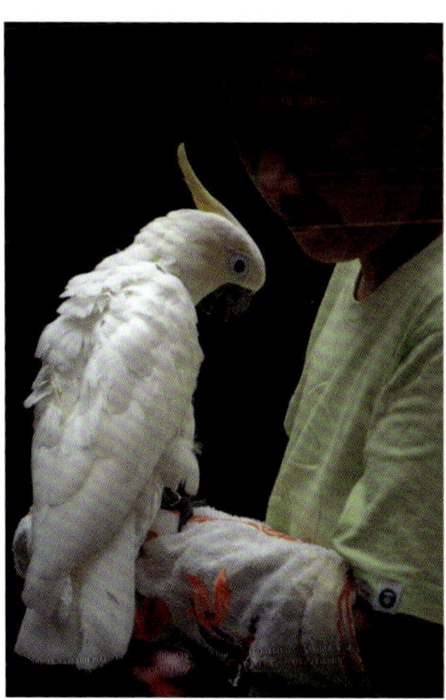

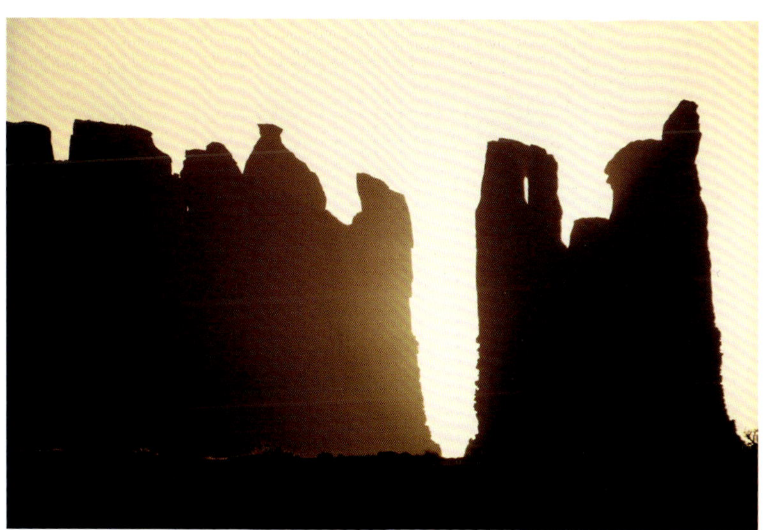

SEMANTIC & LOCAL

O ne of the cornerstones of computational photography introduced by smartphone cameras is recognizing individual subjects so they can be isolated and processed separately; lighter, darker, different contrast, colour changes and so on.

This is known as semantic processing; in other words, not just local areas of the picture, but subjects such as people, faces and skies. Photoshop and other processing software have picked this up, and with the benefit of machine learning, it's now sophisticated, fast and accurate. Before this, making an accurate, sharp-edged mask was time-consuming, demanded skill and always ran the risk of looking artificial, which is why soft-edged masks and particularly radial ones were favoured, as far back as dodging and burning prints in a wet darkroom. A smooth radial ramp fools the eye, whether you're lightening or darkening, because it changes smoothly and towards or away from a centre of attention. Now, however, automatic semantic masking is almost perfect, and will continue to improve.

As described in the text, the bride at a wedding near Shanghai waits with make-up artist in attendance as guests leave for the open-air event.

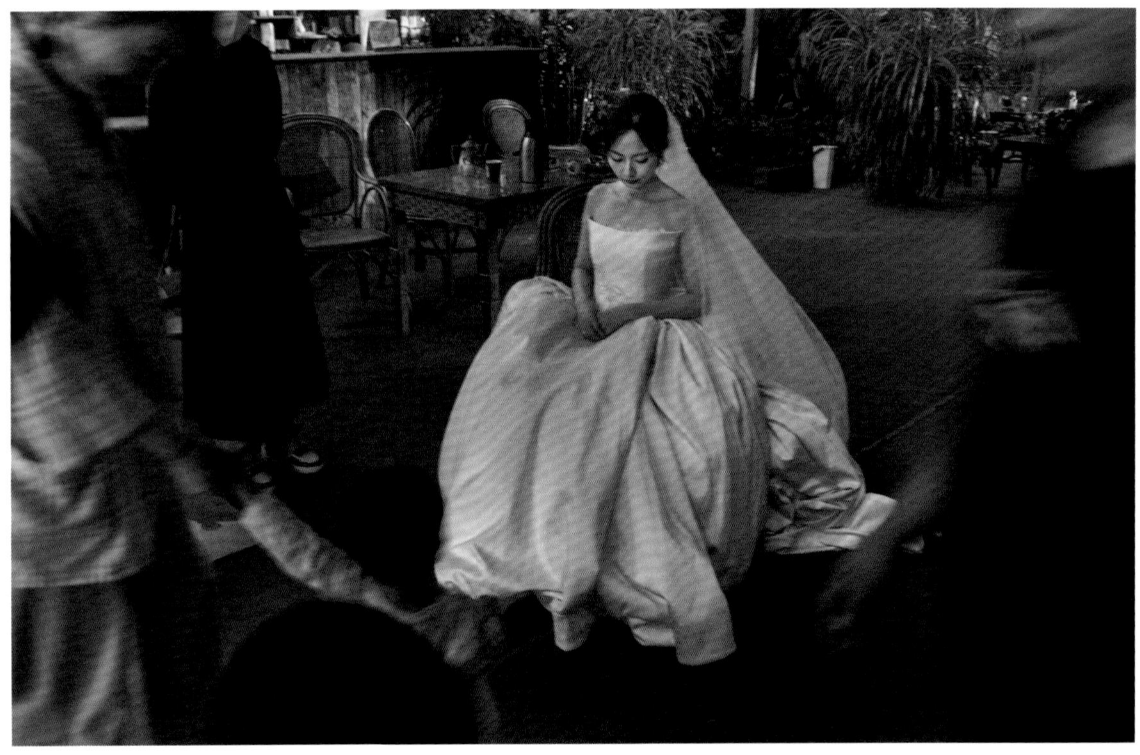

The example below shows semantic processing at work in a reasonably subtle way, and for good measure I've also combined one of the semantic masks with a soft radial one. The occasion was a country wedding near Shanghai, and just before the ceremony was due to start in the garden, the bride was seated alone inside, waiting for the finishing touches of make-up. Guests were hurrying outside, and I liked this moment of contrast between their movement (with motion blur, as I was shooting at 1/20 sec) and her stillness. Even better, she is framed quite neatly by the moving figures, so it's a noticeably centred composition.

It works well enough as shot, but in black and white rather than colour. The colours are insipid, and not only fail to contribute to the point of the picture, but distract, as they take the eye away from the bride and towards the background. The lighting is flat, which is no bad thing, as there are no hard shadows to interfere with the contrast between the still figure and the surrounding movement, but it can be improved greatly.

Using the people-recognition capabilities of ACR (or Lightroom), the procedure was simple. Using a whole-figure mask, both the brightness and contrast were increased. This mask was then duplicated and inverted to select the surrounding area, and further refined by subtracting the outer area with a radial gradient. This mask then allowed a gentle darkening around the bride.

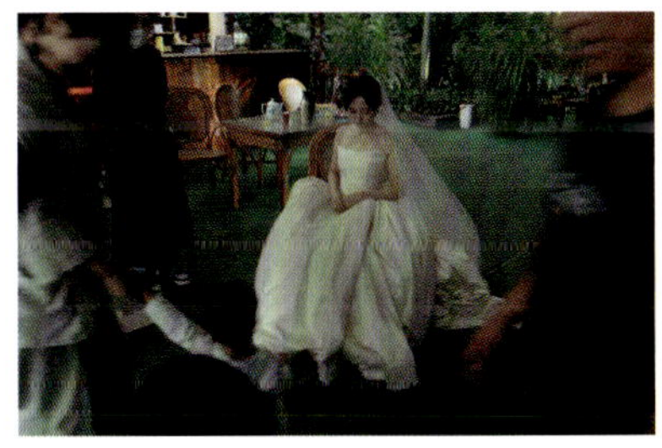
1.

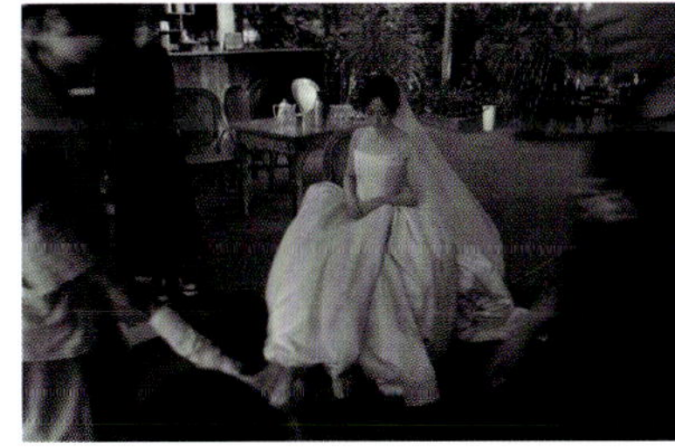
2.

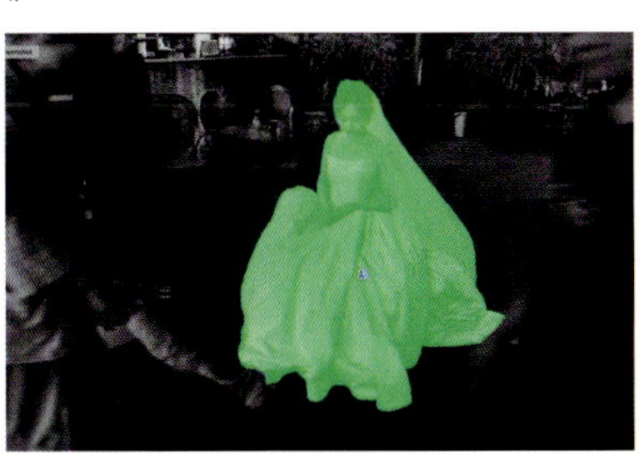
3.

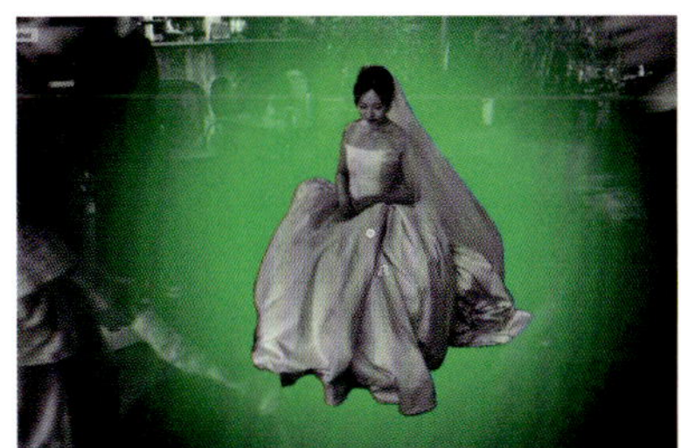
4.

1. Original image

2. Converted to black and white

3. Figure mask for the bride

4. Mask inverted and refined for the background

The picture shown here is of an ancient covered bridge in China's Zhejiang province, which I used in *Michael Freeman on... Black & White* to demonstrate how to make it work in a particular way in black and white. However, I changed my mind about the processing and thought of a new way that I preferred. In the world of black-and-white printing (in a wet darkroom) and digital processing, this happens all the time.

The earlier version, below right, played on the idea of an old-fashioned, period look from orthochromatic film, but the new treatment (opposite) tries to make it rich, dark and strong. For this to work, we need a semantic mask precisely on the bridge, as it has to be a little brighter to stand out from the deep, almost black, wooded background and with a strong contrast that brings out the texture of the wood. The only way to achieve this is to isolate the bridge and give it its own independent processing. Content recognition is the answer, helped along with a roughly guided outline. Specifically, this meant selecting Object in ACR's masking tools, which is a moment's work. Tools such as this, across a range of image processing software, are here to stay and will only get better.

The other subject that needs to be localized is the farmer on the path, who wouldn't survive the dense, rich processing used across the rest of the image – the figure would become lost, but it's an essential human element in the scene. Ironically, perhaps, new-style semantic masking is not what's wanted here, because the figure has to 'emerge' from the background. Instead, an old-fashioned soft radial mask does it, with the precaution that the balance of brightening and the feathering of the radial mask needs to be finely judged in order to appear realistic.

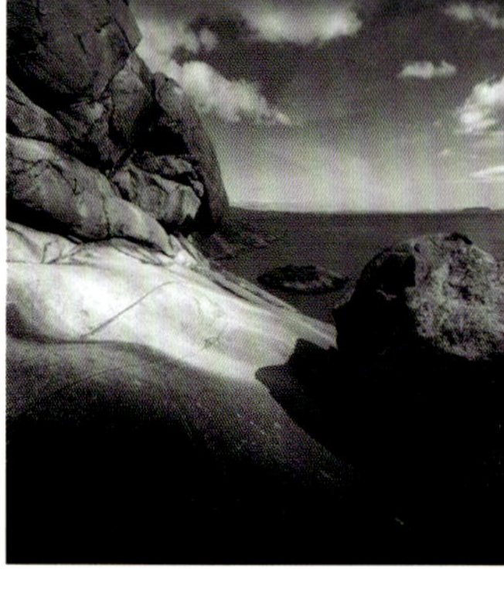

This black-and-white film negative was printed with a much-darkened foreground, to concentrate attention higher in the frame and conceal the unsharpness of the rock that is closest to the camera.

1. Original image

2. First black-and-white version

3. A semantic mask isolates the bridge, and a radial mask picks out the farmer on the path

4. The reworked black-and-white image

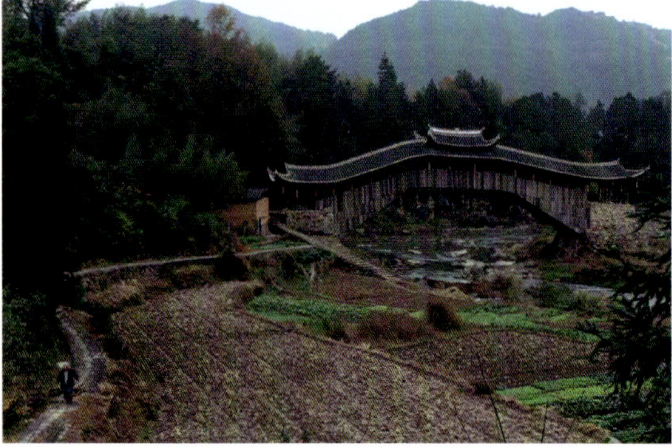

1.

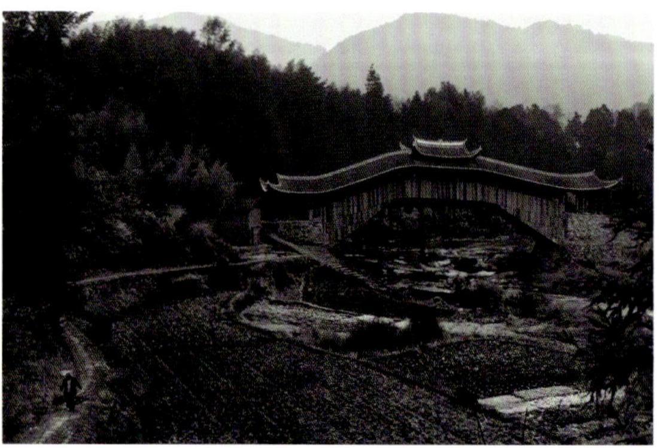

2.

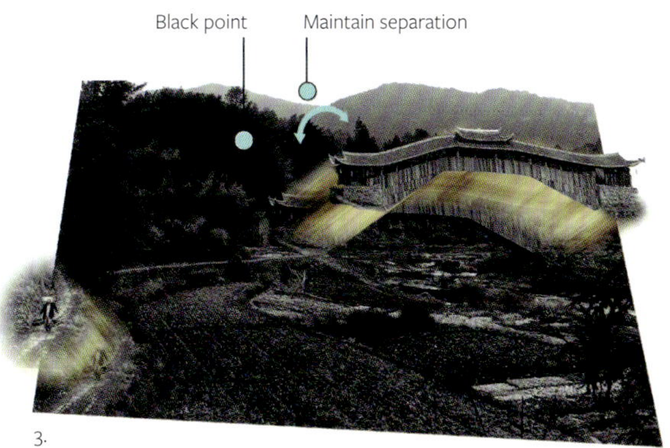

3.

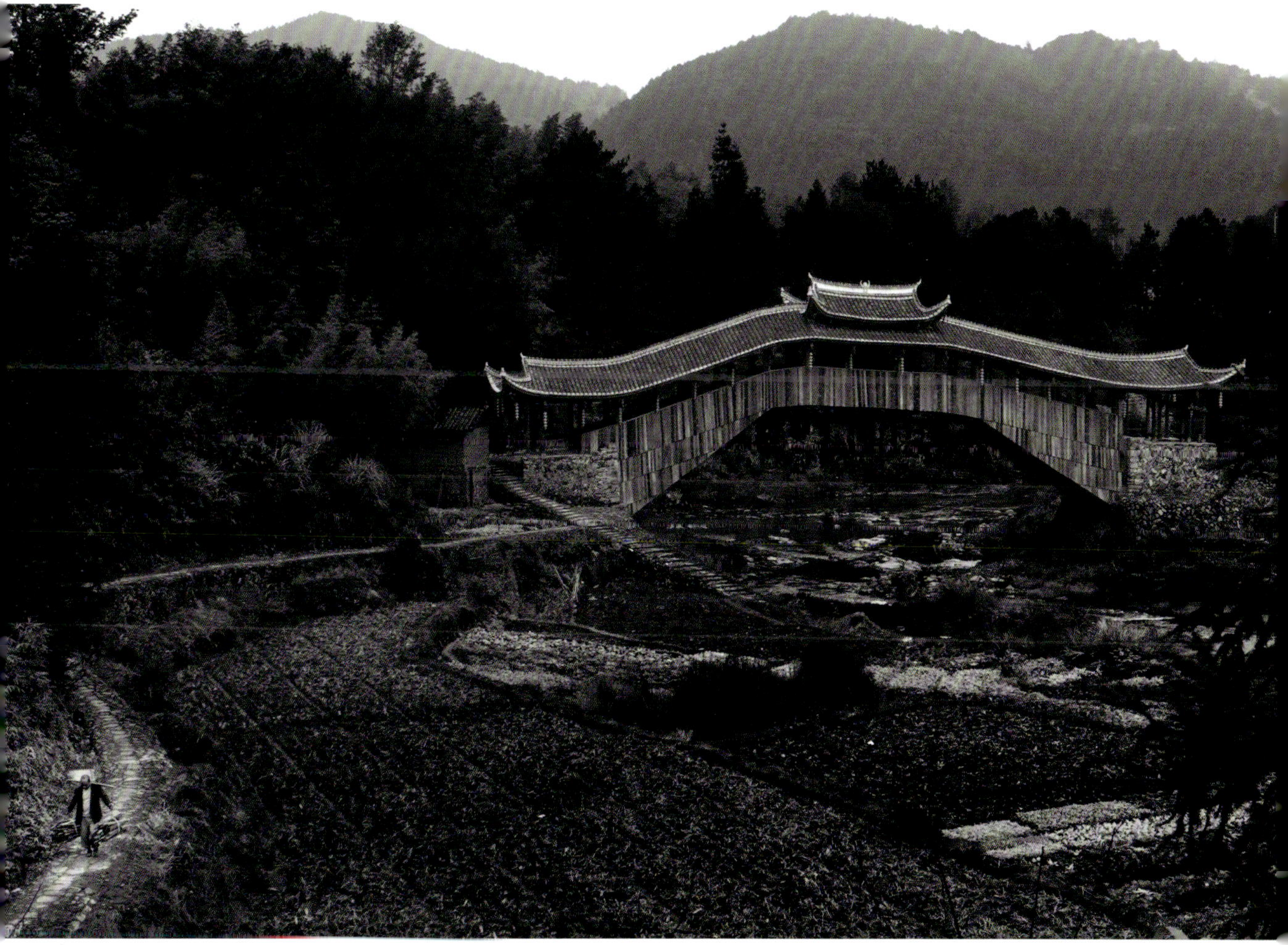

4.

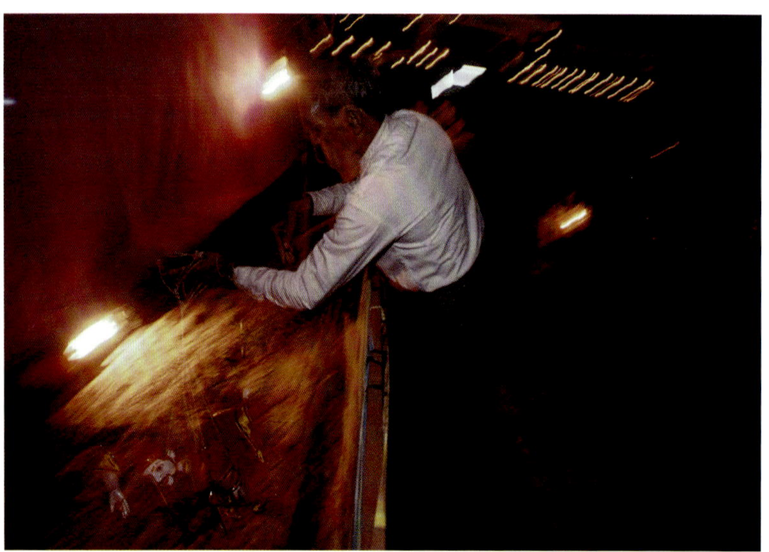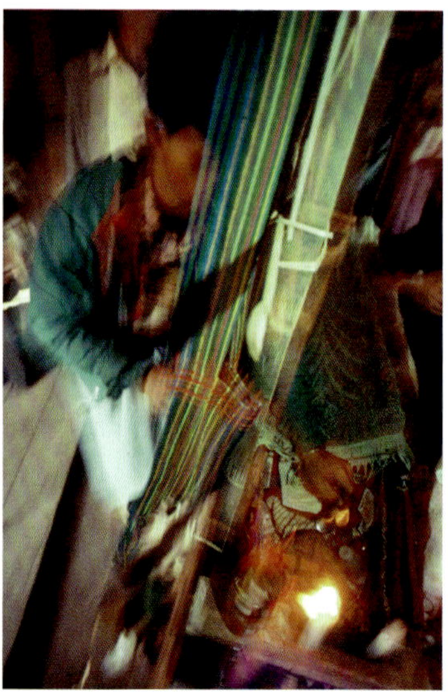

SLOW EXPOSURES

E xposure times longer than usual add another dimension to the look of a photograph – at least when there's movement in the scene. This translates into some kind of blur, usually in the form of streaking.

The variations are endless, depending on the exposure time (which can range from a fraction of a second to minutes, or even hours in the most extreme cases), and on what exactly is moving in the frame, how fast and across how much of the frame. All of this is about creating a visual impression rather than delivering actual information, and understandably divides opinion. There is definitely more of it appearing on social media photo-sharing platforms than before, which shouldn't be a surprise as more and more people search for ways in which their imagery can appear different. One problem is that while it was certainly unusual and eye-catching in the early days of photography (such as the experiments by the Italian photographers Anton Giulio and Arturo Bragaglia in the 1920s and the slow-motion series on rodeos and bullfighting by Ernst Haas in the 1960s), it's now so common as to be clichéd. As with all technique-based looks, it can overwhelm any sense of personality that a photographer might try to inject, which defeats one of its purposes.

These two photographs use a similar technique (both on film) that combines flash with a slow shutter speed while moving the handheld camera. The image on the left is of a Burmese puppet show in Mandalay, while the image on the right shows mourners at a Padaung funeral in Kayah State, Myanmar, passing the open coffin.

Using a tripod or finding some other way of locking the camera keeps the scene steady and sharply focused, so that the streaking is confined to whatever is moving. In the case of the photograph below, the movement is fireworks at a temple festival in Thailand, with an exposure time of three seconds. Longer exposures of some minutes applied to moving water (seashore, river or stream) create a mist-like effect, which I'm intentionally not showing here, as it truly has become a photographic cliché. It even contains well-known sub-clichés, such as bobbing gondolas moored in Venice's lagoon. Nowadays, waterscapes like these go by the name of ND, for neutral density, as strong versions of these front-of-lens filters are typically needed to reach long exposures in bright daylight. This is a well-subscribed area on photo-sharing platforms, as is the even more extreme technique of moving the camera itself during a longer exposure, so everything in the frame streaks. This could be curved or jerky if done by hand, or smoothly vertical or horizontally if the camera is mounted on a tripod with one axis of the head loosened slightly. Doing this in colour rather than black and white adds one more effect-colour blending.

A compromise that works in low light is to use flash together with a longer exposure. With SLRs and DSLRs, this usually took the form of rear-curtain flash, in which the flash is triggered at the end of the time exposure. The effect, which you can see opposite, is that a sharp image overlays a streaked one, and the streaking is 'closed off' by the flash, which looks more logical.

With the camera on a tripod, this 3-second exposure shows fireworks at a temple festival in northern Thailand as a cascading streak against the full moon.

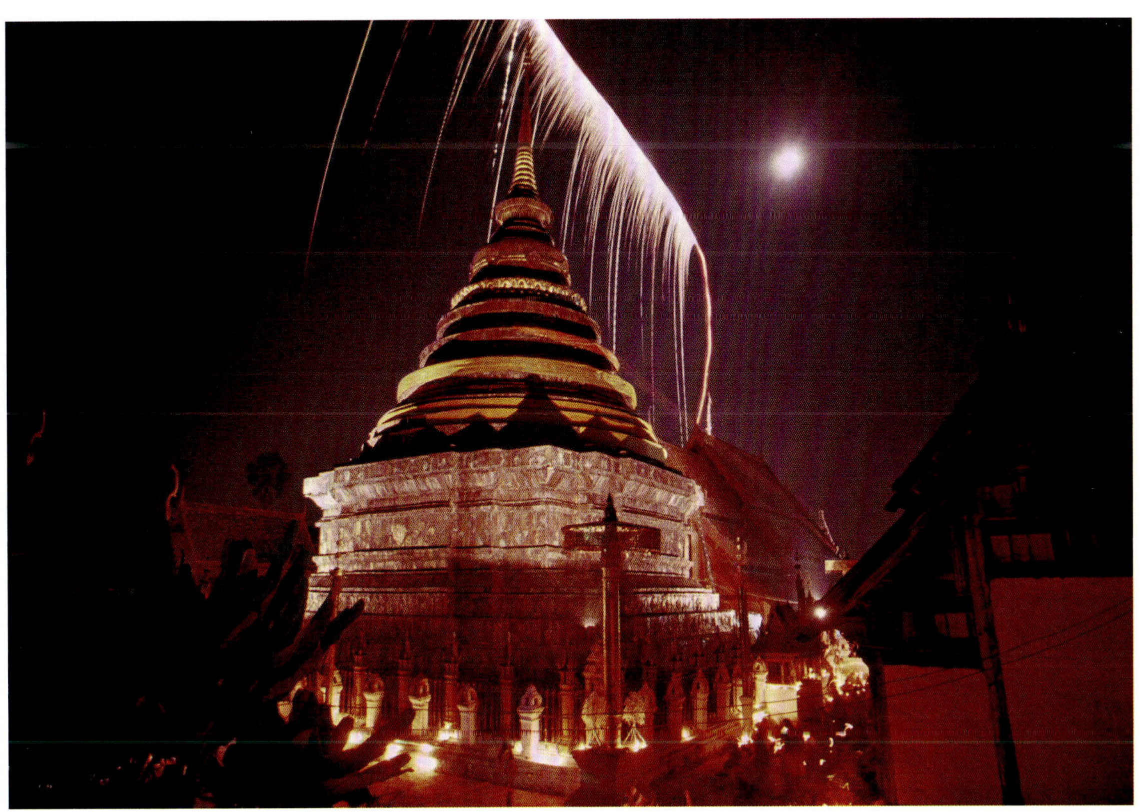

MANAGING EXPOSURE

2

Creative exposure can't exist independently. It has to sit against some notional idea of a standard exposure, which is, I suppose, what most people would do. If there's an 'away from average' (as outlined on pages 20–1) then the average – the standard default – has to come from some sort of best practice. Although this is the territory of my earlier book, *Perfect Exposure*, there are some new things to say about managing and measuring exposure, not least the way that exposure has expanded to include how the capture is processed. This can be done after the event, in-camera or – as increasingly happens with smartphones – during the exposure. Or a mixture of the three.

The paradox is that you can now work with a camera without bothering to measure the exposure. The technology will do it for you, and if the result happens to be off, never mind – you can check it on the screen and re-shoot. Naturally, I believe it's worth the trouble to measure the exposure, not least because being creative with exposure actually demands a good understanding of it. If you want a certain look that depends on the image being brighter or darker, with more or less contrast, then it's a whole lot easier if you're familiar with the starting point.

It also helps if you are familiar with the way the camera calculates the exposure, but the more sophisticated the software inside cameras becomes, the harder this is to predict. Camera manufacturers work hard to give photographers the best results possible, and they're successful at this to everyone's benefit.

However, if you want a different result – one that is more creative – it's not as easy to know how to override what the camera will normally do. It is definitely possible, though. Firstly, we need to go back to a few basics when it comes to understanding light, how it falls and what it does to the subject in front of the camera. Then we need to see how digital capture and computational photography have changed exposure; it is still a simple three-setting task that uses shutter speed, aperture and ISO sensitivity, but there are now more complications.

WHAT DIGITAL DID

It has always been possible to be creative with exposure, and you need only glance at the work of notable photographers such as Edward Steichen, W. Eugene Smith, Roy DeCarava and Brett Weston to see this. But a combination of the latest sensors and digital processing means there are now more opportunities than ever. Without much fanfare (apart from the flurry of excitement over AI), both sensors and processing software have been improving steadily, to the point at which they can now make a fundamental difference to the way we work and how we choose our pictures to look.

When digital cameras became practical in the early years of this century, they were far behind the image quality of film. I had the experience of shooting both at the same time for a large book project on Sudan. It was large in two senses. To start with, I spent two years shooting, making six trips that covered the length and breadth of what was then, in 2003, Africa's largest country (before the independence of South Sudan). It was also a physically large book and some pictures were given double-page spreads. For a 35mm film frame, which scanned to 8,400 x 5,600 pixels, this wasn't an issue, especially as I was using Fuji Velvia film, which was the highest-resolution film at that time.

Digital was another matter. I had a Nikon D100, which produced six-megapixel images, so it was a calculated risk that the software of the day could upscale them sufficiently; there were also things that top printing companies could do, and we took advantage of this as well. For landscapes and other slow photography, I could get large files by shooting pan-and-stitch, but overall, it was a pain trying to compensate for the fact that the sensor simply wasn't big enough, and its dynamic range and colour management was frankly poor (at least by today's standards).

A coffee shop in northeastern Sudan, taken with the camera on the floor. At the right is the processing done at the time, in 2005, which is about as good as could be expected with the tools available. Below is a reprocessed version using the full capabilities of ACR. My taste has also changed.

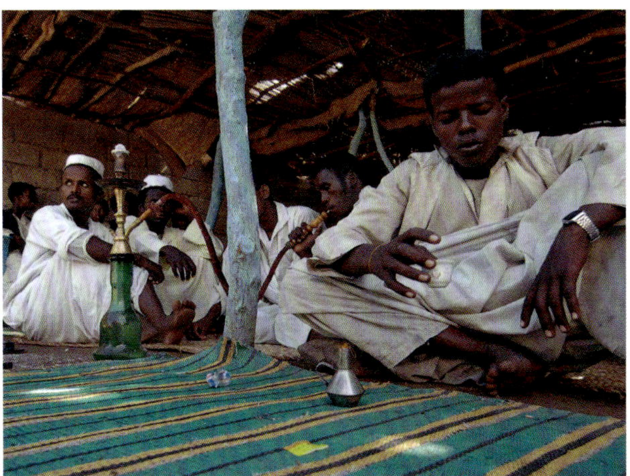
Original

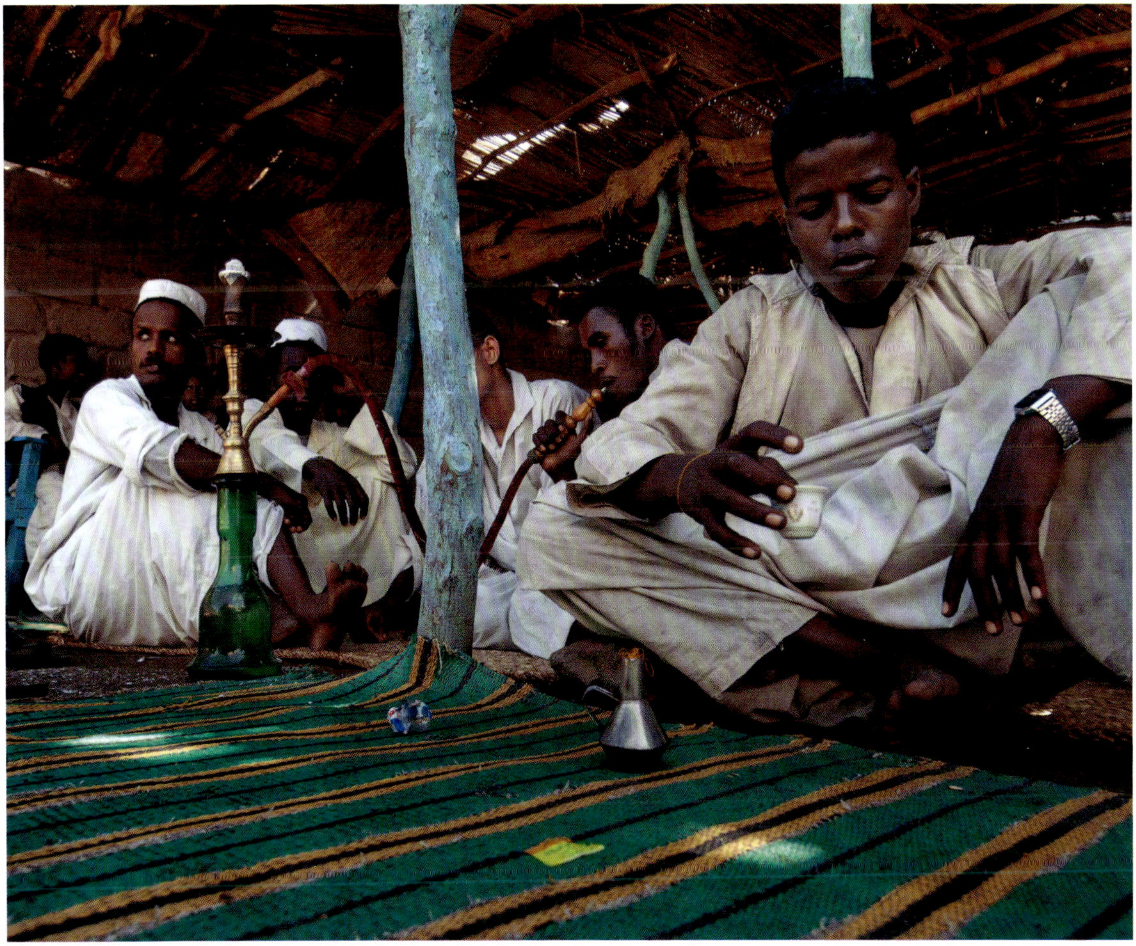

You might wonder why, knowing this, I was committing some of the shooting to digital in never-to-be-repeated situations. The main reason was sensitivity. Velvia had an ISO of 50, which was the price for its wonderful resolution. A fast film was ISO 400 and both grain and weak colour were guaranteed. For this reason, I thoroughly disliked fast colour film and so never used it, but digital was a revelation in low light. Sure, noise is even less likeable than grain, but software can help, and I found that I could work at up to ISO 1000, which was unheard of with colour film. For the first time, I could shoot colour handheld in the evening and in quite dark interiors, and could even shoot landscapes by moonlight. So, when the light was good I used film, and when it wasn't I used digital.

After a while, I also began to try digital in daylight. Optimistically, I knew that digital would take over from film at some point, and I wanted to be there at the start. It seemed logical to me that processing software would always improve, and that eventually I'd be able to revisit the files I was shooting and do much better with them. I wasn't being prescient, it was just logical. Interpolation and recovery would have sounded alien to any 20th-century photographer, but the point I'm making with this diversion into my Sudan project is that exposure is partly for the future – what you do with it later.

It is now two decades since I was in Sudan and, size for size, sensors have surpassed film in all ways. Resolution is no longer an issue for all normal uses, and the quality that matters most for this book – dynamic range – is now so large that it makes exposure flexible and adaptable, so you can revisit it very profitably.

Pan-and-stitch is now commonplace and widely used for creating high-resolution panoramas without cropping the top and bottom of the frame.

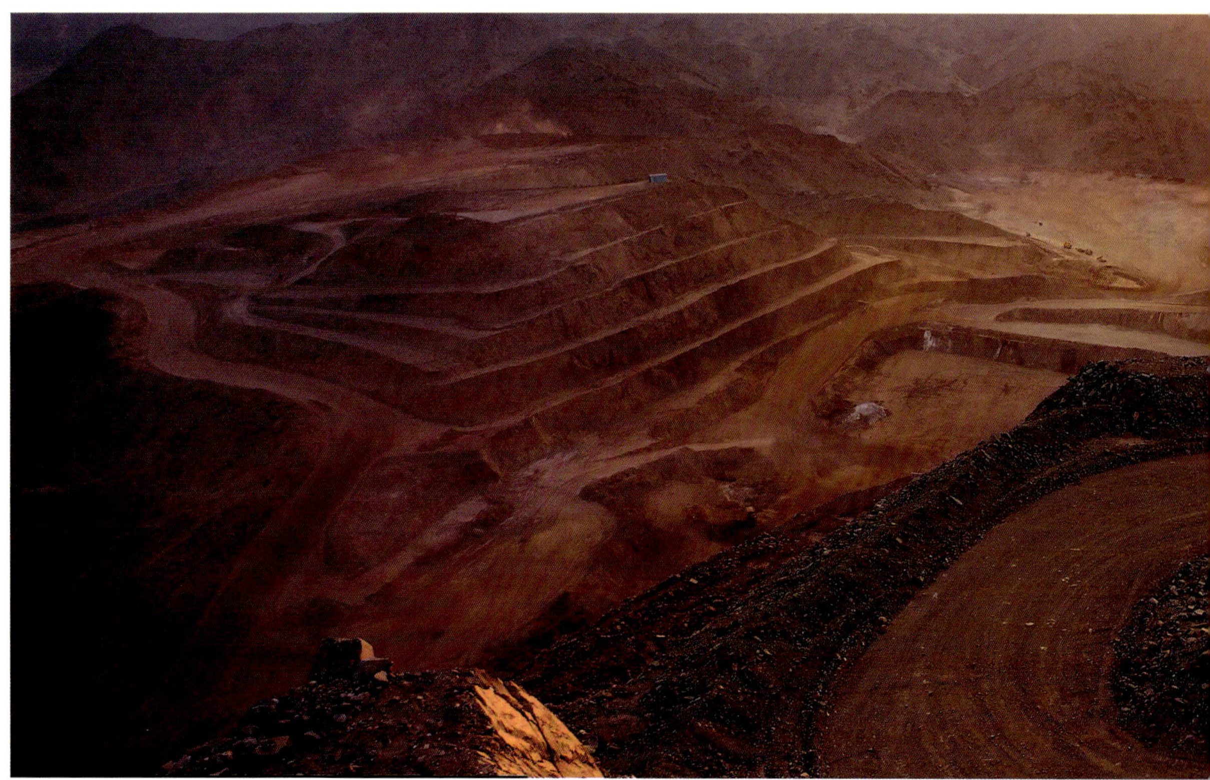

How much larger? We should be cautious about the published dynamic range claims from the camera manufacturers, as most are economical with the truth or are simply coy. The best guide is the independent DXOMARK website, which at the time of writing has the flagship Hasselblad at the top of the dynamic range scale, with a range of 14.8 f/stops, which compares with 9.9 f/stops for my old Nikon D100. Bearing in mind that the dynamic range doubles with each stop, that's a huge industry improvement.

The second part of the equation is processing software. Cameras process images onboard for anyone who wants a simple JPEG, but for quality, the procedure is to shoot Raw and then use a processing engine such as Adobe Camera Raw (that's what I use, although I'm not promoting it over other high-end software such as Capture One and DxO PhotoLab). If we stick just to exposure matters, the important events have been the introduction of highlight and shadow recovery, and most recently, semantic masking in which subjects such as people, faces and skies can be recognized and dealt with separately. More on this last major improvement later, but what shouldn't surprise anyone is that this is already a part of the actual at-the-moment exposure in the computational photography pioneered by smartphones.

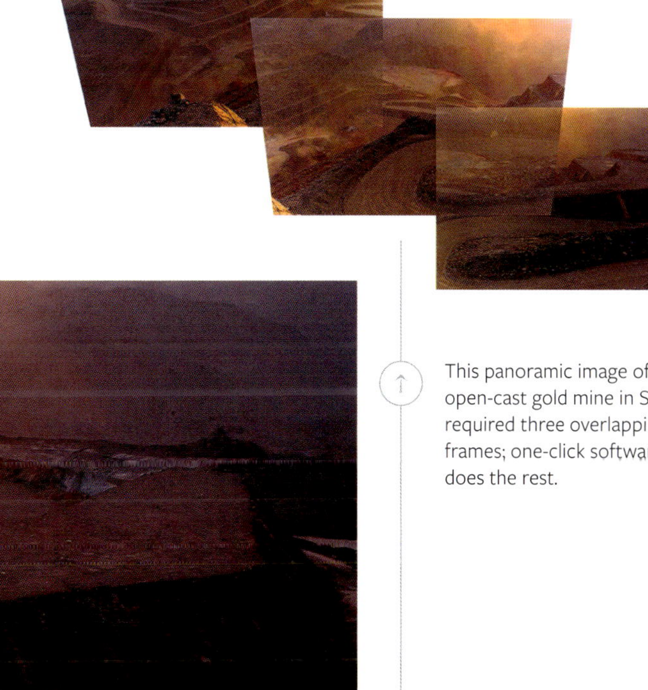

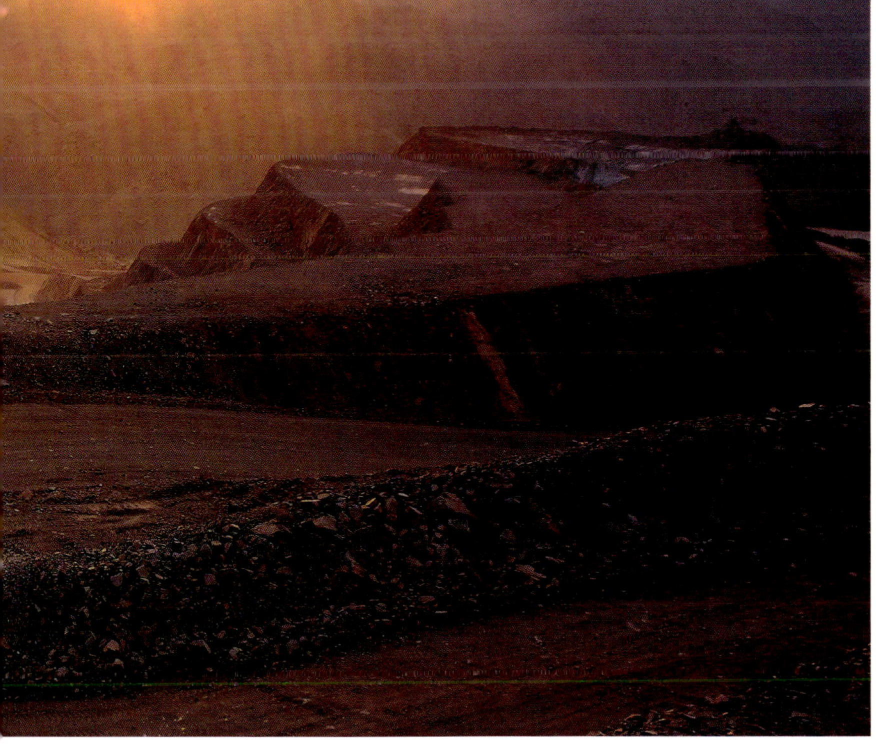

This panoramic image of an open-cast gold mine in Sudan required three overlapping frames; one-click software does the rest.

Continuing the Sudan theme, the product of the gold mine on the previous pages is ingots. The image to the right shows conventional processing to maintain detail throughout. Below is an example of a purely creative decision to expose down for richness and detail in the gold, while allowing the hands and shirt of the man to fade into darkness.

All of this significantly changes the landscape for exposure, and enables us to be creative with it. It also recalls the heyday of black-and-white printing. The timeline of photography – professionally and for publication – went from black and white to colour transparency to digital. Black-and-white negative film has a lot of latitude, which means that not only is it forgiving of exposure mistakes, but it allows all kinds of manipulation when printing in the darkroom. You can hold back the exposure from one part and give more to another – dodging and burning, in other

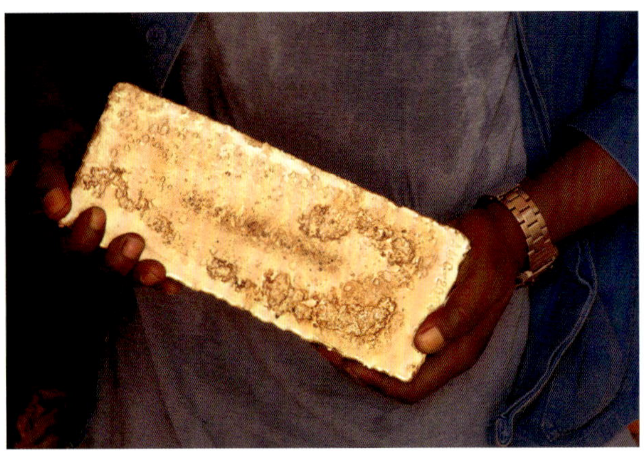

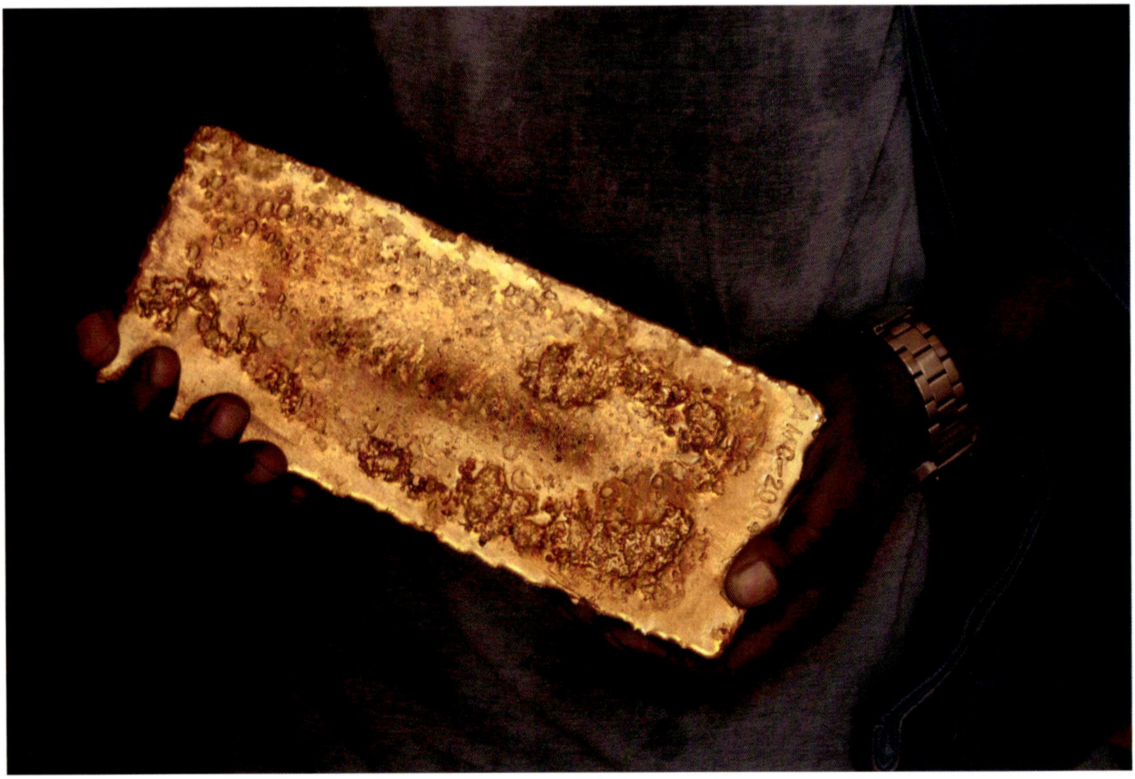

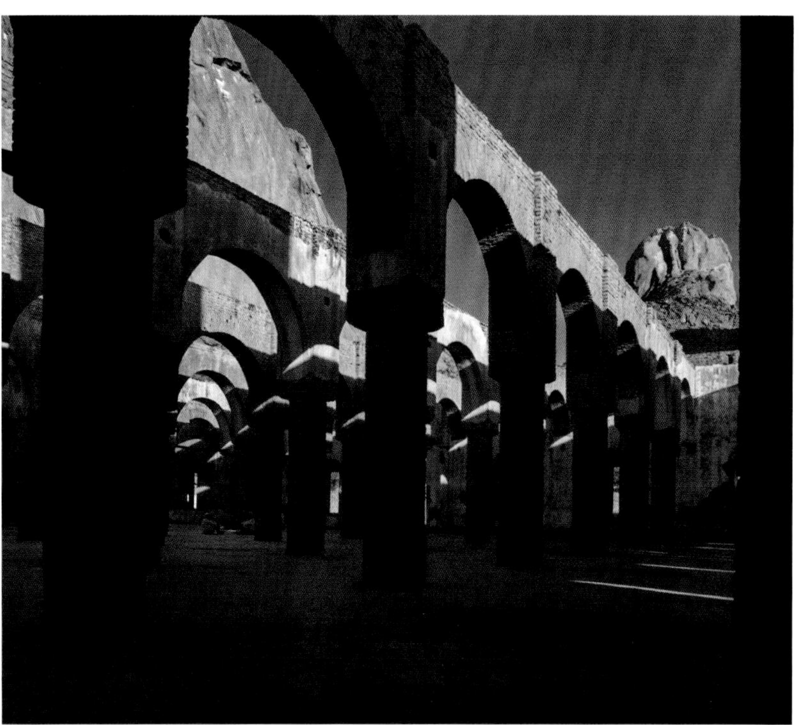

This black-and-white image of a ruined mosque, also in Sudan, was stitched in the same way as the panorama on the previous pages. However, here I used a shift lens at full shift, which I rotated between frames.

words. This created a breed of largely unsung craftsmen who printed on behalf of photographers, and the best were very good indeed.

Then came colour reversal film, which had much less latitude (one stop at most) and no printing stage (there was Cibachrome, but it made little impact). This put paid to the idea of making the final image at leisure. Instead, you shot, handed the roll to the lab and that was it. The early days of practical digital photography were not much better, and a dynamic range of less than ten stops gave very little creative freedom in processing.

Now, by contrast, we're back to the possibilities that were always a part of black-and-white photography. Not only that, but it's more controllable, the range of brightness is greater and it can be in colour.

THE MEASURE OF LIGHT

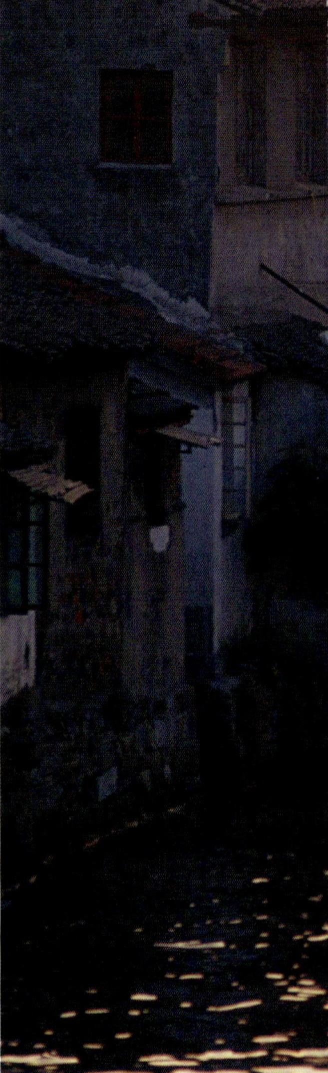

Being imaginative with exposure means a departure from some kind of normality or average. As such, all of the ideas in this book are pushing against expectations, and so it helps to know what, in any situation, that average exposure would be.

There was a time when that would have been stating the obvious, but today I'm tempted to say that few people measure exposure, because every camera does it for us. It's no longer an issue. In-camera metering has been around for decades, and what started as a fairly crude way of choosing which part of the frame was going to be given an 'average' exposure has evolved into a sophisticated system that mimics what most people would want. This is obvious and admirable progress, but what got left behind was the idea that you might want to think about the light.

For that, we need to measure the light, and if you already know how to measure the brightness of a scene, please skip this page. Otherwise, I strongly recommend understanding this basic (if rather unsexy) fact of camera life. The light that matters in photography is the light that's reflected from the surfaces in the scene in front of the camera, which is a combination of how bright the light source is (such as midday sun or heavy cloud) and how reflective the surfaces are (snow, brick, skin, dark foliage and so on).

Enter the light meter. The earliest – and arguably the simplest – uses a selenium cell that conveniently needs no battery power, as the light activates it. The most widely used of all was the Weston Master, which I still use – it still works and also underlines that not much has changed in the measurement of light. I simply have to point it at the scene, and it takes in more or less§ the view that I can see (around 30 degrees). The reading it gives is of the average luminance of the scene, which is a good starting point, because it's how the photograph will be seen at first glance.

As this is photography, the reading needs to be practical, which means a shutter speed and aperture value for whatever the sensitivity of the sensor or film is. If it's a bright sunny day and the sensor or film ISO is 100 (quite typical), and I have the shutter speed set to 1/100 sec, the reading will be about f/16 for the aperture.

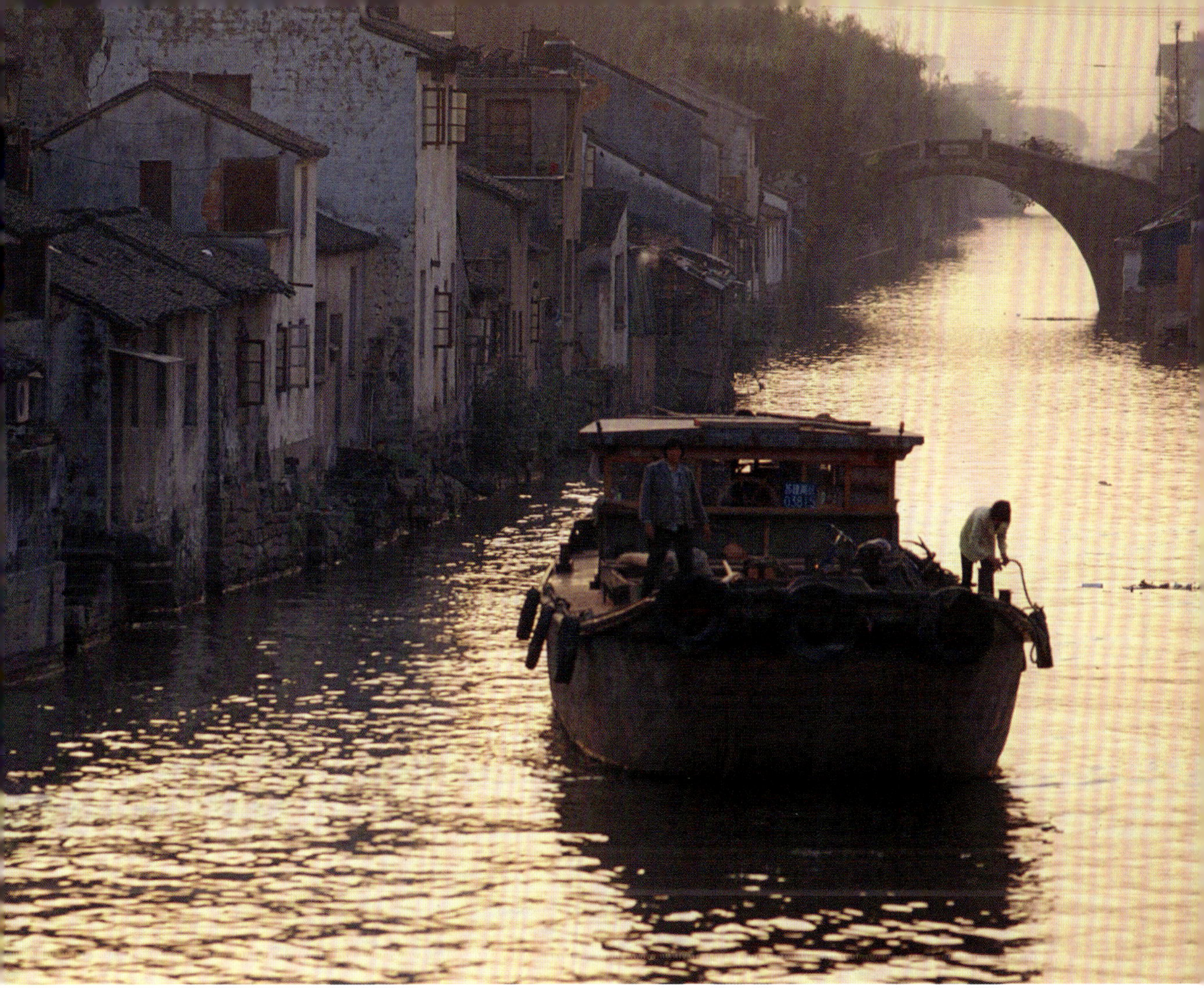

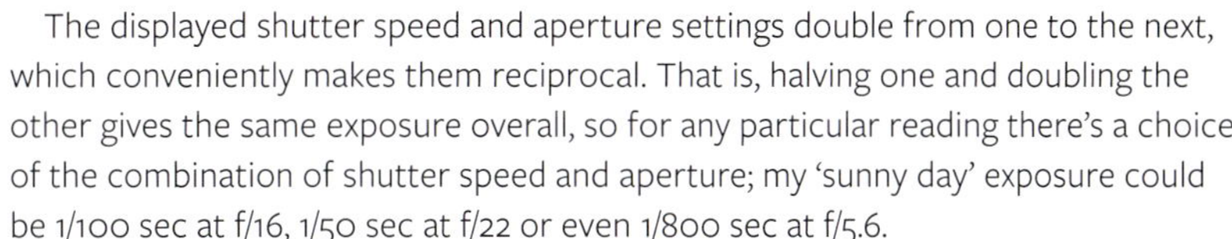

The displayed shutter speed and aperture settings double from one to the next, which conveniently makes them reciprocal. That is, halving one and doubling the other gives the same exposure overall, so for any particular reading there's a choice of the combination of shutter speed and aperture; my 'sunny day' exposure could be 1/100 sec at f/16, 1/50 sec at f/22 or even 1/800 sec at f/5.6.

None of this sounds exacting, but that's because there's a fair amount of tolerance in the system. It's enough to know that you could be around one stop over or under with a digital sensor and still be okay. Black-and-white negative film and colour reversal film have more and less latitude respectively, and the dial of the Weston Master anticipates this with two sets of markings: U and O (for under and over) are each four stops away from the arrowhead reading, and they represent the extremes for black-and-white negative film. The A and C markings are each just half a stop on either side of the arrow, and they represent the much narrower latitude of colour reversal film.

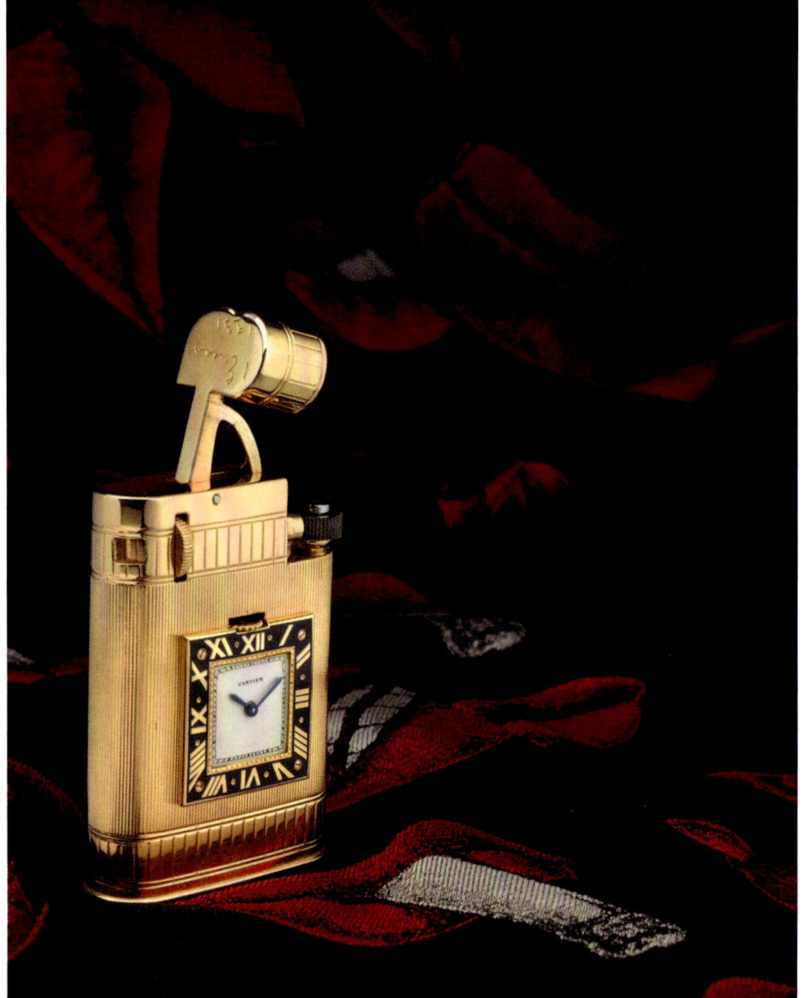

All of this is based on reflected light readings, which is naturally how in-camera metering works – it measures what's contained in the viewfinder. This is fine for most situations, unless the scene is unusually bright or dark, such as a polar bear in snow or a black cat in a coal cellar. The other exception is surfaces that are going to be finely judged, such as skin in a portrait. If you take an exposure reading close to a face, it will suggest a mid-tone, whatever the actual skin tone might be, so a Japanese geisha in white make-up and black skin would both be mid-grey (or the colour equivalent).

This is where incident light readings come in. Rather than measuring the light being reflected off the subject, an incident reading measures the light falling onto it, which ignores differences between surfaces. It means fitting a special cover over the light meter (usually a white dome) and aiming it back towards the camera, and while this is not necessarily convenient for street photography, it is still widely used in studio settings.

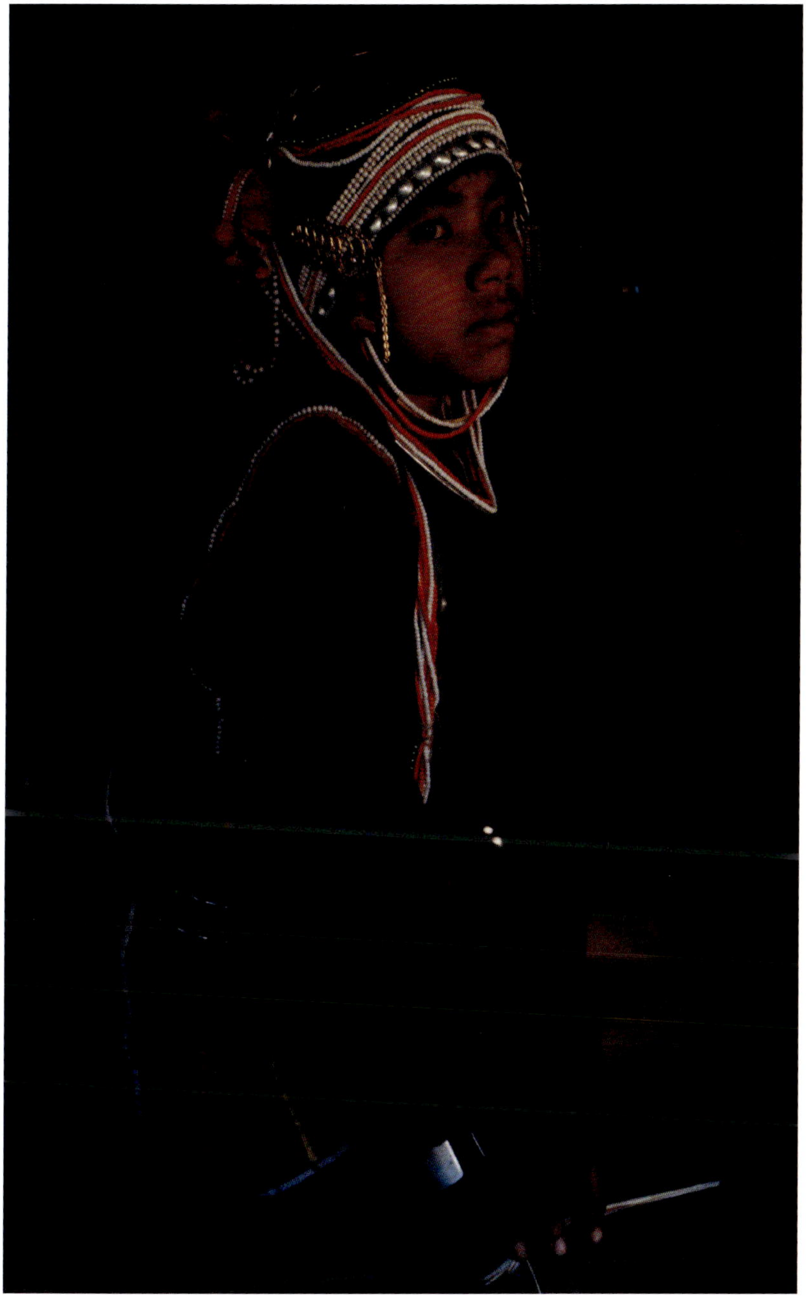

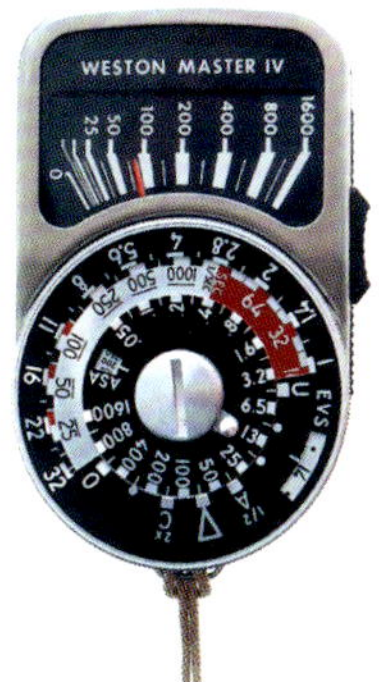

A handheld Weston Master light meter. When there is time, measuring different parts of the scene and taking an incident light reading will improve accuracy.

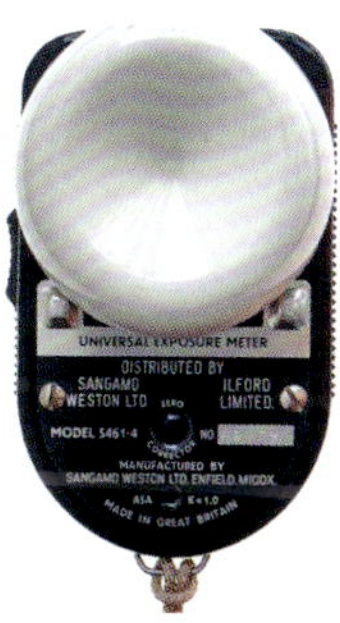

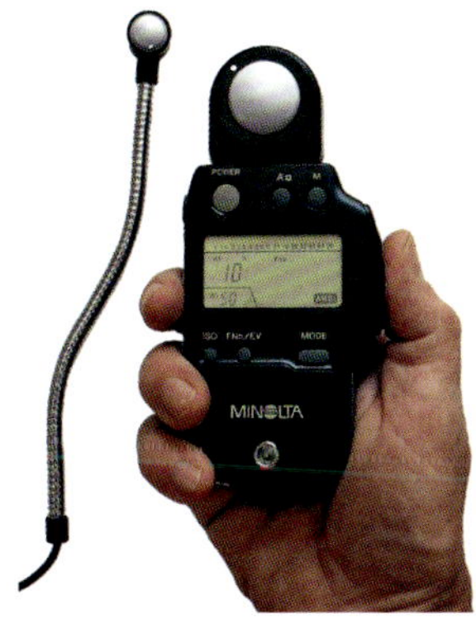

A digital handheld light meter fitted for incident light readings, alongside a probe for taking the same kind of reading in small spaces.

EXPOSURE TRIANGLES & DONUTS

Exposure in a camera requires a combination of three variable settings: the shutter speed, the lens aperture and the sensitivity of whatever's recording the image (sensor or film).

In other words, exposure depends on the length of time the light is allowed in for; the amount of light allowed to pass through the lens aperture; and the ISO setting. The more that you, the photographer, take part in this mixture of settings, the more important it is to have a simple way of visualizing the choice. Dedicated cameras have auto modes of one kind or another, from completely automatic to asking you to prioritize either shutter speed or aperture, while smartphone cameras are by default completely automatic.

Many cameras will also let you work completely manually, setting each of the three exposure parameters yourself. This isn't quite as mad as it may sound, as working manually forces you to stay aware of the light and the priorities of capturing movement with a particular shutter speed, or of getting a shallow or deep depth of field through your choice of aperture.

In any case, the decision over how these three settings are balanced depends on the other effects that each setting has on the image, *apart* from controlling the brightness. Shutter speed affects how the movement of elements in the frame appears, on a scale from sharply frozen to streakily blurred. Aperture affects depth of field, which is how much foreground-to-background sharpness there is, from very shallow (helping the focused subject to stand out) to everything in focus. Sensor sensitivity, measured in ISO, allows less light to form an image if you dial it up, but at the cost of noise, or the best image quality if you leave it at its lowest setting. Conventionally, most photography aims for an absence of blur and strong depth of field, but if creativity is important, convention doesn't matter.

When you adopt a creative approach to exposure, it's inevitable that the three exposure settings are going to need more attention than when aiming for an average, standard exposure. As we'll see, there are going to be more instances of raised and lowered exposures: high-register and low-register pictures. All of the above pushes us towards thinking about exposure settings, so it helps to have a simple overview.

One way of linking the three is with the long-established exposure triangle, while a more modern approach comes in the form of a torus, or donut. In this, the three settings appear as variable sections of a ring. Lengthening one or more of the three sections closes the brightness circle from dark to an averagely bright picture, while going further with them results in 'overexposure', which could be intentional or not. This seems more intuitive than the exposure triangle, as the length of the sections can be taken in instantly.

A three-dimensional rendering of the exposure triangle described in the text. In order to maintain the same exposure, if one of the three settings is raised, one or both of the others needs to be lowered.

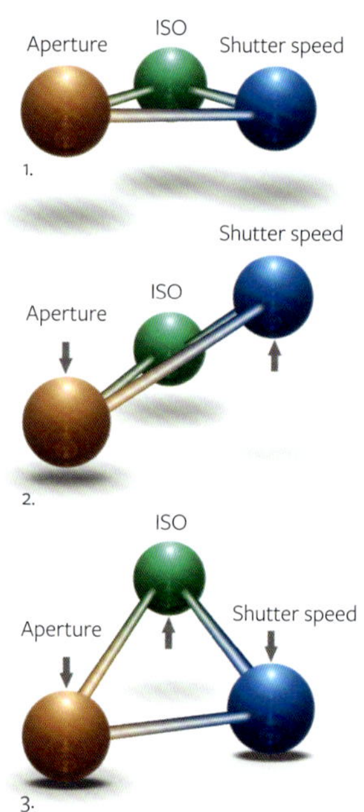

A proprietary alternative to the exposure triangle is Expodo (from 'exposure donut').

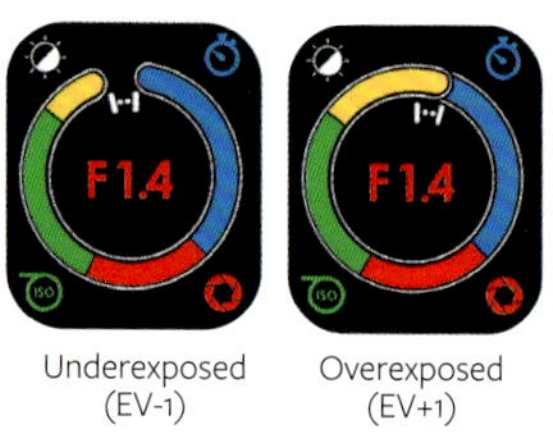

Underexposed
(EV-1)

Overexposed
(EV+1)

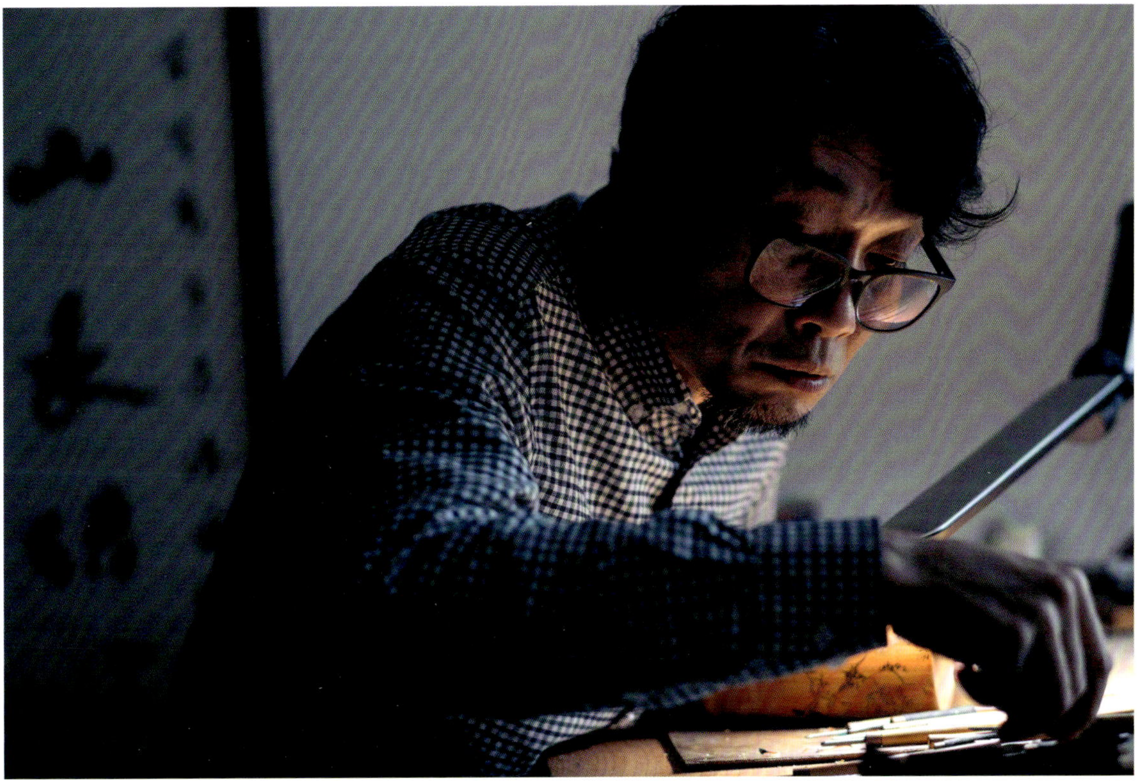

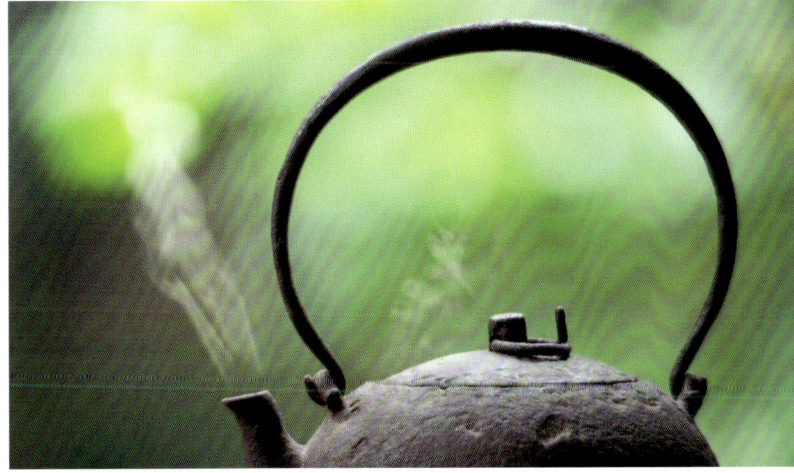

Low light is one condition that forces some kind of compromise. Here, the craftsman's movements are slow, so 1/80 sec is fine, and the lens is fast enough to allow an aperture wide open of f/1.2, needing just a modest increase of ISO to 320.

Rapid movement across the frame also puts pressure on the settings. Here, a boiling kettle needs a minimum 1/160 sec shutter speed to halt the steam at f/1.2 and ISO 320.

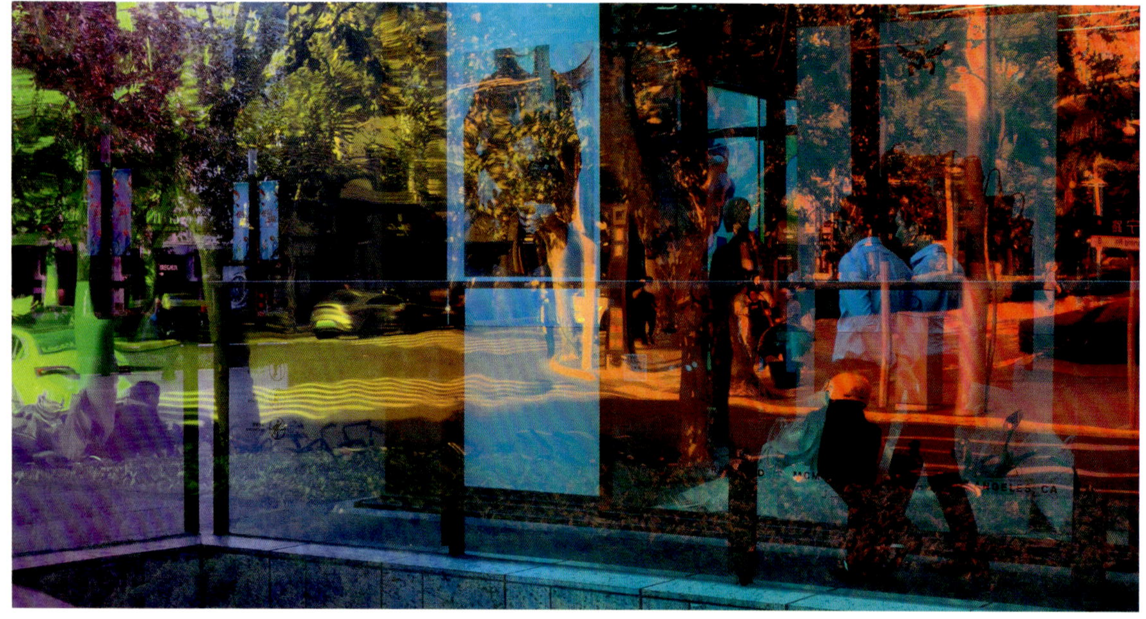

COMPUTATIONAL EXPOSURE

S martphone camera systems increasingly use computing to deliver photographs to users. This is partly to compensate for the problems posed by their tiny lenses and sensors, and partly to leverage their computing power.

The results are now ramping up, with impressive performance that improves year by year. Dedicated cameras may or may not adopt and catch up, but in any case, the entire camera world is so dominated by phone cameras that computational photography is the future. There are more things involved than just exposure, but it's very much at the heart of computational photography.

The principle is simply analyze-and-adjust, which means that, by default, the camera system will first bring the overall exposure into line with what the manufacturer believes is a good-looking, acceptable brightness and contrast. More than that, the camera is trained to recognize certain features, such as faces, the human body and sky, and can use this information to adjust the exposure separately for each subject. In tricky situations, such as an overly bright sky or a heavily backlit face, the picture can be balanced in much the same way as you would make selections when processing on a computer or tablet.

A kaleidoscopic scene in downtown Shanghai, photographed with the 5x lens of an iPhone.

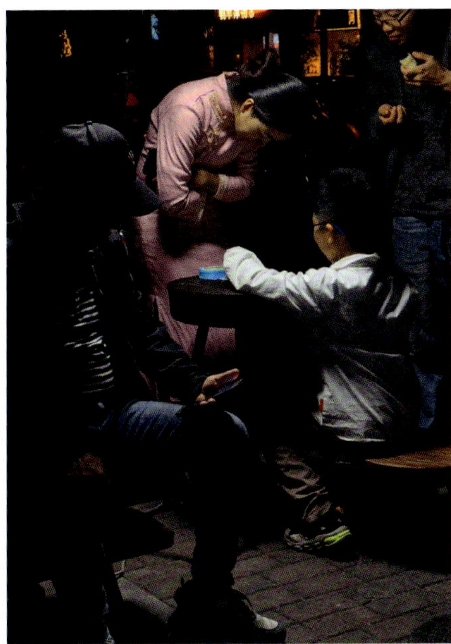

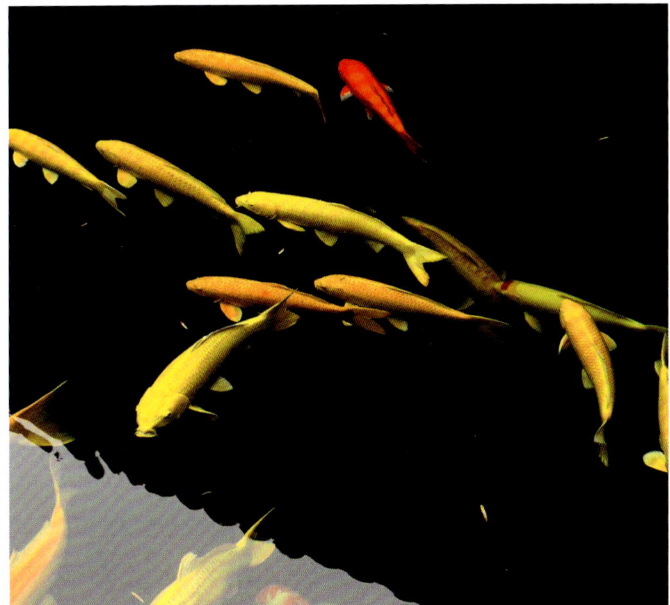

A night market in a Chinese town, with high-contrast street lighting and dense shadows. The computational exposure on an iPhone (using the Raw option for a DNG file) and adjustments in processing handled the dynamic range perfectly.

A third iPhone shot, this time of a carp pond that had a surprisingly high dynamic range. The exposure needed almost no later adjustment, maintaining rich blacks and deep colours.

This type of selective processing is nothing new. It can be traced back to old-fashioned dodging and burning in a wet darkroom under the enlarger, but doing it more or less at the moment of capture is more efficient. Machine learning is also refining the recognition of elements in the frame, so in principle this looks to get better and better. The problem, however, is that the camera system takes charge more and more. While this is perfect for most phone-camera users, for anyone who wants to keep control over the way their photographs look, it means there is more to override, so for creative exposure you are starting with an intricately optimized picture, rather than an untouched one.

Therefore, whenever you are shooting with a computational camera (which includes all phone cameras), the first precaution is always to choose the Raw option. This will preserve the full bit-depth of the capture, although not all the computational adjustments that went into it. Whether or not manufacturers will enable access to these adjustments at any point in the future is yet to be seen, although most smartphone manufacturers now have a model aimed at serious photographers, with features and adjustments aimed at people like us.

3

LEARNING FROM FILM

While film photography (or analogue photography, as some people like to call it) is enjoying a revival, it's still niche, so why would it be important to look back at an era of photography that all but ended almost a quarter of a century ago? Because there were some desirable qualities in film that are absent in digital photography for awkward technical reasons, and also because the chemistry of film created a particular bounded world of tone and colour within which photographers learned to work as best they could. One of the funny things in creative arenas like photography is that it's the constraints that push people to find imaginative solutions rather than the freedoms. The very limitations of films such as Kodachrome (narrow latitude and bad behaviour in the highlights) led skilled photographers to find ways of exposing them that were distinctive and creatively successful.

Whether it's Ektachrome, Kodachrome, Velvia or something else, transparency film reacts differently to light when compared with a digital sensor, and a whole suite of exposure effects spring from this. A photograph on film is also different perceptually to a digital image. In its 'raw' form, unscanned, it has a different look to the pictures we normally see on screen, and there are some useful qualities we can learn from this, especially if we want to build up a personal repertoire of looks.

First, film reacts differently to exposure than a sensor, particularly at either end of the tonal scale (the extreme brights and darks). As the interest here is in being creative with exposure, rather than aiming at some idea of 'correctness', it doesn't matter whether film or sensors are superior at capturing shadow or highlight detail – I'm concerned much more with how a photograph looks.

It's in the shadows and highlights where you can be the most expressive in a photograph, and it's worth taking a detour to see why. Almost all pictures are built around the mid-tones, because that's the average brightness we expect to see, and we're fairly sensitive to what seems 'right'. The result is that we have many fewer expectations about how shadows and highlights ought to look, which means there's room to play creatively here.

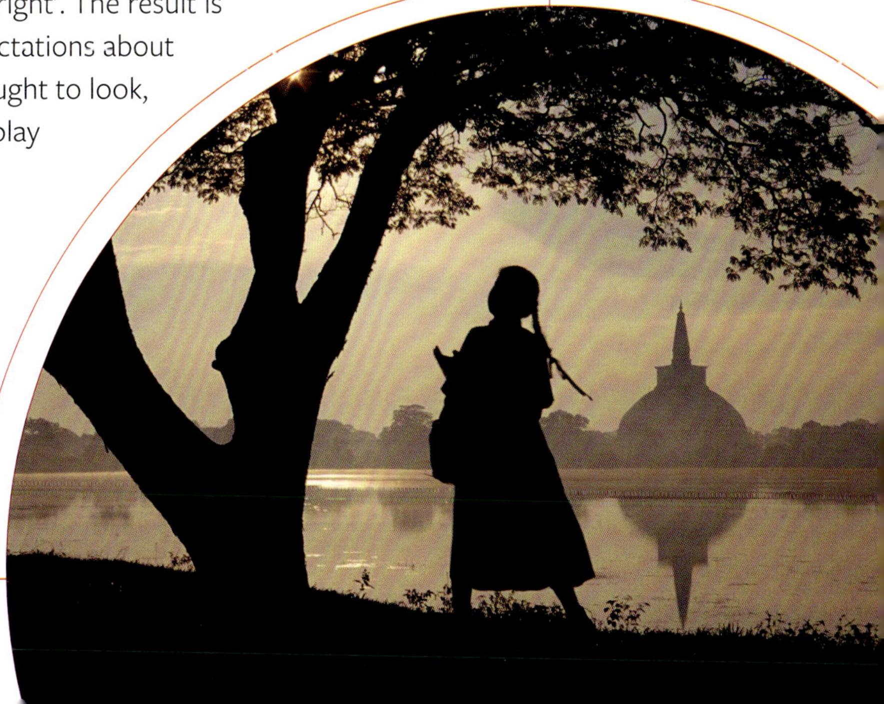

TOE & SHOULDER

The key to understanding the special way in which film reacts to exposure is that at either end of the scale – small amounts of light in the shadows and large amounts in the highlights – it 'slows down'.

I'm taking some liberties here with terminology, but that's the practical effect. More accurately, and graphically, you can see the behaviour of a film brand in its response curve, as shown opposite. This is called a characteristic curve, and from left to right, it shows what happens as the emulsion receives an increasing amount of light. For a sensor, this would be a straight line and very simple – twice the dose of light gives twice the brightness, anywhere along the scale. Not so with film. Very small doses of light have very little effect. What's happening is that the first few photons have trouble overcoming the inertia of the emulsion. This slowness to start appears as the 'shoulder' of the curve in colour slide film, and this is where the deepest shadows in a typical image are in colour transparency film. With increasing light, the slope straightens out, and most of the curve is straight, as for a digital sensor. Unsurprisingly, this is called the straight-line section of the curve, and the broad range of mid-tones lie here. Then, approaching featureless white, increasing the exposure starts to have less and less effect on the film. This is the 'toe' of the curve, where all the highlights lie. For negative film, the slope is reversed, starting low at the left and rising to maximum exposure at the right.

This is the basic difference regarding exposure between film and digital, and there are various ways of describing it. One common description is that the shadows and highlights get 'crushed' or 'blocked', and not in a complimentary way. More objectively, they are compressed, and it's easy to see this as a technical problem that would be good to overcome.

Digital sensors do indeed overcome this, which is surely an improvement? Well, yes and no, because there are other things involved. One term that was used with film but has all but disappeared is 'latitude', meaning that you can underexpose or overexpose it somewhat and still have a useful image. The 'somewhat' was generally around one stop over or under.

A scene in southern India shot on Fuji Velvia, looking into a misty rising sun. The gradual tailing off in the highlights towards the centre is in contrast to the clipping problems of digital sensors.

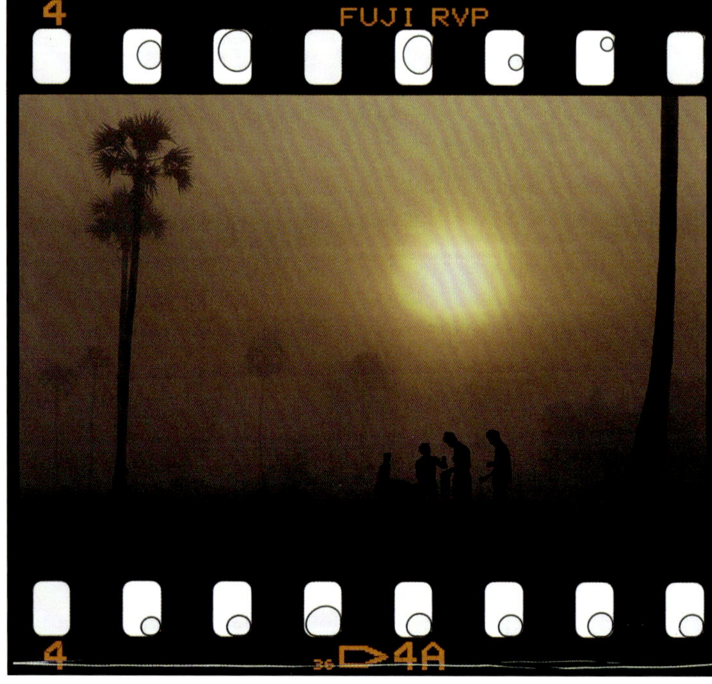

The shadows in this 1990s street view in Shanghai, also shot on Fuji Velvia, are all held nicely, with no absolute blacks (compare with the fullest black possible in the sprocketed rebate).

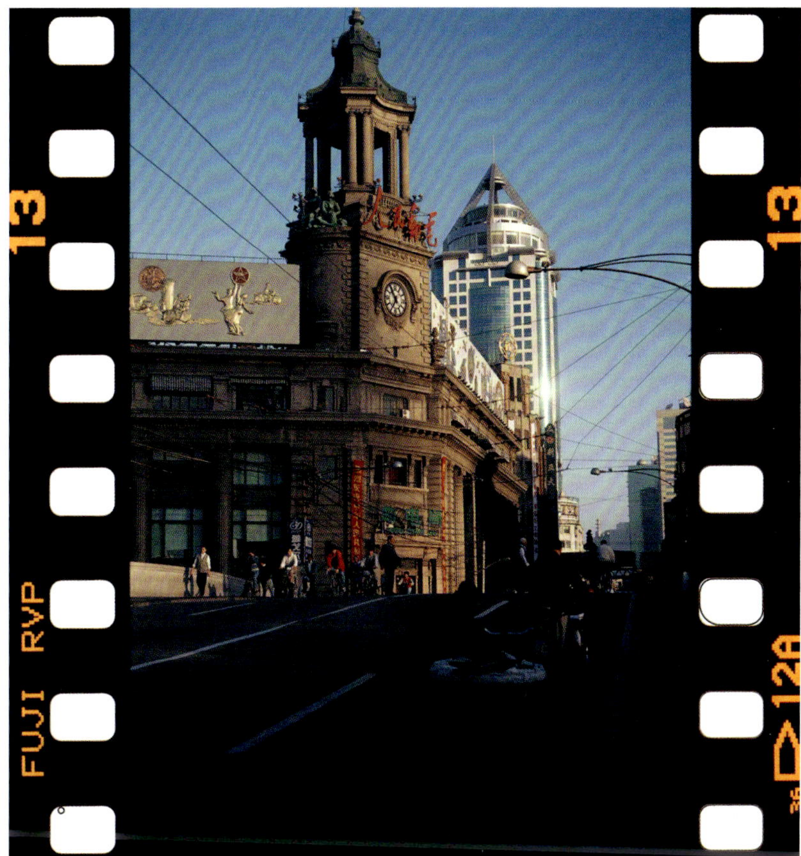

The characteristic curve of transparency (slide) film, as explained in detail in the text. The slopes at the top ('shoulder') and bottom ('toe') are responsible for film's gentle treatment of shadows and highlights. This is the curve for Kodak Ektachrome 100.

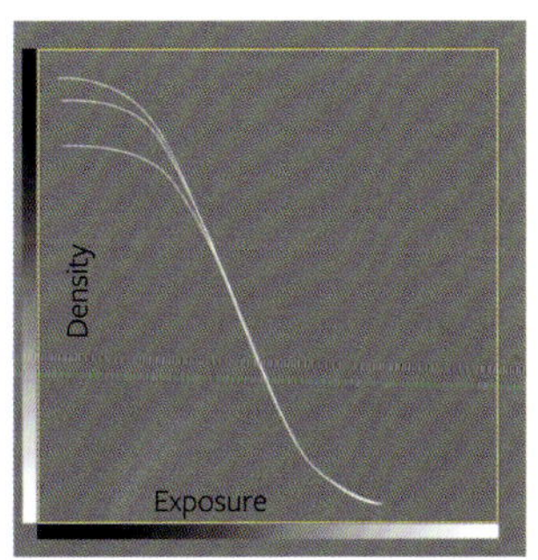

At the same time, highlight compression has a positive effect in some images by smoothing out overexposed areas. Consider what happens when you're shooting towards a light source and it's in frame, such as the sun in a slightly hazy sky. Spatially, part of the image grades from bright to highlight to blank white. Digitally, this is a problem, because the photo site for each pixel fills up steadily with more light until it's suddenly full. 'Suddenly' means there's a break between just a little tone and none at all, and that's called clipping. This appears as a band with an edge, and because each of the three channels reacts a little differently to light, there's also usually a band of a different hue. Although these things can be dealt with to an extent in-camera and by processing the Raw file, it is not easy.

Film bypasses this because of the slope in the shoulder of the curve. The ramp from bright to white is naturally smooth, without a break, which means film doesn't clip. Given that clipping is an artifact that has nothing to do with the actual scene (and has no redeeming qualities), this is very much in film's favour. As you'll see, you can overexpose film as much as you like and there are never any sharp breaks in the highlights. To go overall pale, almost to white, is an artistic choice that's been used by numerous photographers, including Jeffrey Conley, Henry Wessel, Paul Graham and Koo Bohnchang.

LOOKING AT FILM

An issue that gets less attention than I think it deserves is how we view an image – the display, in other words. Since the advent of digital photography, this has been overwhelmingly screen-based, with most photographs processed, sent and viewed on the screen of a mobile phone, tablet or computer.

Backlighting gives a brilliance to a picture that is accepted as normal, with screen technology improving to increase this sensation of brilliance, and approach what in the engineering world is seen as the holy grail: full HDR. The world of film is more complex. Negative films need to be printed as contact sheets so that we can assess them and decide which to print, while transparency (colour reversal) film provides ready-made images with a double life.

Earlier on, I said that transparency film is a limited process: you expose, you process and that's it. There's no essential darkroom work later. There is with a black-and-white (or colour) negative, though, and this means you are always thinking ahead at the time of capture to how you're going to handle the printing.

What was once normal is now rare. From around the 1960s through the 1990s, photography intended for print publication – magazines, advertising, books – was shot primarily on reversal film (aka slide film, transparencies or chromes). Everyone, from photographers to art directors and picture editors, would judge the pictures on a light box.

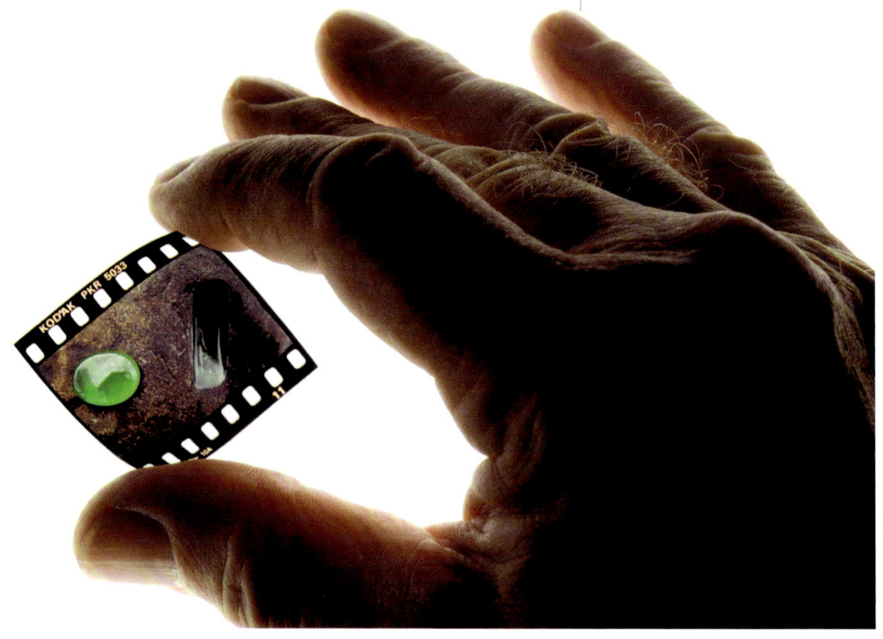

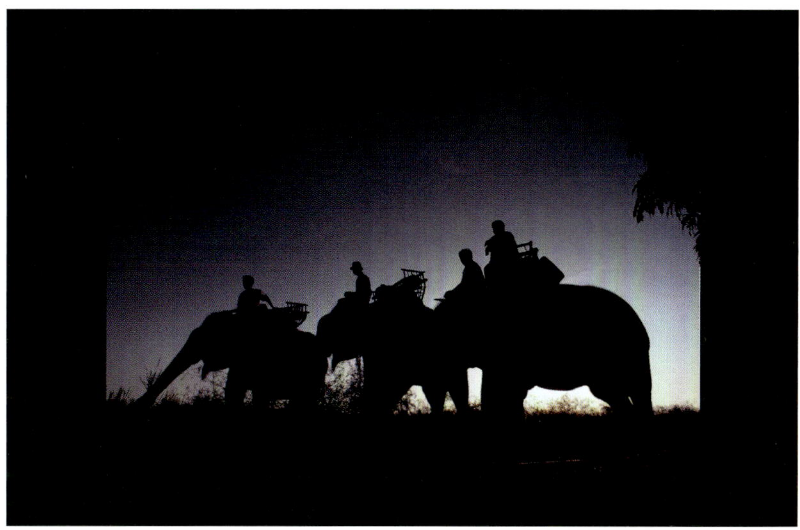

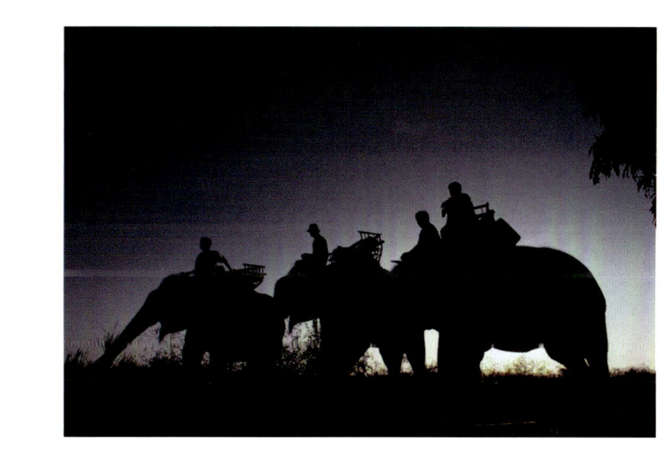

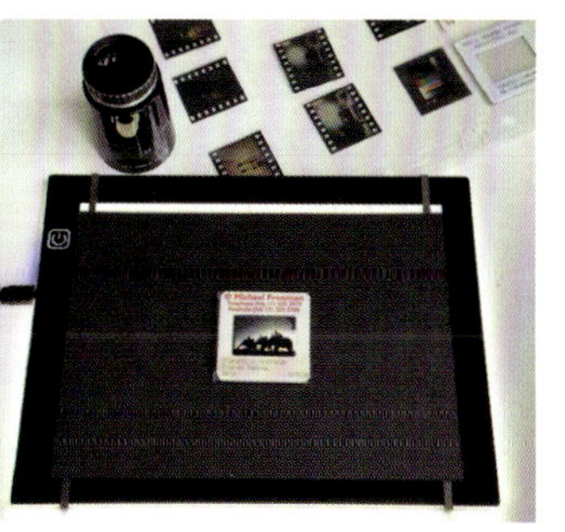

However, while a transparency is a finished image-in-an-object, at a professional level, it will be used, typically in print. That means it will be scanned, which is another step and another complication in how the image will look. A lot of people believe that photography became digital at the start of this century, with the advent of the first digital cameras, but in reality, photography went digital in the 1970s with the invention of drum scanners. These were the first scanners that were designed to work with computers, and they had a profound impact on professional photography. Colour magazines were still powerful media, with new titles such as *Smithsonian* and *GEO* being launched, and the high resolution and colour quality of these scanners meant that 35mm slide film could be printed at a large size and still look very good.

Much of the mythology and misunderstanding about the 'special' look of
transparency film stems from the varied ways of actually viewing it. I spent half my
photographic life looking at and selecting my pictures on a light box under a loupe,
as did everyone else in the business. Occasionally (and reluctantly), photographers
would load 35mm slides into a projector and pray they didn't get damaged or
exposed to the projector lamp for too long, in order to present work to a client,
but for the most part, film was viewed in magnification from just a few inches away.

All judgments, from editorial to repro, were made in this manner, and film looks
very different when it is seen like this. As it's backlit, that means a high dynamic
range display, so paradoxically you have a medium dynamic range image displayed
in HDR. Because you're examining it in detail, you can see into the deepest recorded
shadows and view the subtle roll-off of highlights as they merge into the near-white
of the film base – almost like real life! And that is the point: you look *at* a normal
photograph, but you look *into* a transparency.

Consequently, well-exposed (meaning slightly underexposed) Kodachromes
acquired a near-mythical reputation because when viewed like this, they are
exquisitely sharp, smoothly toned and grain-free, with subtle hints of detail deep
into the shadows. Professionals who worked regularly with Kodachrome learned
to lower the exposure by ⅓ to ½ stop to keep the highlights under control (blown
highlights were anathema to everyone), and for this reason, everyone got used to

While digital imagery is
always viewed on some
kind of screen, colour film
is a physical object, usually
mounted in card for ease of
handling. Doing a large edit
involved a lot of clutter.

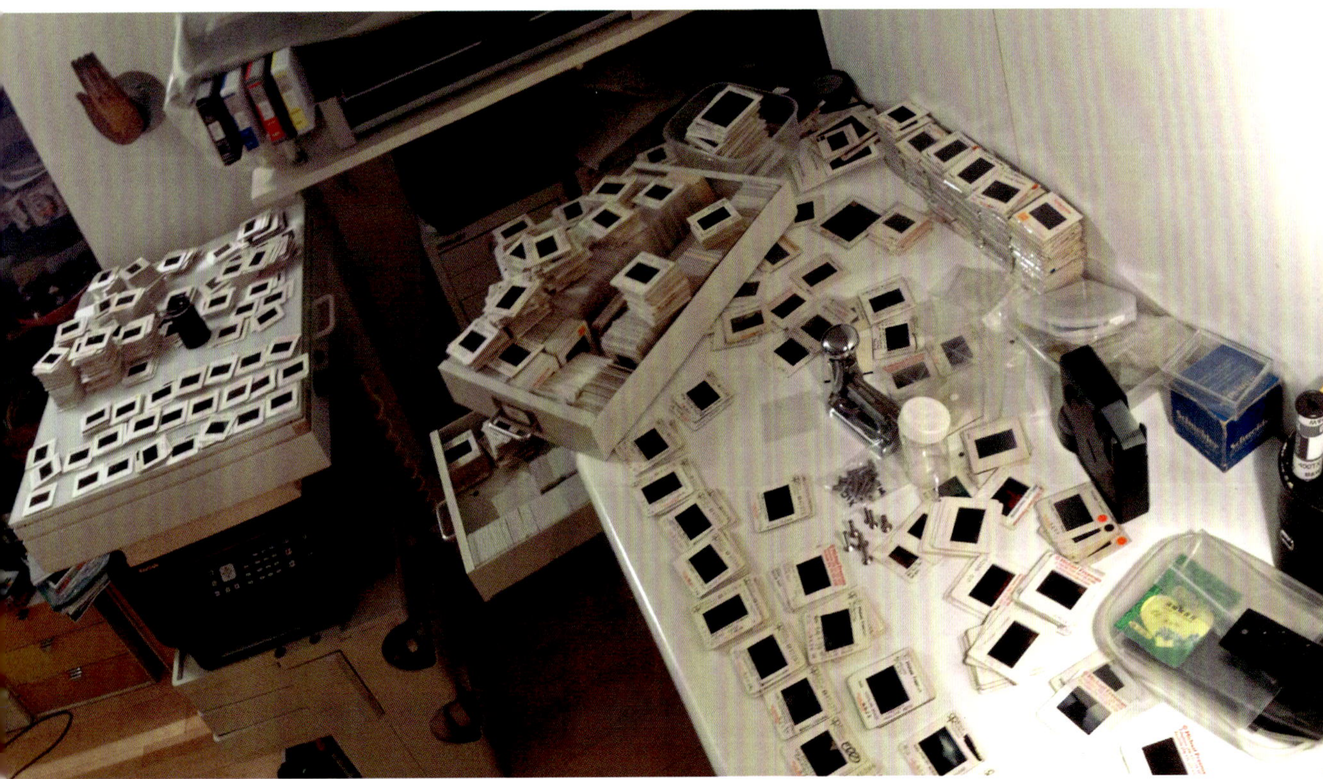

A backlit view of cargo being loaded onto a ship. I intentionally underexposed the Kodachrome, which exhibits an exceptionally smooth blue-grey gradient from the sun to the clear sky.

them being rather dark – or 'rich', as we preferred to say – which just encouraged everyone to look a little further into the transparency. Well, almost everyone. I got hauled up for consistently darker-than-average images by the picture editor of *Smithsonian* magazine, who handed me a photographic book by a Japanese photographer whose name I don't recall. The pictures were so dark that it was hard to make out what they were about. 'This is an extreme example,' she said. 'I want you to keep it and look at it, because your pictures are in danger of going that way, and it makes life difficult for Production.' Duly chastised, I reconsidered my 'dark phase', but I'll revisit it later, because it makes for an interesting creative exposure.

KODACHROME & VELVIA

Of all transparency films, Kodachrome acquired the most special reputation, as it had three measurable qualities that set it apart from all other films. First, it had very high resolution, because the emulsion was thin and the colour was added later in the processing (unique in the world of film). Second, the colours tended to be natural, meaning not so highly saturated, and professionals generally liked this. Third, the shadows were deep.

Lake Atitlán in Guatemala, shot on Kodachrome. This image displays good handling of highlights (without clipping), a smooth sky gradient, natural greens and rich shadows.

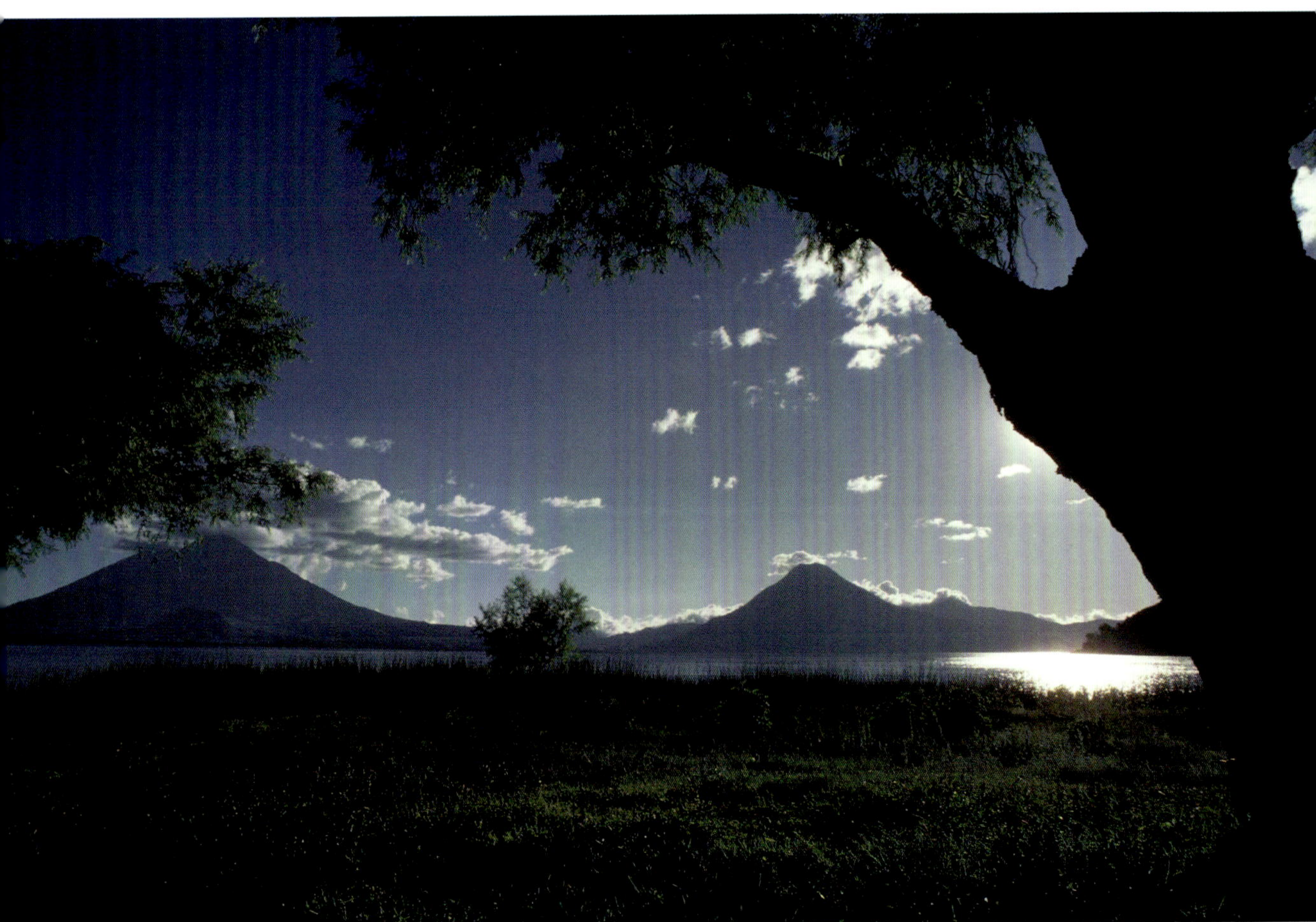

This calls for some explanation, because transparency film was actually contrasty, meaning it had little latitude and little detail in the shadows. Indeed, among transparency films, Kodachrome had a special reputation for the density of its darkest areas, which are known in the film business as its Dmax. The Dmax of any film never reached absolute black, but Kodachrome's was as close as you could get. Viewed on a light box, a good Kodachrome looked rich. This is one important way in which perception parts ways with measurement, as it was a quality admired by most professional users, provided the exposure was exact and no highlights were blown.

Less well known (and I must admit I paid very little attention to it during the 20 or so years I used Kodachrome), is that there is a blue colour cast to shadows, although this is not noticeable in shots taken in golden light, such as sunsets and warmly lit interiors. This is because the order of the red, green and blue layers is reversed in comparison to every other transparency film. With Kodachrome, red is at the top, meaning that the deeper the shadows, the denser the red layer is, which makes the blue more visible.

This density, and the visibly high resolution, especially along edges, is the key to understanding the Kodachrome 'look', which was always at its most distinctive in the darker areas. The shadows just above the Dmax were crushed, which was not at all a good thing from a film chemist's point of view, but visually it was interesting. The lowest 10–20 percent of the density scale had higher contrast because of that lower Dmax, which not only made shadows look rich, but also made deliberate underexposure look 'deep', rather than just getting uniformly darker.

Should you be tempted from all of this to take a deep dive into the reputation of Kodachrome and its appearance, you'll find a mass of online contradictions, which I suppose ought not to surprise, given that few people today have ever shot the film, or even seen it. Reputation has largely taken over from reality, and it's important to be aware that the special qualities of Kodachrome, or of any other make of reversal film, will be lost in digitization. You need either to look at them under a good loupe on a light box or, as a distant second best, reproduce them in print with a good knowledge of how and why the film was shot by the photographer. In fact, some of the most reliable places to see Kodachrome at its best are well-printed magazines and books of the 1970s, when production departments handled the film day in and day out. You could do a lot worse than look at Ernst Haas's acclaimed book *In America* (1975). We've tried to keep the same sensibility here in the printing of my Kodachromes in this book.

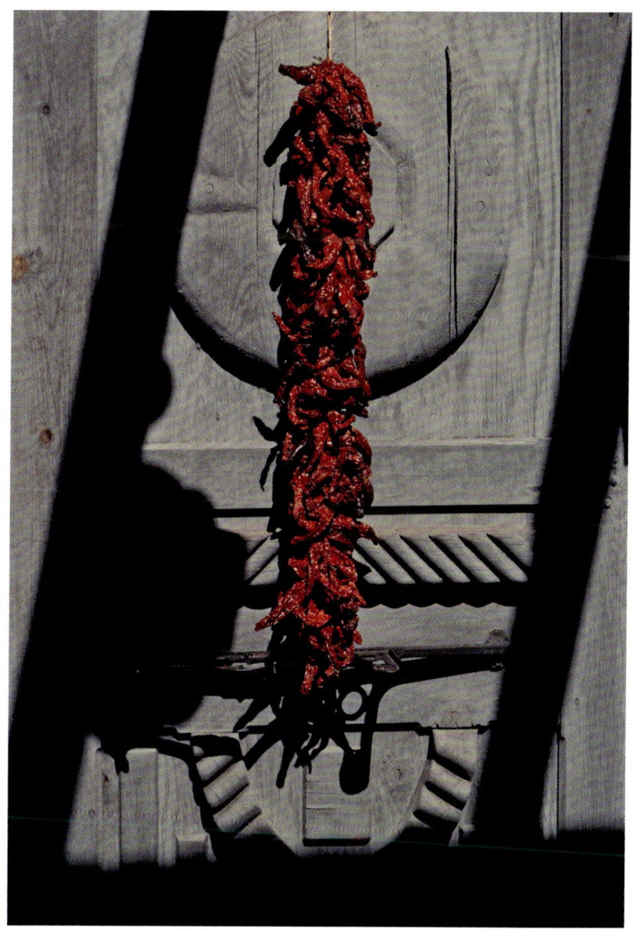

Chili peppers hanging to dry in New Mexico. Shot on Kodachrome, which was underexposed slightly to achieve rich reds, while still displaying neutral tones in the wood.

An old monastery in Ayutthaya, Thailand, shot on Velvia (main image and below right) and on Kodachrome (upper right). The Velvia is more saturated in all colours, and in particular has vibrancy in the green foliage.

Part of Velvia's appeal is its high overall colour saturation, especially its vibrant and slightly warm greens, which are evident in this picture of an Indian tea plantation in the Nilgiri Hills.

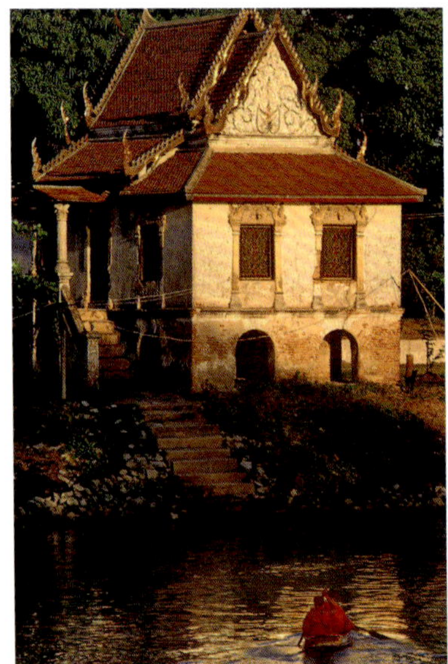

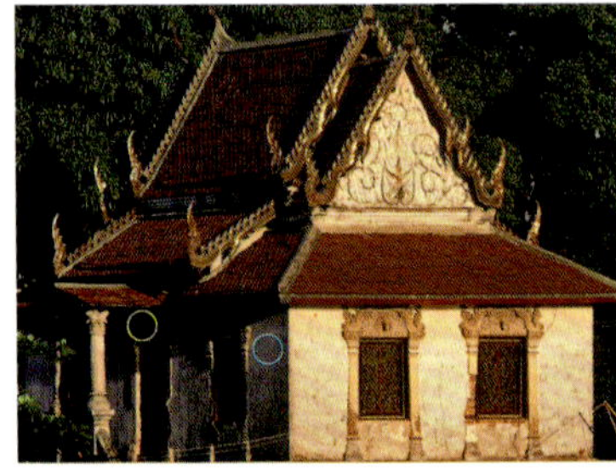

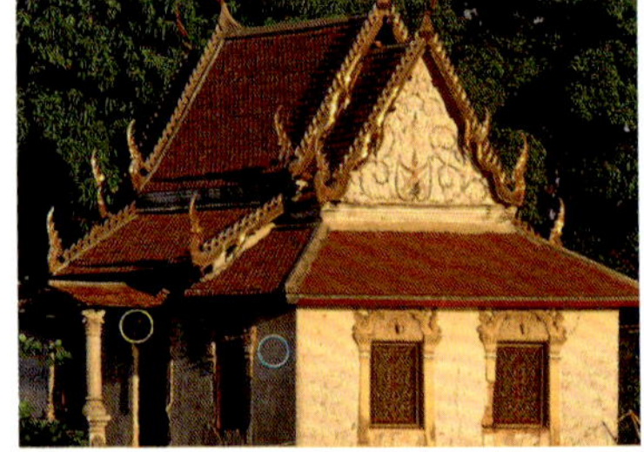

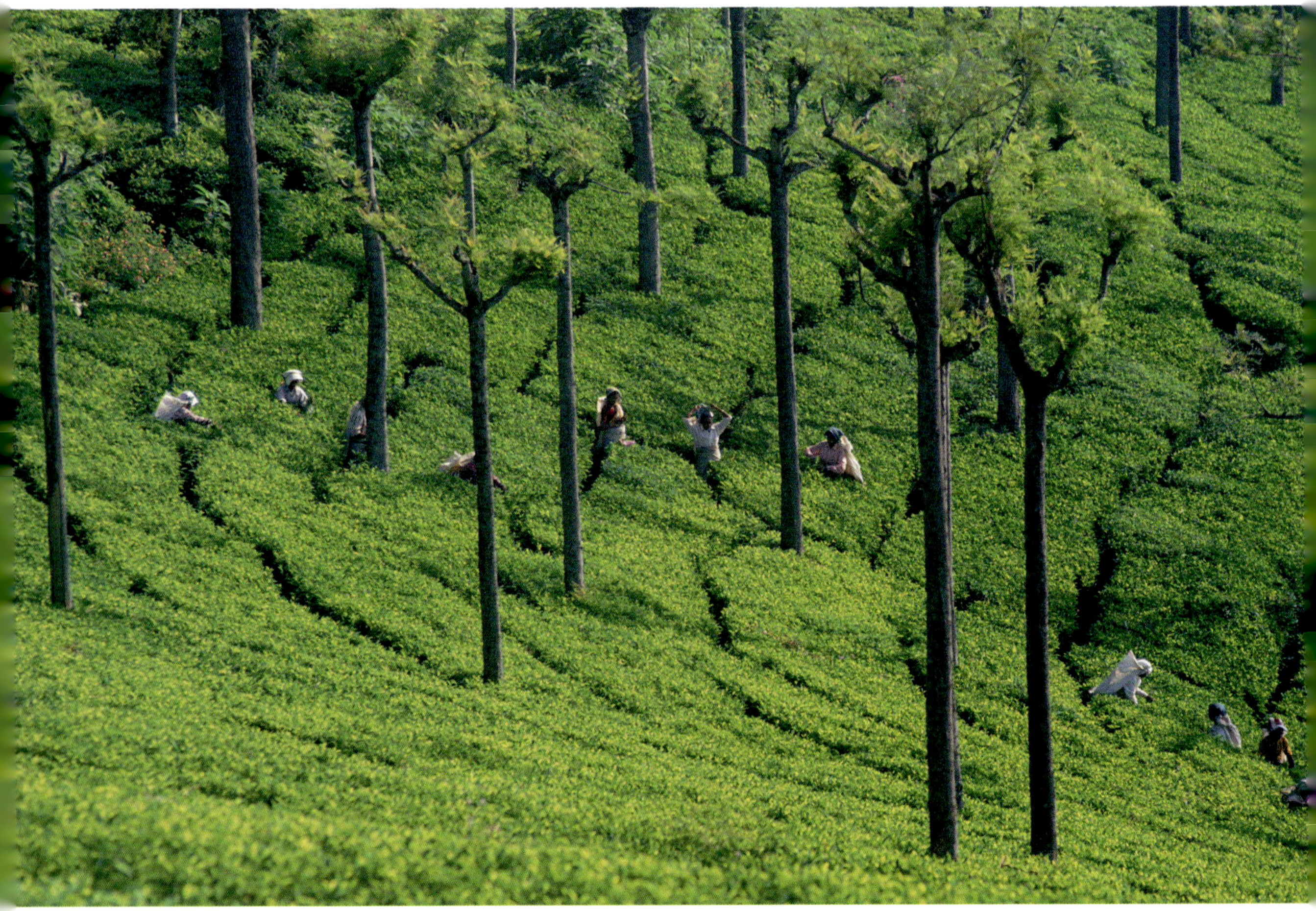

For most of the Kodachrome era, which was essentially the second half of the 20th century, the film stood apart from the workhorse films that used the E-4 and later E-6 processing chemistry – various types of Ektachrome (also made by Eastman Kodak) and Agfachrome. These were films that were designed to give a more natural appearance to skin and commercial products, had more latitude (meaning they were more forgiving of exposure mistakes) and could be pushed and pulled in processing to play with contrast. Consequently, most commercial photographers used them, and if you wanted to play creatively with overexposure, they were a more reliable choice than Kodachrome, which started to look rather harsh towards white.

Then, in 1990, Fujifilm launched Velvia (the name comes from 'Velvet Media'), as a direct challenge to Kodachrome. Velvia's Dmax was deeper, the sharpness was better, it could be processed in the simpler and more widely available E-6 chemistry and the colours were more saturated – and a lot of film photographers wanted more colour. Maybe not everyone, but as Velvia's success (and Kodachrome's decline) showed, most people enjoyed the vibrant greens and blues for which Velvia became famous. Think palm fronds waving against a gorgeous tropical sky and you have the perfect 'Velvia moment'.

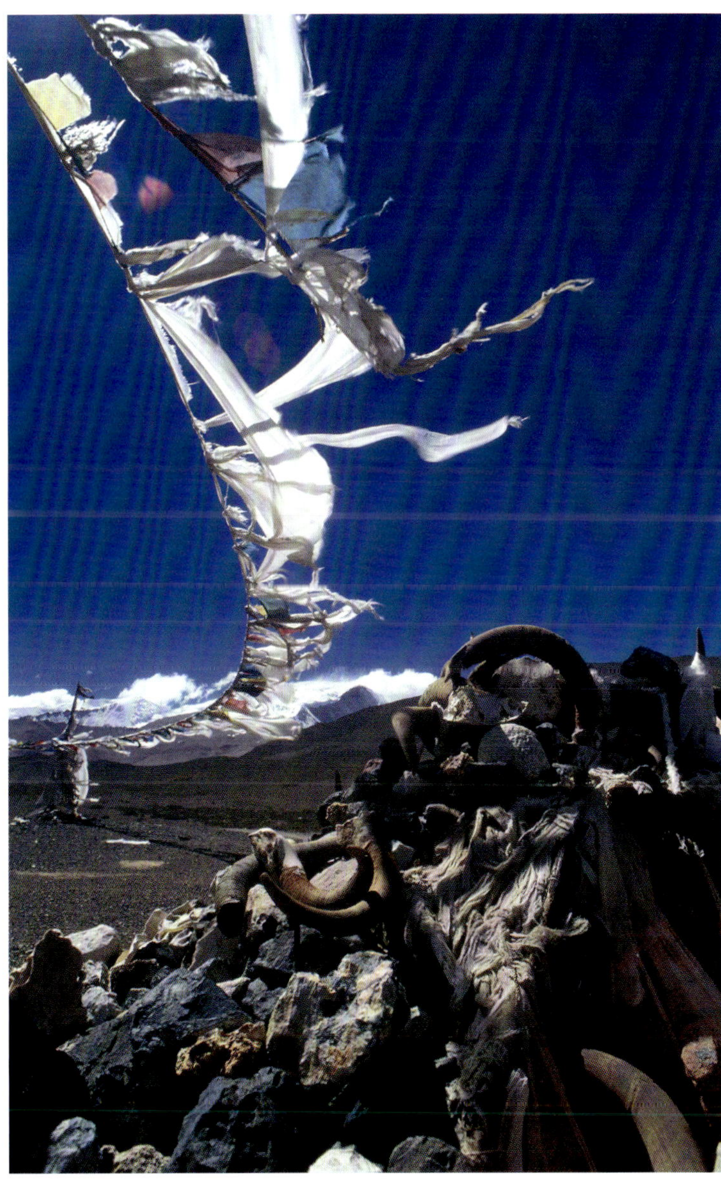

Blues were also targeted by the Fujifilm chemists developing Velvia, but drew some criticism for creating excessively saturated skies. Here, it is more obvious than usual on a high-altitude Tibetan plateau.

COLOUR FILM CREATIVE STRATEGIES

While there are important differences in the way that film and digital sensors record light, any film effect can be reproduced when you process a digital image, albeit with varying degrees of difficulty. The essential issue is whether you *want* a film look.

Technically, modern sensors – particularly the larger ones – win hands down on the range of tonal information they can collect, but aesthetically it's still an open question. There's a Kodachrome story that illustrates this well. The original film was improved in 1961 with the launch of Kodachrome II, which the company boasted was '…sharper than regular Kodachrome. The emulsion is thinner and scatters the light less'. It was also less contrasty: 'Shadow areas are softer and more "open", and dark areas don't go dark so fast with underexposure.'

However, one year later, an inter-office correspondence at Eastman Kodak revealed that despite its overall good reception, there was some criticism from 'salonists and other camera club detractors' who said that Kodachrome II lacked the 'Rembrandt blacks' of regular Kodachrome. 'In other words, Kodachrome II has been criticized for not having some of the glaring faults of Kodachrome film.'

Fast forward more than 40 years to the launch of Photoshop's Shadows/Highlights tool and evangelist Russell Brown's lyrical enthusiasm for opening up any shadows. Why wouldn't you want such a cool feature? Well, you might want the image to look mysterious and expressive, for one. The engineer's arguments tend to be based on having lots of accurate data, whereas creative photography is concerned with how much information to show and how much to withhold, and not just the overall quantity.

Kodachrome, even when it was improved, had serious limitations in contrast and exposure latitude. However, as has been the case throughout photography's history, imaginative people not only found workarounds, but also how to turn those limitations into advantages. I started my photography in the early 1970s, when Kodachrome was universally used for magazine work in 35mm, and just about everyone came to like Kodachrome's way with shadows – and also its way

Looking vertically down into a gold refinery's furnace where ingots are being smelted – a seriously hot camera position. I was using Kodachrome and exposed down in order to retain richness in the oranges and yellows.

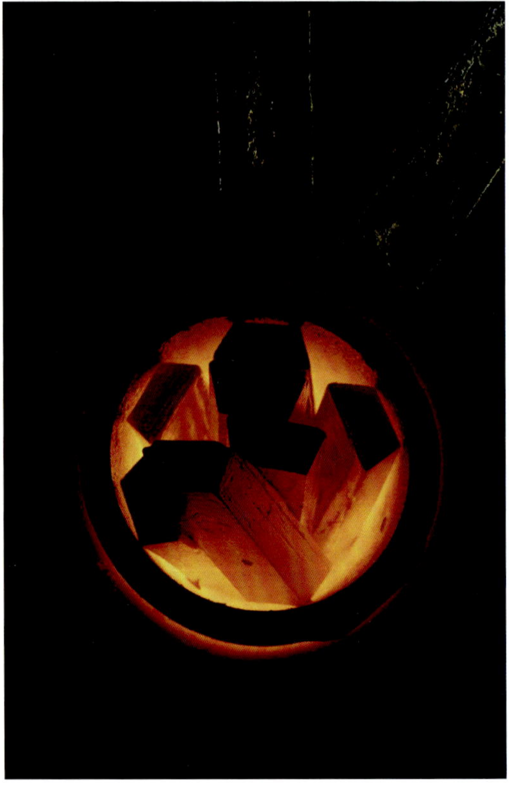

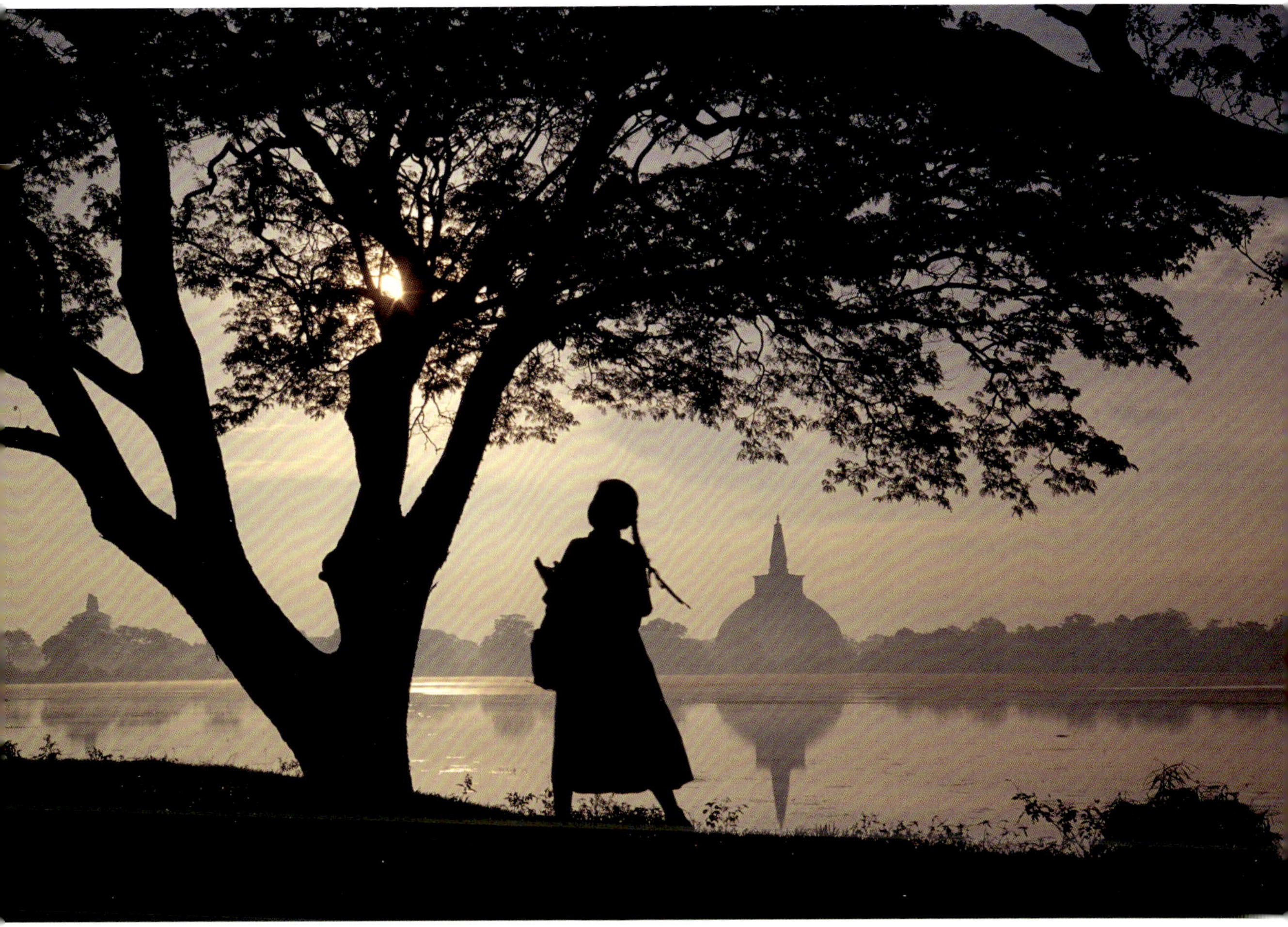

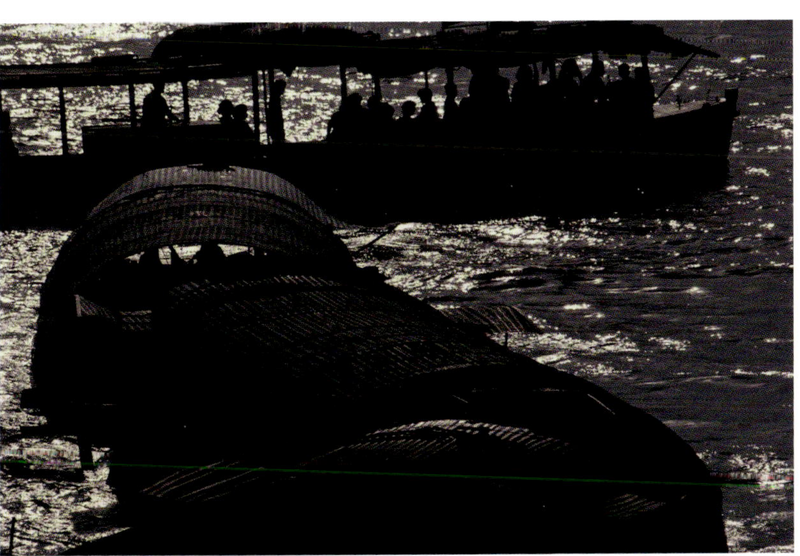

A Sri Lankan schoolgirl walks silhouetted against the sunrise over the Basawakkulama tank (an artificial body of water) and the Ruwanwelisaya Dagoba in Anuradhapura, Sri Lanka.

Rice barges and a ferryboat pass each other in late-afternoon sunlight on the Chao Phraya River, Bangkok.

with underexposure, however strange this may seem now. One thing that everyone agreed on, from photographers to printers, was to never allow the highlights to blow out through too much exposure. If blown, they looked terrible and the image was unusable, and this alone drove exposures downwards. It became interesting to see what happened to the darker tones. How dark could a slide be and still look good? It turned out that on a light box and under a loupe, it could be one or two stops darker and look unusually interesting.

I should say that all of the above applied to photographers who were trying to express themselves and be distinctive in the way they saw, framed, composed and exposed – trying, in other words, to impose their personality on a photographed scene. Although this sounds very much in tune with today's social media-driven photography, where self-expression is totally accepted, 'subjective' photography at that time was at odds with the Neue Sachlichkeit (New Objectivity) movement that started in the 1920s.

The philosophy of the New Objectivity movement was to let the mechanics of the camera and optics dictate the imagery, with the individual photographer taking a back seat. It stemmed from a growing fascination after the First World War in the aesthetics of machinery, industry and construction. After the Second World War, as colour photography became a practical possibility, an interest in 'objective', dispassionate styles of photography resurfaced, but so too did 'subjective' photography, which was promoted by the Fotoform group of photographers.

Although Ernst Haas was never a member of Fotoform, he was definitely in the subjective camp. In a 1961 interview with the Swiss arts magazine *DU*, he wrote: 'Bored with obvious reality, I find my fascination in transforming it into a subjective point of view. Without touching my subject, I want to come to the moment when,

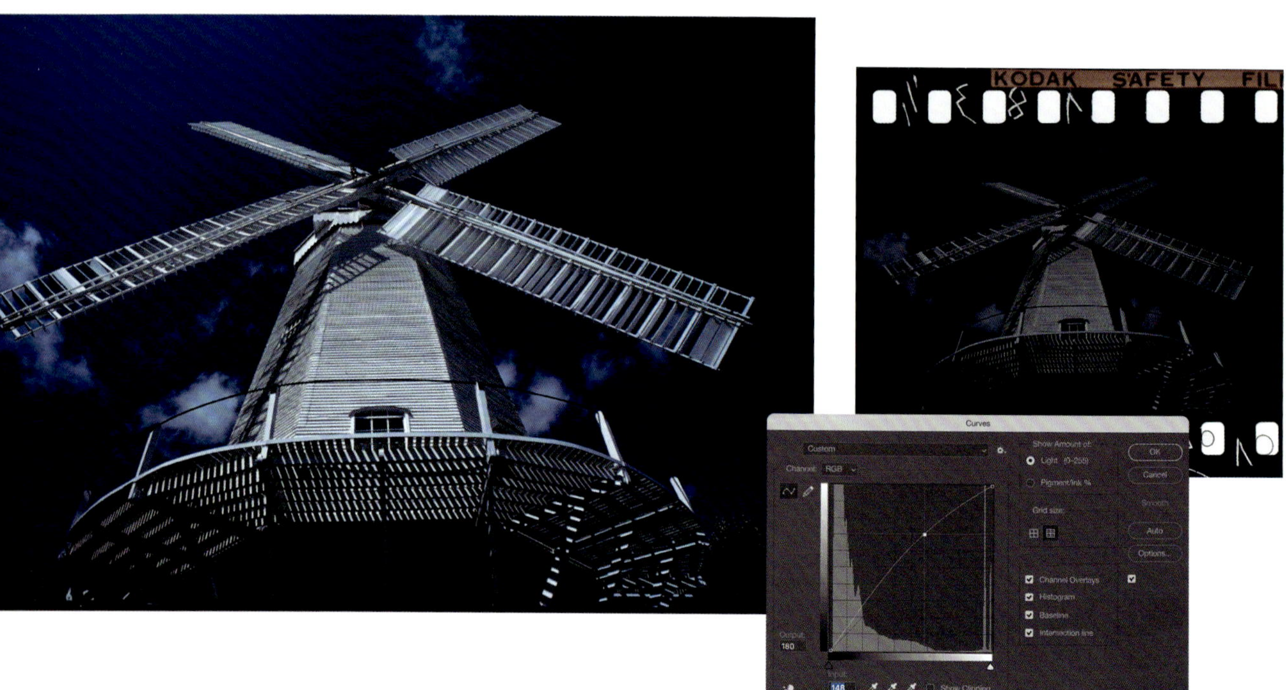

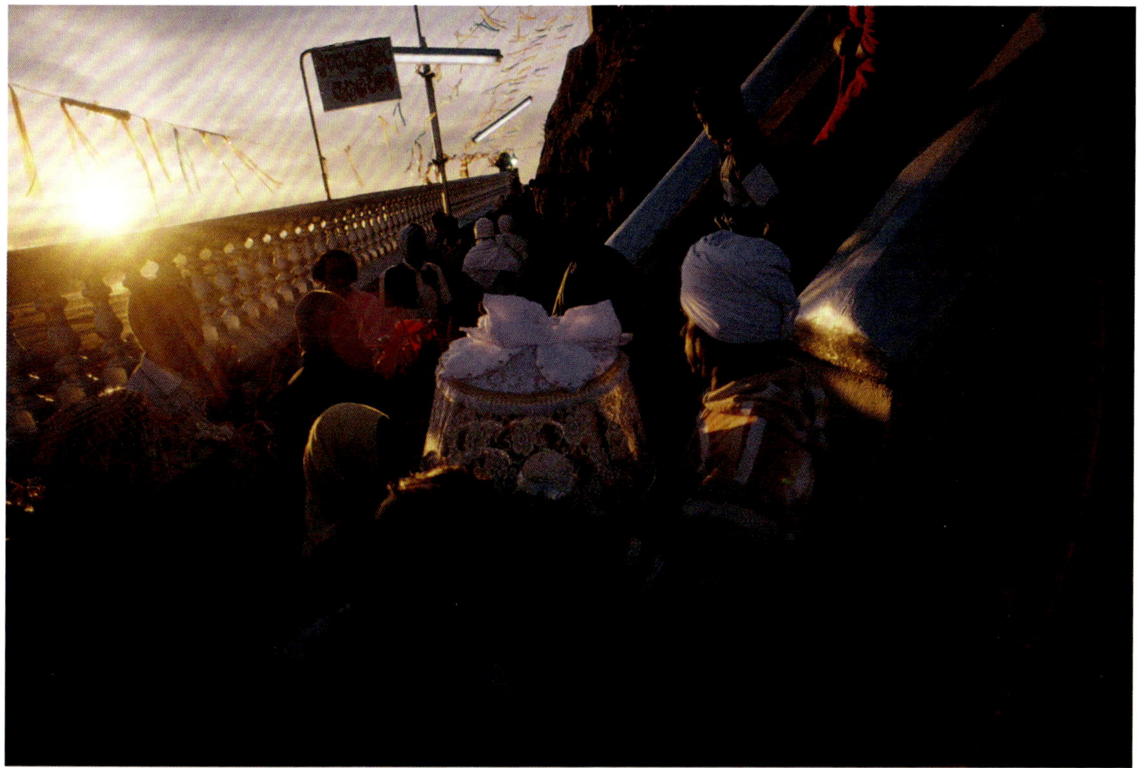

A sunrise festival at the summit of Adam's Peak, Sri Lanka. Shooting on Kodachrome, directly into the sun, naturally challenges the film's dynamic range, but highlight compression ensures that the highlights are held.

through pure concentration of seeing, the composed picture becomes more made than taken.' This was a self-imposed challenge.

For decades, there had been expressive ways with photography that involved double or multiple exposure, retouching and compositing different images together. Surrealist photography, for example, had taken this route. However, Haas and other 35mm colour photographers of the time, such as Saul Leiter and Erwin Fieger, stayed 'straight' in that they photographed only what was in front of them – as Haas said, 'without touching my subject'. This meant they had to work hard to find images that qualified as being 'uniquely seen'. Exposure was an important tool, but it was combined with new ways of composing, different camera angles, alternative lens focal lengths, unexpected reflections and so on. In the end, everything photographed was of a real place at a particular moment, and so stayed 'real', which added to the challenge.

The 1970s in particular were an inventive time for colour photography, both editorially, with colour magazines at their peak, and in advertising, which was enjoying a vogue for visual entertainment in New York and London. There were more new lenses coming out than at any time before or since, including dramatic wide-angles (20mm and 24mm), long telephotos, fast telephotos and catadioptric mirror lenses. It was a time of breaking out and of experimentation, and everyone wanted to be different. That meant unusual compositions, underexposure, overexposure, motion blur and so on. This wasn't the first time, of course. There was the post-war 'Beat generation' rebellion centred largely in New York, then the

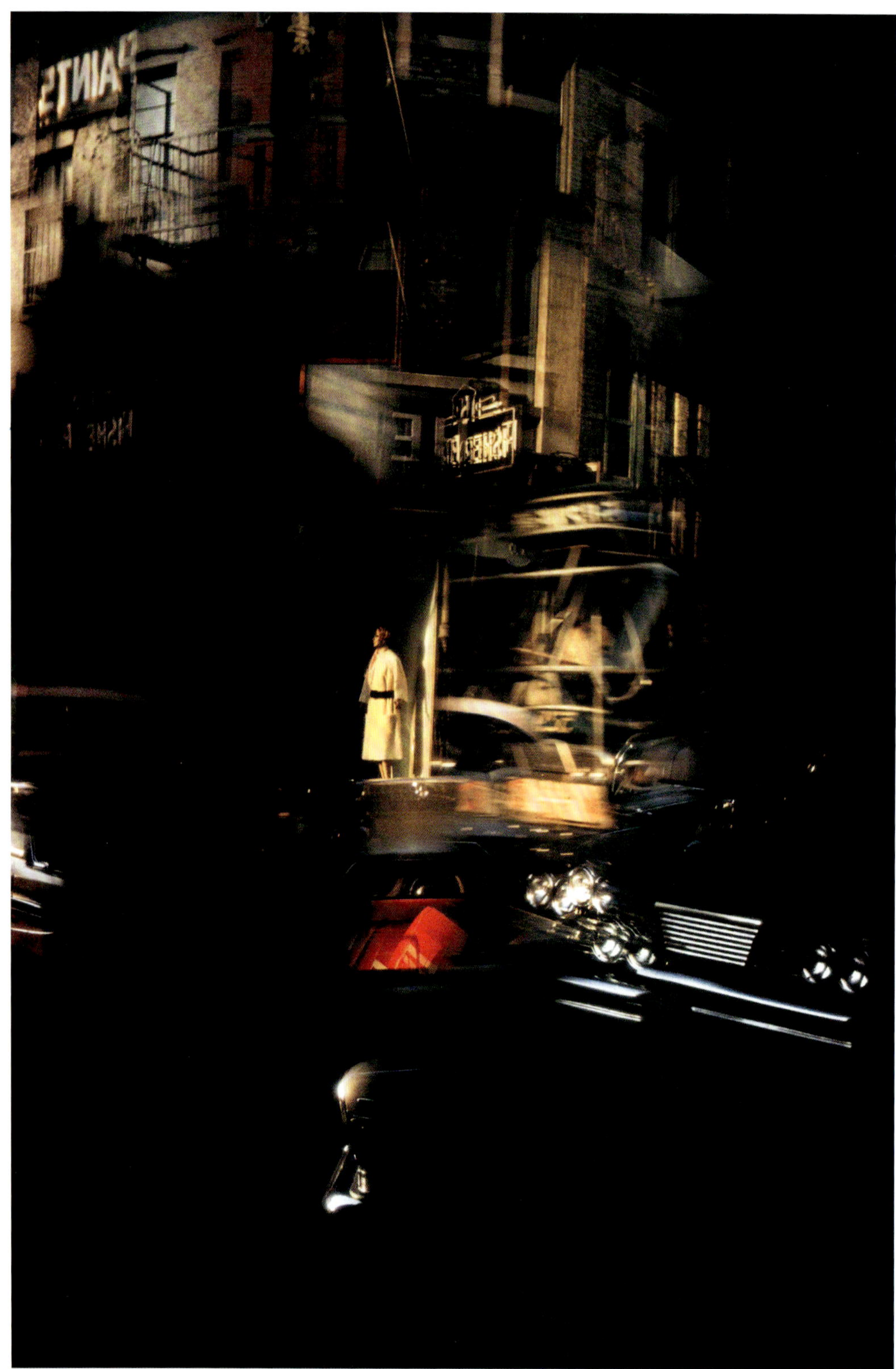

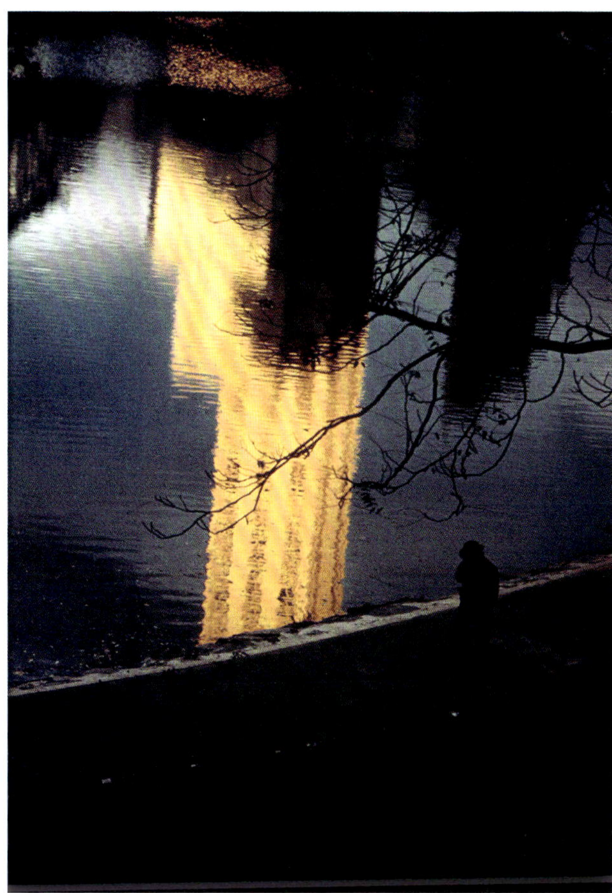

'Swinging Sixties' in London, but the 1970s were very much in colour and had all these new lenses.

The rationale for underexposure was a combination of visual drama (often between small, bright subject or elements and extremely dark background) and the unexpected (a traditionally normally exposed scene shown very dark). Since the 1950s, photographers such as Harlem-based Roy DeCarava had experimented with unusually dark, low-register images in black and white. However, colour added a new dimension, because it challenged the realism that was normally associated with colour photography. This alone made it more exciting for creative photographers to play with extremes of tone and to be different.

If there was time, what often happened was that the photographer would bracket their exposures, and in a high-contrast situation with some strong highlights, they might throw in some significant underexposure for a frame or two, just to see what would happen. These exposure experiments were then judged on a light box when the film came back from the lab, and there were occasional happy surprises. There was also experimentation at the opposite end of the scale – overexposed, washed-out images with hints of pastel colours – but Kodachrome didn't handle highlight compression as well as other films.

What follows is a suite of six creative strategies that are inspired by film in general and Kodachrome in particular. In subsequent chapters, we will explore ways of applying these strategies to modern digital photography. In particular, I'm anxious to show that while it was film that motivated photographers to shoot like this, these are still valid exposure styles, regardless of the recording medium.

Two Kodachromes of New York by the Swiss photographer Ernst Haas, who took an impressionist approach in his editorial and private work. These were shot for his 1953 picture story, *Magic City*, which ran over two consecutive issues in *Life* magazine. This was the first time the magazine ran a major feature based entirely on photography.

TEXTUREGROUND SILHOUETTE

Textureground is a word I have invented to set this style of shooting apart from the more ordinary kind of silhouette that is taken against a bright backdrop, such as the sky. Here, instead, the background against which the silhouetted shape stands is a properly textured surface in its own right.

Creative silhouettes in photography are nothing new – Edward Steichen made a powerful image of the sculptor Rodin in his studio in 1905, silhouetted against a lit sculpture – but colour film created new possibilities. Ernst Haas used this technique in his *Canyon de Chelly, Arizona, 1960*, where the spreading branches of a tree frame the White House cliff-dwelling ruins beyond. My copycat version from 1979 (opposite below) is similar in principle, and was taken at Point Lobos on a brilliantly clear late afternoon – clear skies and strong sunlight are what makes this kind of picture.

It was a useful strategy. In 1957, Gordon Parks was assigned by *Life* magazine to photograph a major series on crime, which was later published in book form by Steidl as *The Atmosphere of Crime*. Parks used the early 'Rembrandt black' version of Kodachrome, often at night and frequently with silhouettes. They added to the dark and uncertain tenor of the story, and also conveniently helped with the film's slow speed. By shooting silhouettes against bright street lights and displays, manageable handheld shutter speeds were possible.

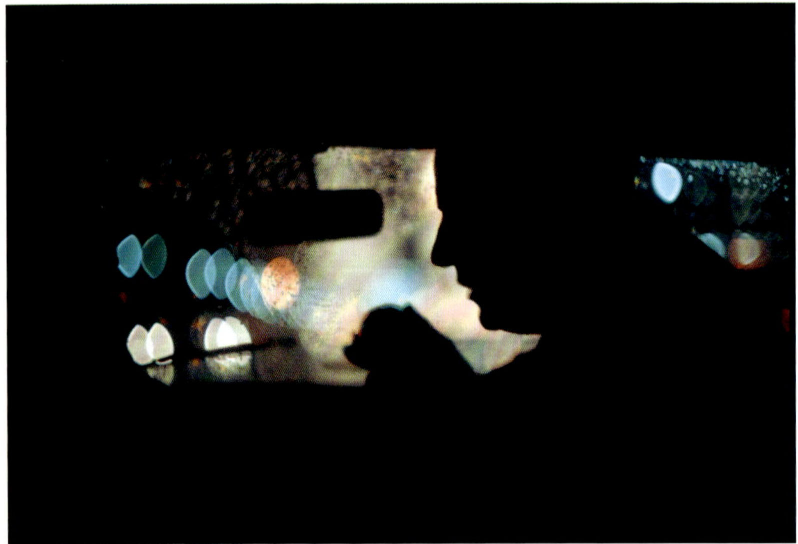

From Gordon Parks's 1957 series *The Atmosphere of Crime*.

A bull moose in the Gardner River, Yellowstone National Park, Wyoming, silhouetted against reflections of the afternoon sun.

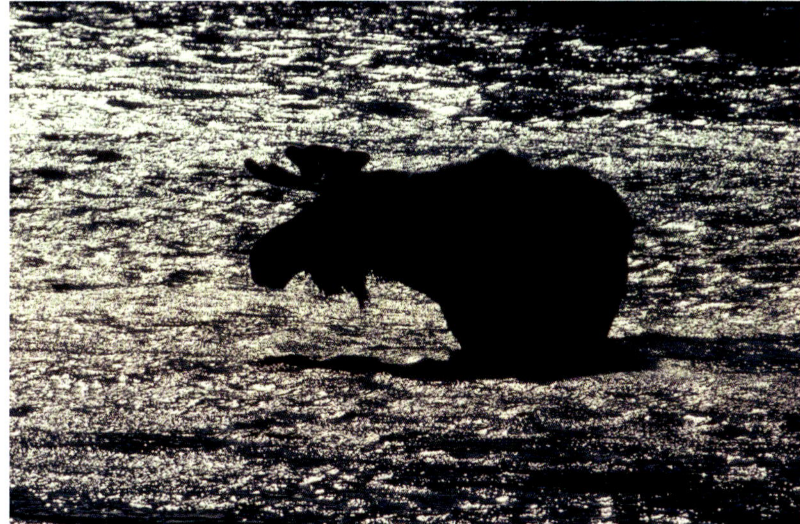

Deep in shadow, the silhouette of an old cypress tree against a sunlit wall at Point Lobos, California. Full depth of field is important for this kind of picture.

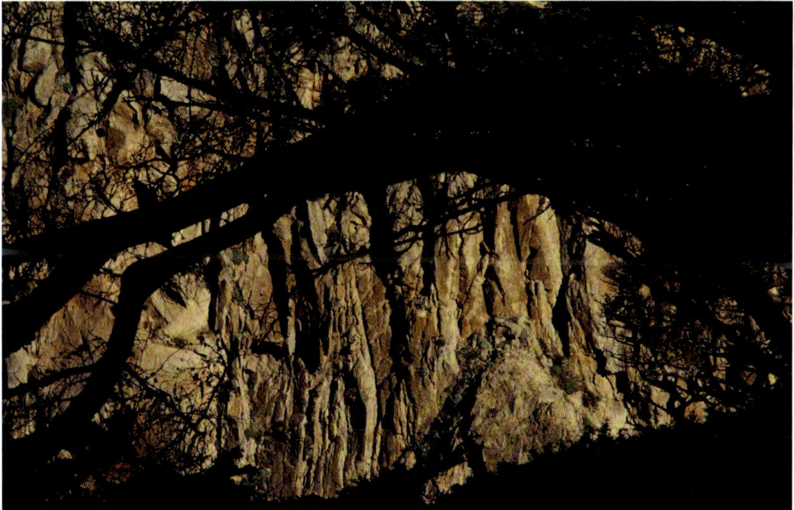

I mentioned that the key to this style lies in the background, which itself should be rich and well textured. Ordinarily, that would preclude a sky, but with the right conditions, even a cloudless day could yield possibilities with Kodachrome. On page 51 is just such an example, which I took at the Greek port of Piraeus. A ship was being unloaded by crane (these were pre-container days), and I realized that if I could get the sun obscured briefly by the pallet, I'd get a soft, spreading halo. The experiment here was to see just how dark I could go and still have a readable image. As with all of these underexposure styles, there's a deliberate element of being a little mysterious, challenging the viewer to work out what's happening and above all to simply eliminate information from the darkest shadows. Note that the blue sky is not at all saturated, as it would have been with Velvia, but that particular film was a long way off. Besides, I *liked* that subtle only-just-in-colour effect.

HARD AXIAL SUNLIGHT

Axial or near-axial sunlight, from behind the camera, has a reputation for being flat and for being the opposite of atmospheric. It certainly runs the risk of being monotonous, a little like a sunlight version of on-camera flash. However, here again, Kodachrome handled it differently from other emulsions, just as long as there was good natural contrast within the subject and the film was slightly underexposed. By 'good natural contrast' I mean that the surfaces of the subject have a wide range of reflectivity – light and dark next to each other – and possibly contrasting colours next to each other as well.

Boom, Belgium, 1988, by Harry Gruyaert.

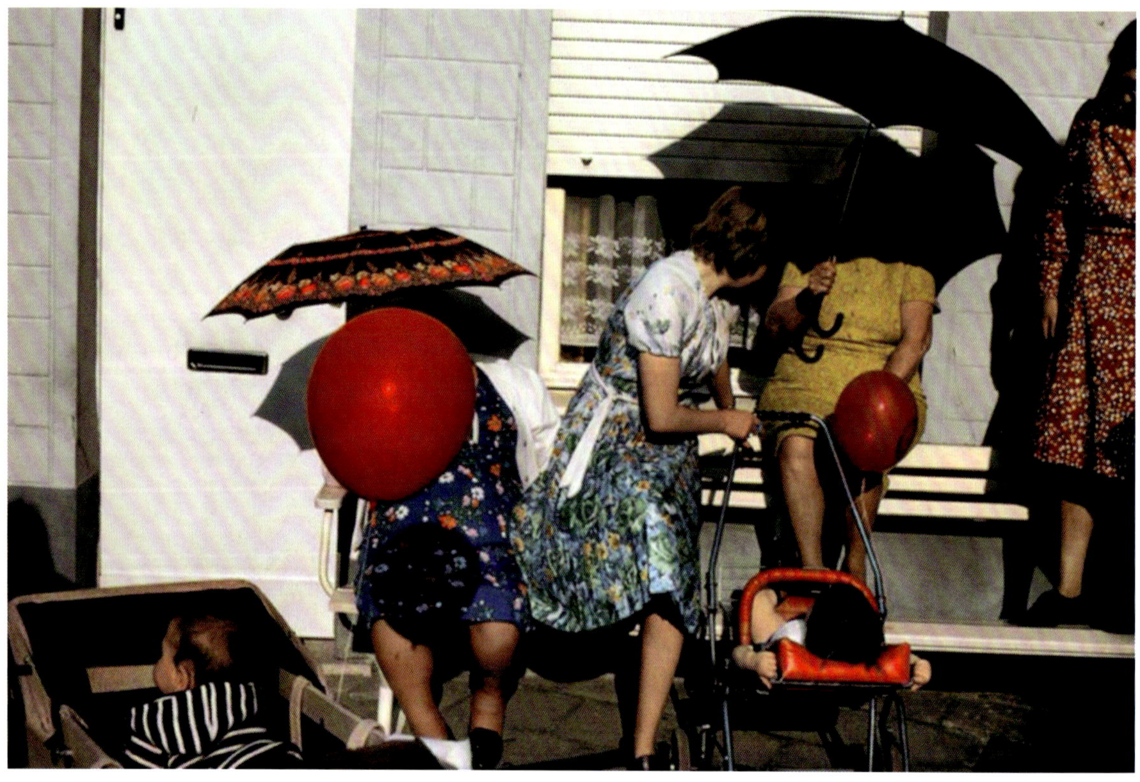

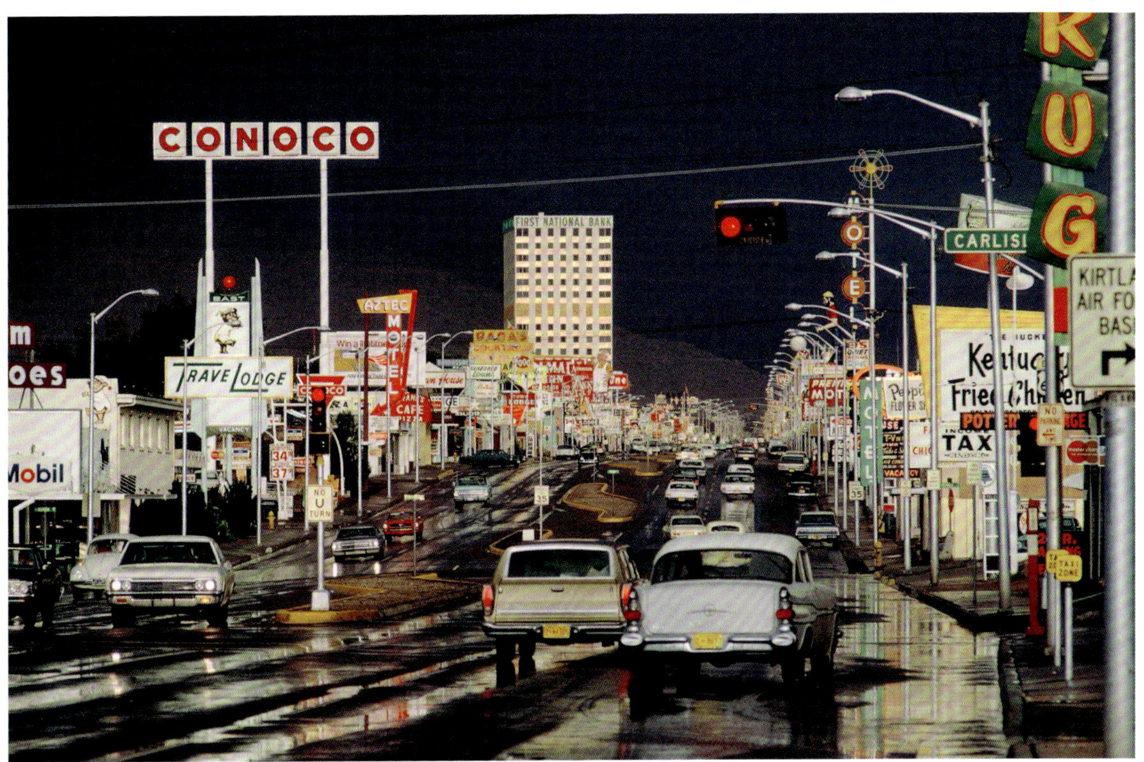

Route 66, Albuquerque, New Mexico, 1969, by Ernst Haas. A clearing storm provides a dark backdrop in this classic image with the low sun behind the camera.

The Belgian photographer, Harry Gruyaert, was very much a colourist. Like many who grew up in photography in the 1960s committed to Kodachrome, he frequently used this viewpoint in hard, low sunlight as a way of getting rich, deep colours. In *Boom, Belgium, 1988* (opposite), red balloons overlap with the printed dresses and umbrellas of mothers with children, while every face is turned away. It's a picture about colour, and the Kodachrome colours are deep; although there's a white door in shot, in Gruyaert's exposure, it's darker than white.

However, one of the most spectacular photographs using this style of exposure is Ernst Haas's *Route 66, Albuquerque, New Mexico, 1969* (above). This is one of his best-known images, which was taken after a storm with the sun very low and behind the camera. The automobiles and hundreds of billboards (Haas used a medium telephoto lens that compresses them) stand out in rich colour against the almost black sky of the receding storm clouds. This image was included in Haas's 1975 book, *In America*, and was later included in *Ernst Haas Colour Photography* in 1989. In the more recent title, it is printed with a little less contrast and a not-quite-so-deep black sky, while on the photographer's estate website, the shadows are opened up even more. I wonder what the actual transparency looks like, and what Haas's preferred version would have been, although I strongly suspect it would be the original printing, which the photographer would have had a say in.

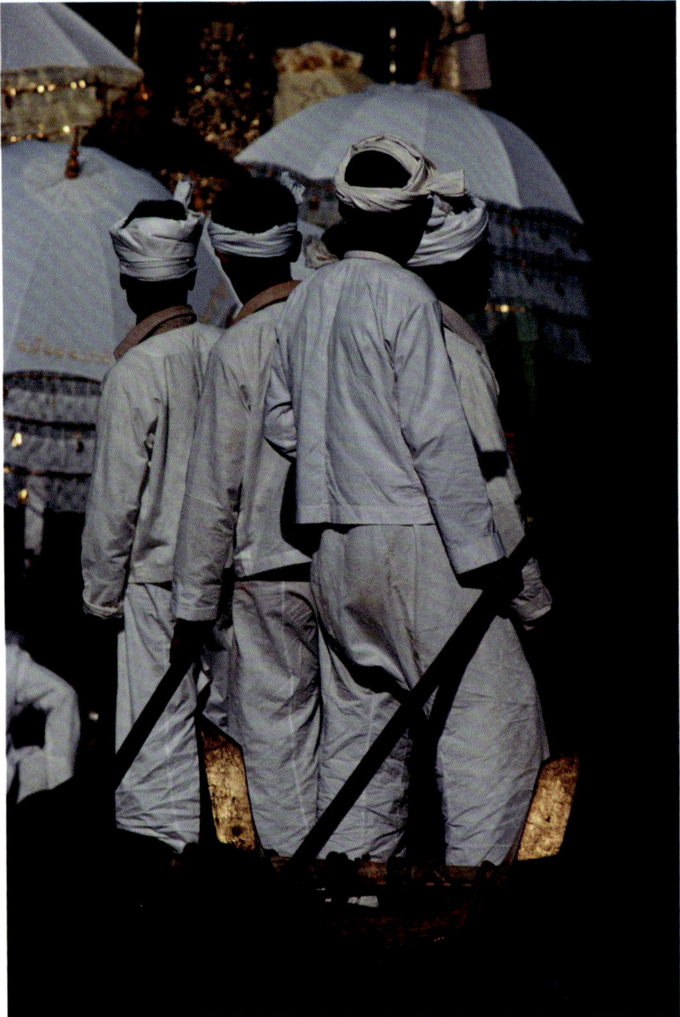

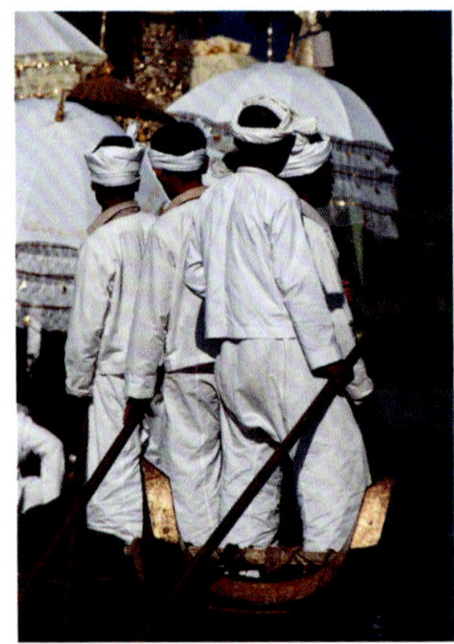

2.

My Kodachrome images here are personal choices, and by no means to everyone's taste. The men in white attire (left and above) were leg rowers on Inle Lake in Myanmar's Shan State. This was a ceremony I was covering in which some particularly sacred Buddha statues were rowed around the villages on the shallow lake. This was a moment when nothing much was happening, so I took time off to experiment. Normally in an editorial context you would be looking for scenes that explain what is going on, but this is the opposite. I was happy that all of the rowers' faces were turned away, as even one facing the camera would take over the picture by attracting attention.

1.

Leg rowers dressed in white for the annual Phaung Daw U festival on Lake Inle, Myanmar. These images show the original shot on Kodachrome, which was deliberately exposed down (1), and the same image opened up in digital processing for a more conventional version (2).

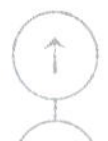

Using the selective view of a telephoto lens, the photograph is intentionally about gold against white cloth. For this reason, I exposed down in order to strengthen the richness of the two gold boat panels at the bottom of the frame, knowing that Kodachrome was especially good at holding the saturation of warmer colours like these when darker. This also maximized the texture of the white cloth.

I've included a second variation after having the transparency drum scanned, just to show what a more 'normally exposed' version would look like. This latter image, while 'normal', appears completely different, because the water and sky at the right of the frame add a sense of depth, and the patches of gold no longer dominate. The eye goes more naturally towards the brightest parts of the picture.

The second picture (below) was taken at a livestock market near Peshawar in Pakistan, and is very much about texture – of skin and of the well-worn cotton clothing. Again, it was a deliberate and personal choice, and my reasoning was that a 'normal' exposure of about one stop brighter (inset, adjusted in ACR from a drum scan) would appear more contrasty overall, with the man's shirt attracting more attention. As I exposed it, the textural detail dominates and appears more similar between skin and cloth.

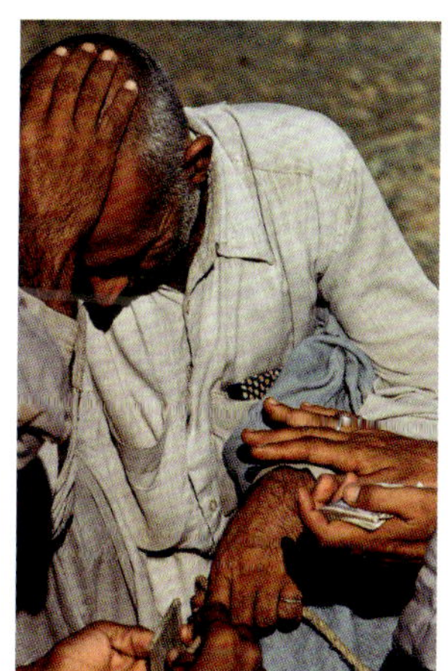

2.

Negotiations at a livestock market in Peshawar, Pakistan, also on Kodachrome. Shown as shot (1) and opened up digitally by one stop (2).

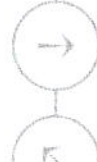

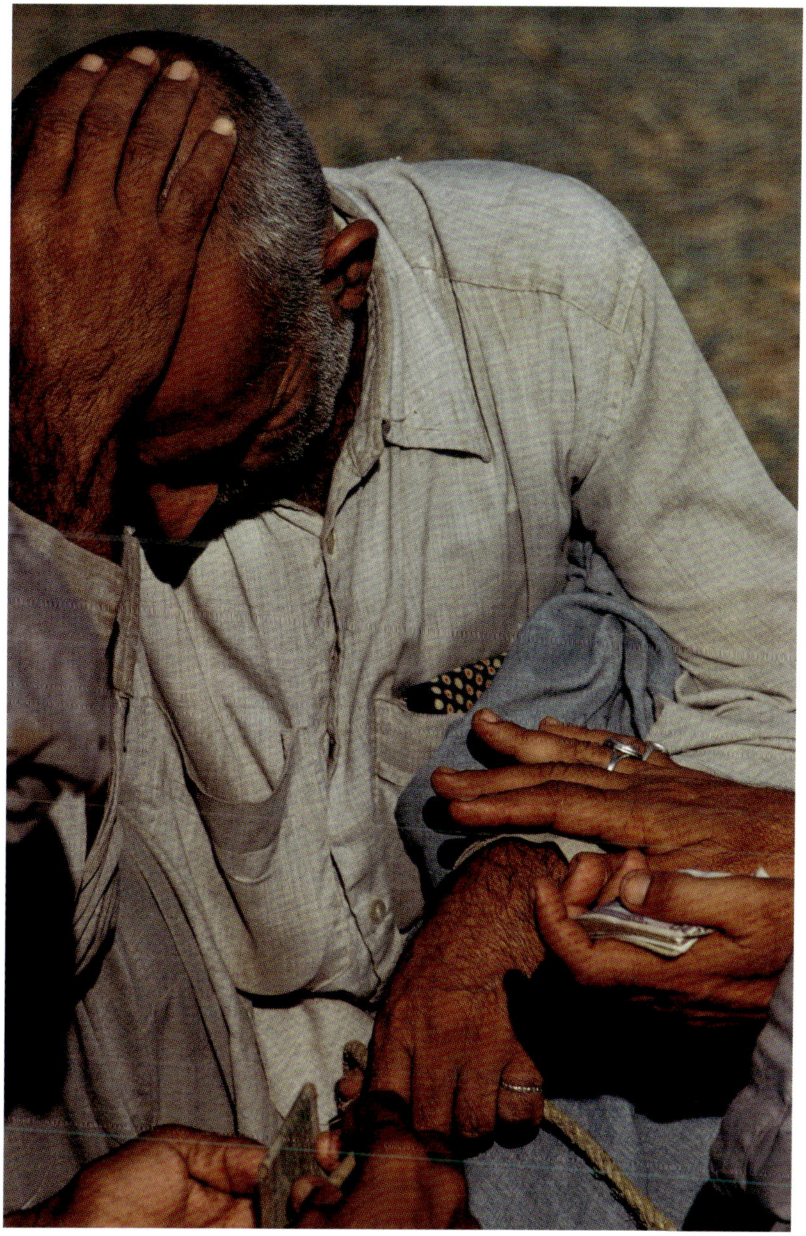

1.

RICH SPECULAR HIGHLIGHTS

Specular highlights are bright, sparkling reflections, which are generally very small. It's an accepted convention that they are excluded from any exposure calculations; as they're small, they can just blow out and no one minds. In fact, having them very bright and tiny often helps the sense of contrast in a picture.

However, this is a different, more extreme approach. If you expose *for* the specular highlights, you will end up with a photograph that is very dark overall, but the creative question is whether that will yield anything interesting. It's experimental in that you expose and compose to hold a few bright elements, and then wait and see what happens to the rest of the picture. Kodachrome, remember, was a film that needed a complex processing line, of which there were very few (often one per country), so popping round to the local photography shop wasn't an option, and you had to wait. As with any extreme exposure, the uncertainty of how it could turn out on film usually meant that you reserved this option for when there was enough time to take a few frames, some of them more normally exposed and then one or two for experiment.

This really is one of the most extreme underexposures that you can give, as mid-tones are usually where most of the meaning and action of a photograph takes place, so those areas would usually be prioritized on colour transparency film. By comparison, specular highlights are usually just reflections of the sun, and are so much brighter that they would always blow out.

Nowadays, digital HDR sequences allow you to hold everything and squeeze it into a normal-range photograph, but this wasn't possible with colour film. However, film has the advantage of rolling off smoothly towards white, with no clipping, and this certainly helped everyone accept overexposed small, bright highlights. It also means that underexposing by, say, a couple of stops – as in the case of the L&C building, opposite – made it look like the specular highlights had been fully recovered. Nevertheless, it's an unusual choice and almost completely abstracts the scene. That, of course, is the idea.

L&C Building, downtown New Orleans, photographed on Kodachrome 25.

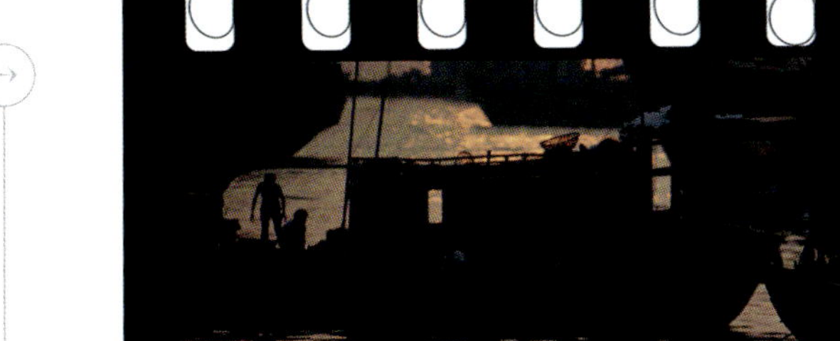

Cheung Chau harbour, Hong Kong, photographed on Kodachrome 25.

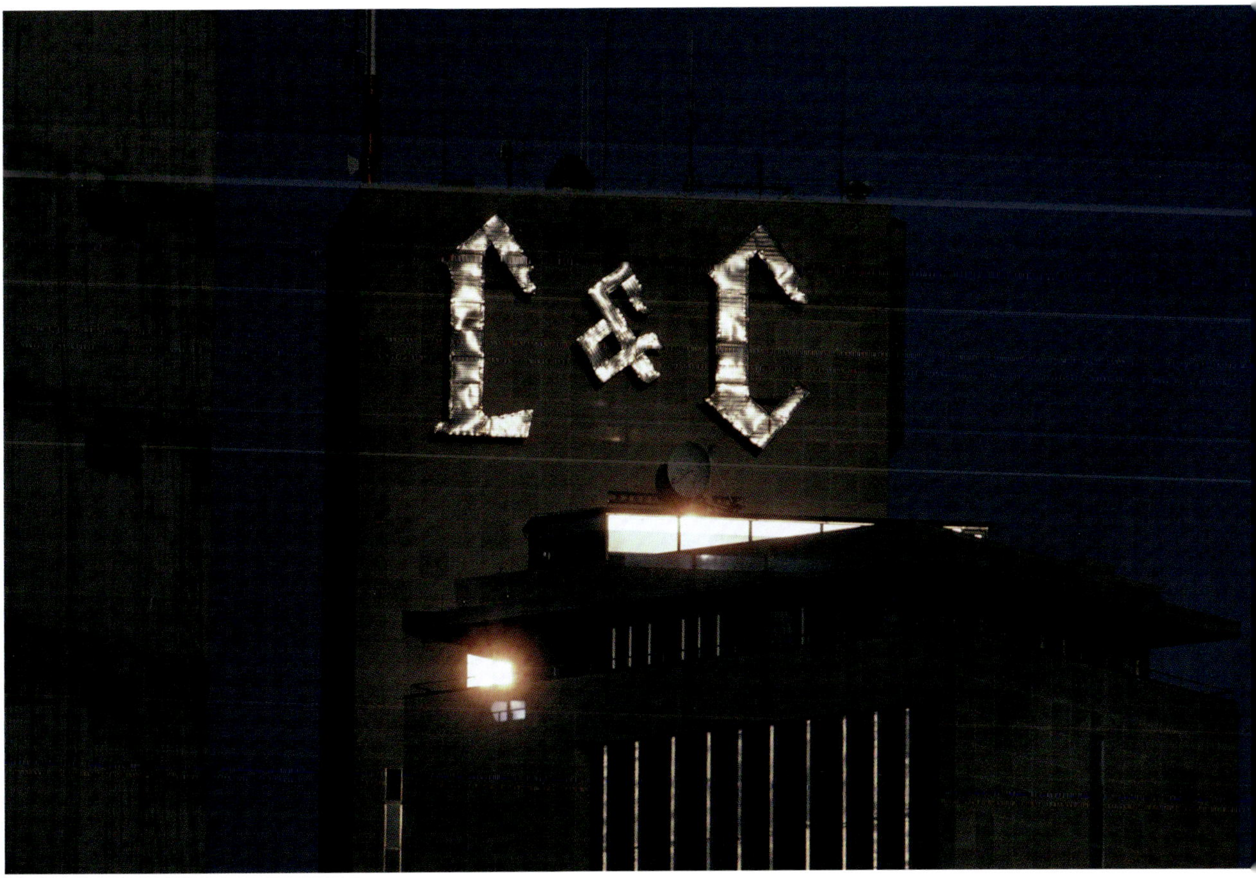

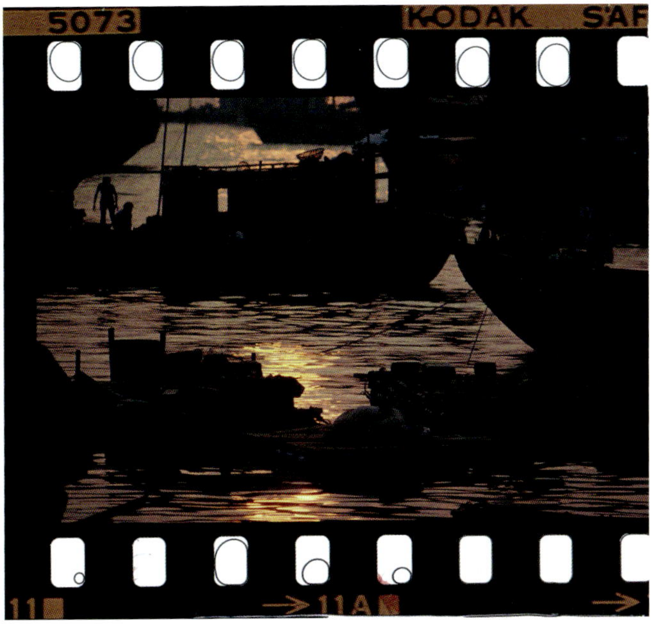

DEEP SHADOW BLOCKS

Of all the styles here, this is the quintessential solution to Kodachrome's shadow-detail crushing, and it was used a lot by Ernst Haas. Very simply, when you had hard shadows from bright sunlight and they were prominent because the sun was to one side, you embraced the fact that they were inky and featureless, and used them as graphic blocks.

I photographed this Buddhist temple on Ektachrome film. I exposed for the lit wall to maintain a reasonable exposure for the view outside, which inevitably meant that the interior shadows would be very dark and become a key element in the composition.

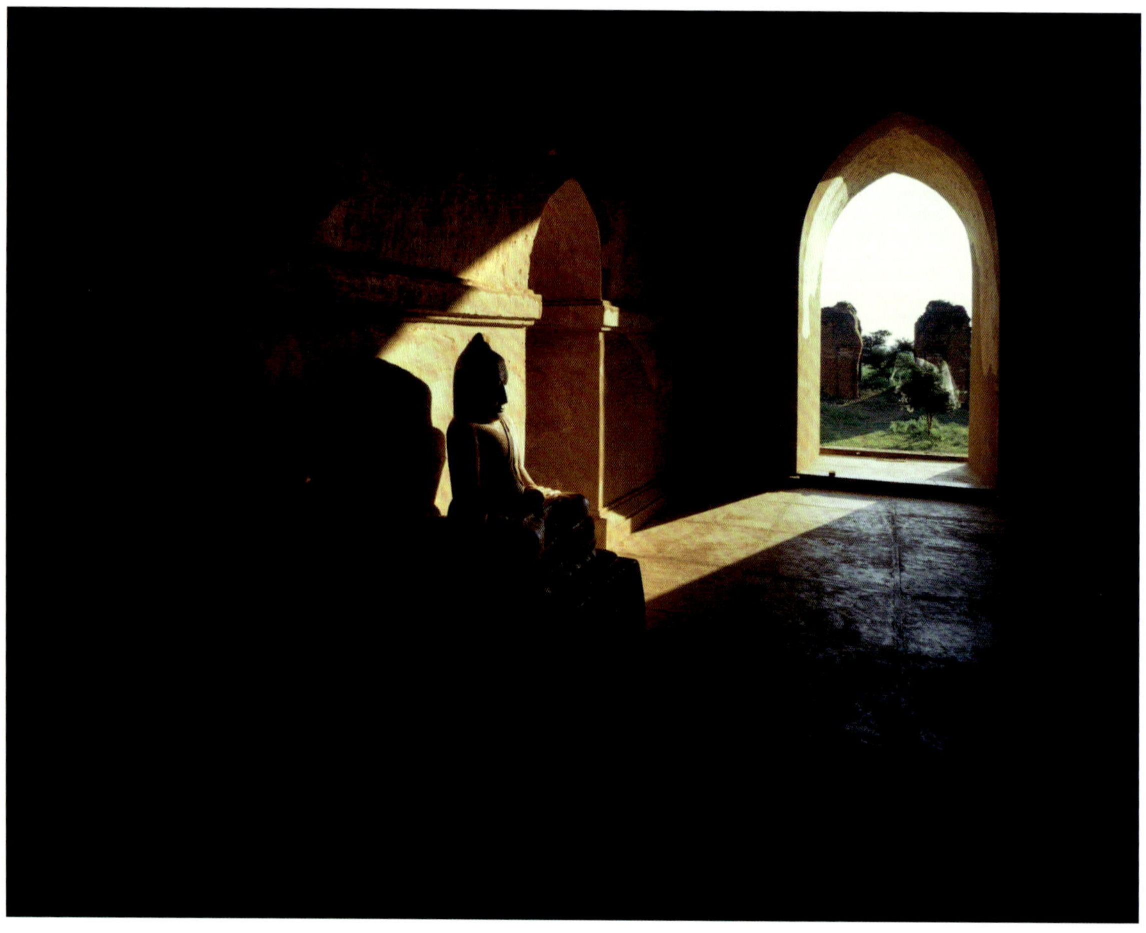

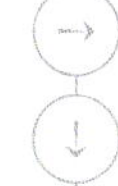

Ernst Haas's *Grand Canyon at Dawn, 1963*, which appeared cropped in his book, *The Creation* (below).

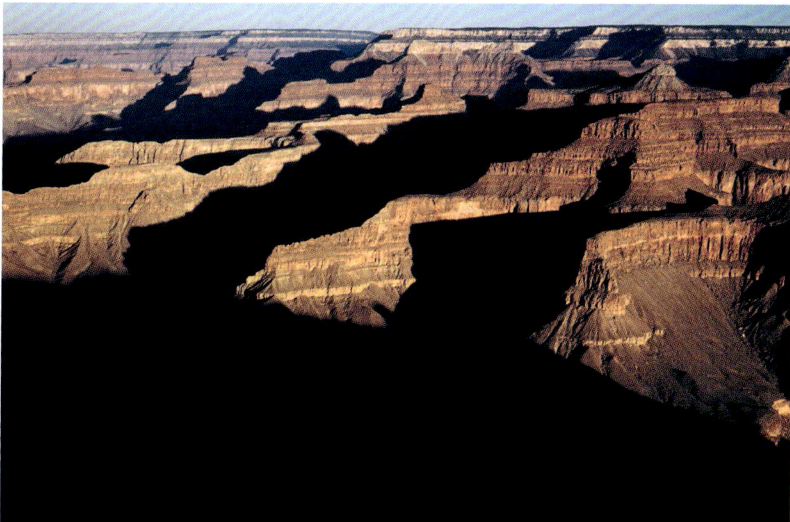

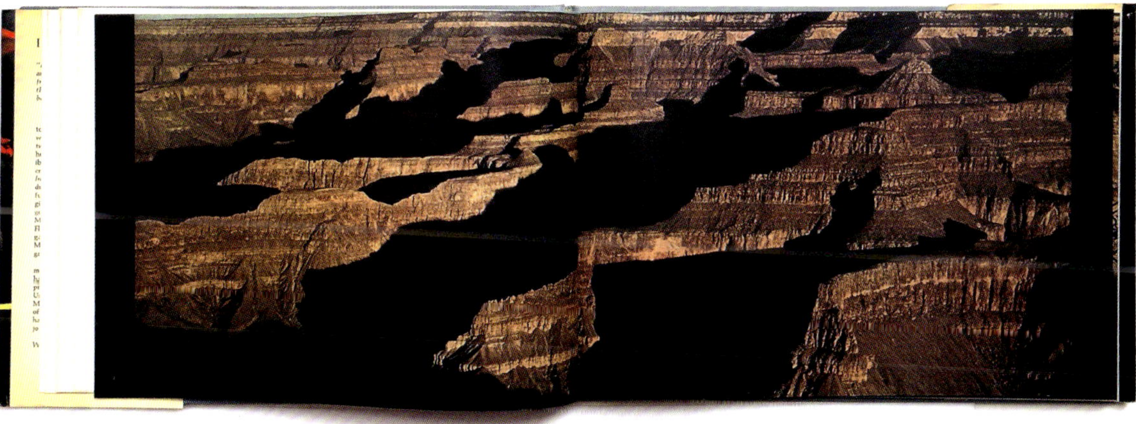

This is a two-dimensional treatment, almost like a woodblock print, which is exactly what the chemists and engineers at Eastman Kodak worked hard to avoid and 'correct'. That again is part of the point: trying not to be realistic, even though photographing in colour. Haas used this deliberately in *Grand Canyon at Dawn, 1963*, making a flowing diagonal pattern of the inky black shadows thrown by the cliffs. They are solid shapes that take up half of the picture, making it a kind of binary image in which the solid blocks are a more powerful element than the actual sunlit rocks. As Haas wrote in a 1961 interview, this treatment is 'less descriptive, more creative; less informative, more suggestive – less prose, more poetry'. Essential for this is the way the picture was cropped for publication, removing the skyline to keep it abstract.

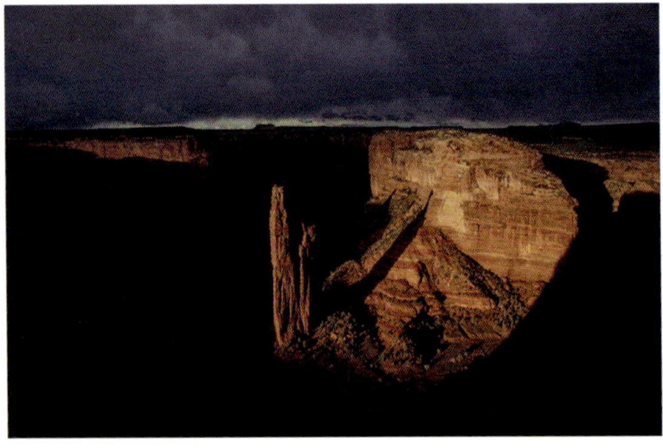

1.

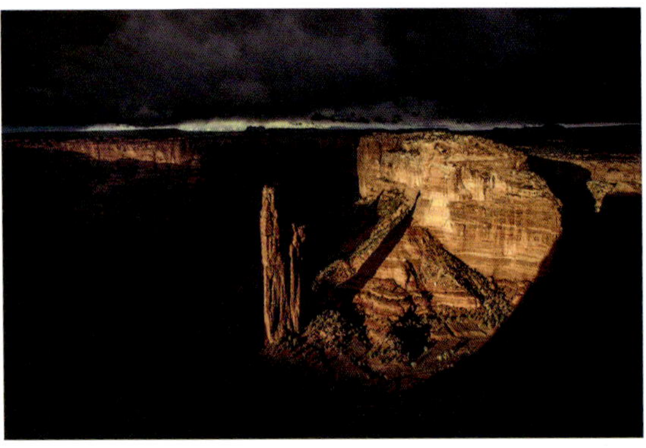

2.

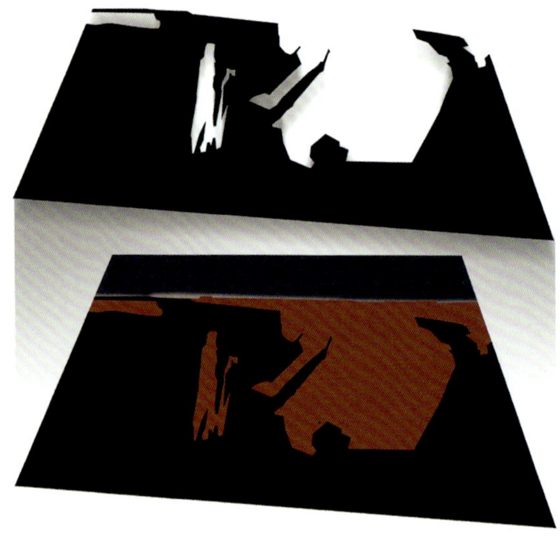

3.

My 'shadow block' version (shown here) is also from the American Southwest, and I was extraordinarily lucky with the light. It was very cloudy and thundery, as you can see from the horizon, and we were minutes away from sunset. I had no hopes at all, and thought that the long drive to this location was a waste. There's a convenient overlook that many people use, so I set up my camera out of habit – or possibly duty – and took a very dull picture as a record of a wasted day.

Suddenly, the light began to change a little. I couldn't even see the sun from where I was standing, so there was no indication that there would be what we all hope for in situations like these – a break in the clouds. But it came and it was intense. I shot only Kodachrome in those days, and knew that the mixture of very bright, low sunlight and underexposure would turn the shadow areas – which took up half of the frame with the 35mm lens I was using – solid black.

It's worth pausing a moment here to think about what that means to the picture. Spider Rock and the right canyon wall pop out of a totally black space that has no depth, no detail, no features. This is just the kind of 'unrealism' that Kodachrome could offer – it certainly wasn't what someone like Ansel Adams would do with the scene, no matter how much he might have liked the conditions. He would have made sure that there was mysterious detail lingering in those shadows. I too like that mysterious treatment of shadows, but not here. This is not 'obvious reality'.

1. The scanned file, processed in ACR using Auto settings

2. The scanned file processed in ACR with the shadows lifted

3. The shadows are treated as two-dimensional blocks

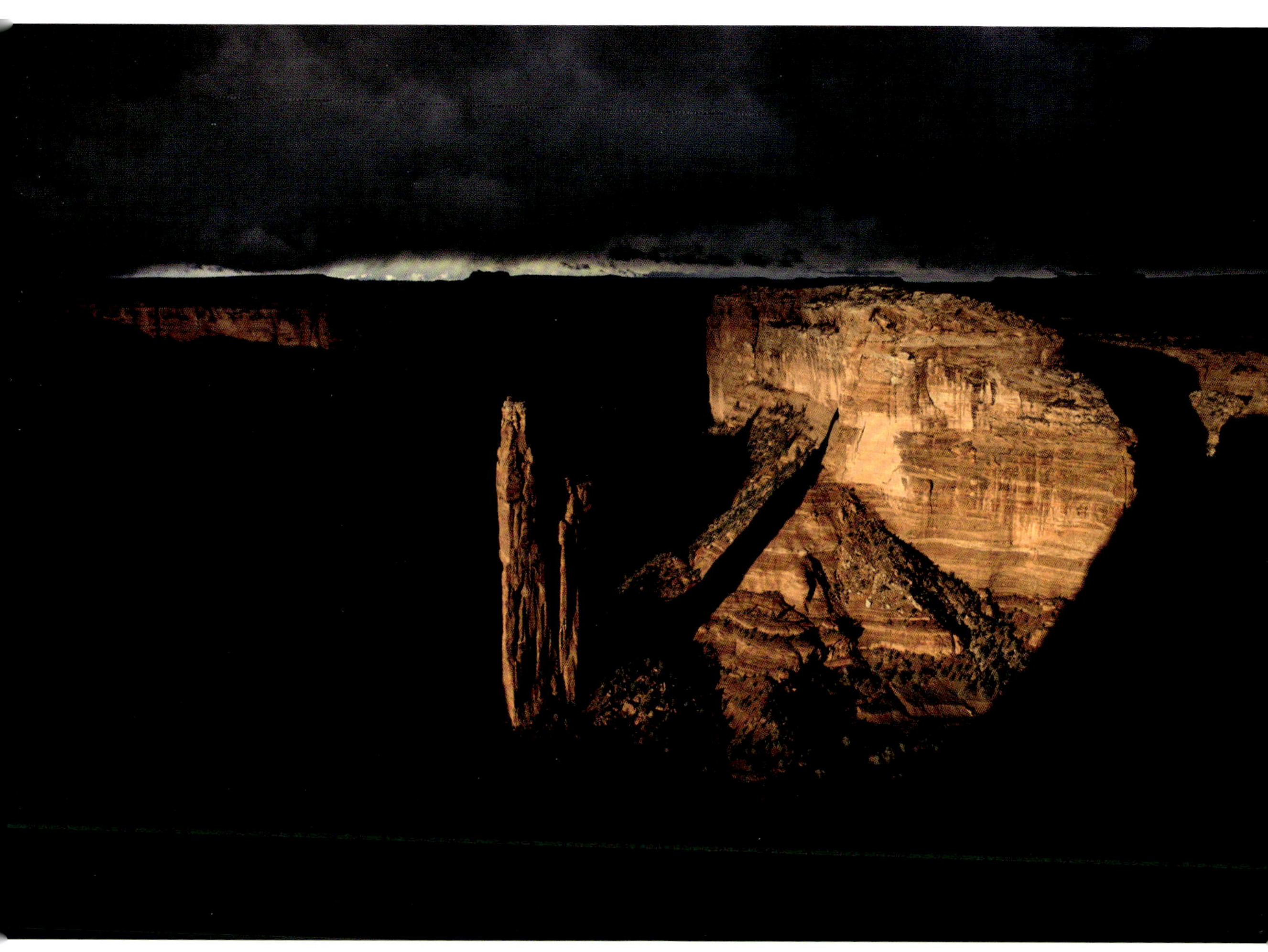

Spider Rock, Canyon de Chelly, Arizona, during a short break in late-afternoon storm clouds. As shot on Kodachrome, drum scanned.

FLAT LIGHT DOWN

aving come on strong about underexposing (as long as you've got hard and contrasty light), it may seem that I'm doing an about-face here. The picture below was from a series of pictures taken one afternoon in a market area in Peshawar, North-West Frontier Province, Pakistan, in the 1970s. It was overcast and there were areas roofed over with cloth, so the lighting was very flat.

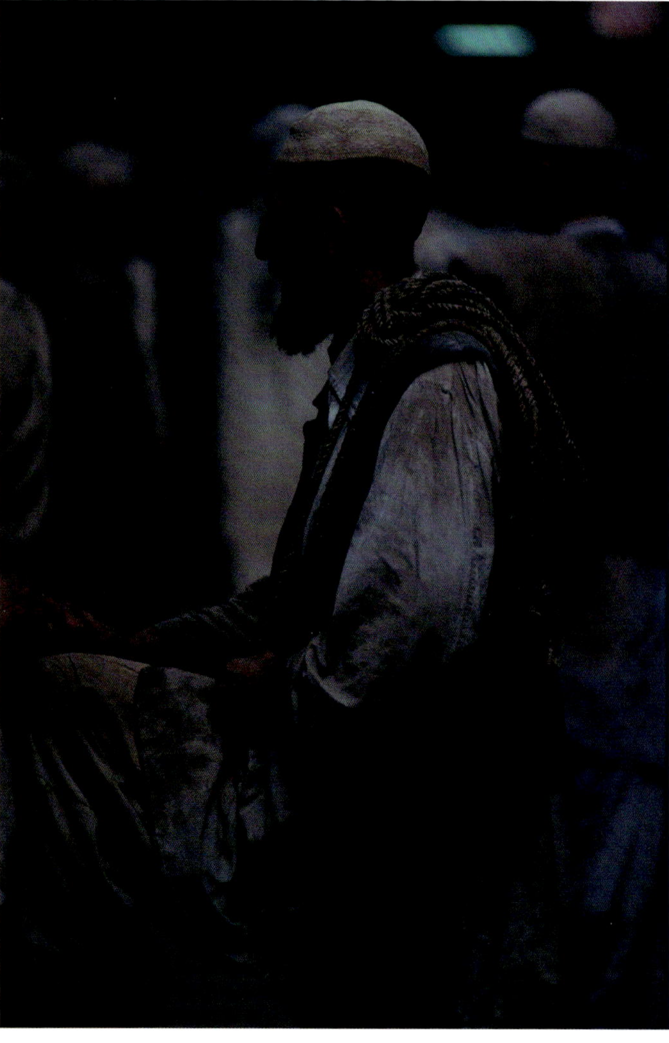

Market, Peshawar, Pakistan, shot on Kodachrome 64.

If you're looking for contrast in a situation like this, it has to come from the surfaces, but there was none of that here; the tones were similar, as were the colours, which were universally drab. That doesn't sound like a recipe for much, but it was, in its way, extreme. There are not too many situations like this, and in any case this was a reportage assignment, meaning showing how things are was a priority. Again, Kodachrome came to the rescue of what could have just been a dull image (I realize some may still think it's just dull, but it's a matter of taste). The 'shadow-crushing' effect of underexposing Kodachrome increased the contrast, while introducing an unrealistic appearance. That sounds like something many people would try to avoid, but it was what I hoped for. Hoping was in fact a part of the experience, as it was a few weeks before I could have the film developed, but for me, the underexposure worked.

Another case that both I and the art director stand by was the stormy coastal view in Wales (below), which was again exposed down significantly. Perhaps paradoxically, it was shot for a motorists' guide to views in the British Isles, and under more pleasant conditions this bay is popular with tourists. I had no choice about the storm, other than returning another day, but perversely, I liked the result. Exposing in this way added an undeniable drama, and took out any sense of colour, making for an unusual, almost monochrome picture.

As I mentioned earlier, photographers shooting editorially for the printed page knew that the printers and their drum scanners could pull the tones back up, even if we made life a bit difficult for them. In other words, there was an informal option for the look of a photograph that was essentially 'expose down/scan up', with drum scanners extracting details that were previously only visible if you looked at the transparency under a loupe on a light box. One way of looking at this is that the scanners were in effect able to 'straighten out' the shoulder and toe of the characteristic curve, which provides us with two possibilities for scenes like these: we can bring up the brightness and contrast during scanning (or these days, processing), or we can simply appreciate and embrace the underexposed result.

A stormy sea at Port Eynon Bay, Gower Peninsula, Wales, shot on Kodachrome 64.

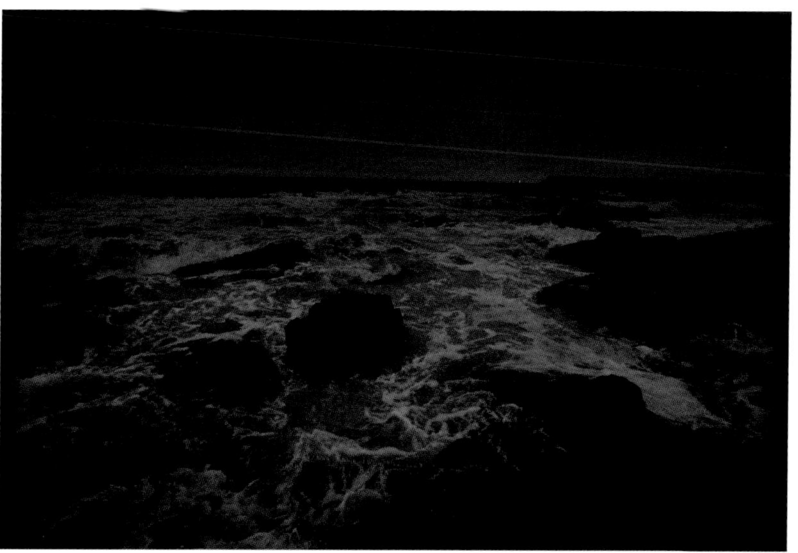

RED RICHNESS

Kodachrome had a reputation for rich colours, but this needs qualification. It was formulated by Eastman Kodak for 'natural' colours, and this meant that when normally exposed, the saturation was by no means high.

When Fujifilm released its Velvia film in 1990, the saturation difference was marked, and it effectively put paid to Kodachrome, as most people preferred high saturation to accurate colour. However, the way in which we perceive colours depends on much more than measurements like hue, saturation and brightness, and the words we use are far from precise. In theory, making a colour brighter makes it more vivid, but as it becomes even brighter, the colour starts to look pale and washed out, although this depends very much on *which* colour and *how* bright it is made.

Kodachrome's reputation for richness was largely based on reds, which stayed strong in appearance even when underexposed, especially when viewed on a light box under a loupe. This almost certainly had to do with a well-known effect in which a mid-toned red looks brighter than a mid-toned grey, and brighter than any other mid-toned colour (known as the Helmholtz-Kohlrausch effect). Therefore, underexposing an image leaves the reds looking relatively stronger than other colours. It does not, of course, change the saturation, but it *looks* rich and dense. The Harry Gruyaert image shown on page 64 is a good example of this red richness: the two balloons pull the eye and dominate the picture.

My Kodachrome red pictures (opposite) were taken at a small town in Venezuela, San Francisco de Yare, on Corpus Christi day, when the Dancing Devils parade from the centre of town to the church. I photographed at different exposures to see what would happen to the intense reds, and the bottom image is one of the darkest frames. It is probably too dark, and I never selected this frame at the time, but now, with the best film drum scanners and modern processing, it makes an interesting version, even if it is unrealistic in a way. To me, this density of red seems to have real depth, particularly set off like this against the man's face, which the underexposure has made extremely dark, in startling contrast to the white of his eye. The second frame (top) is more conventionally underexposed.

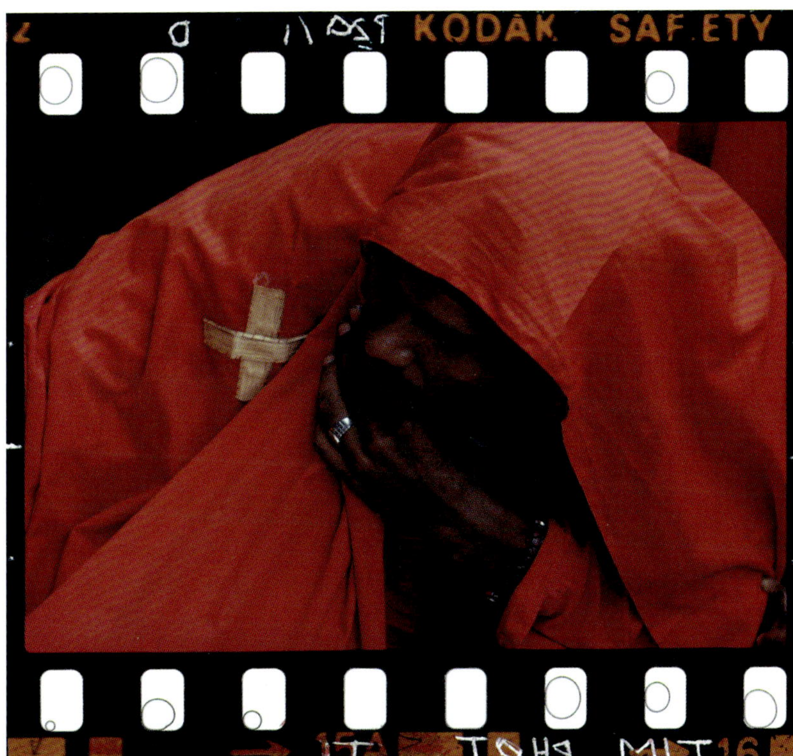

Kodachrome 64 was used for both of these pictures, and delivered exceptionally rich reds. The top picture here was exposed normally.

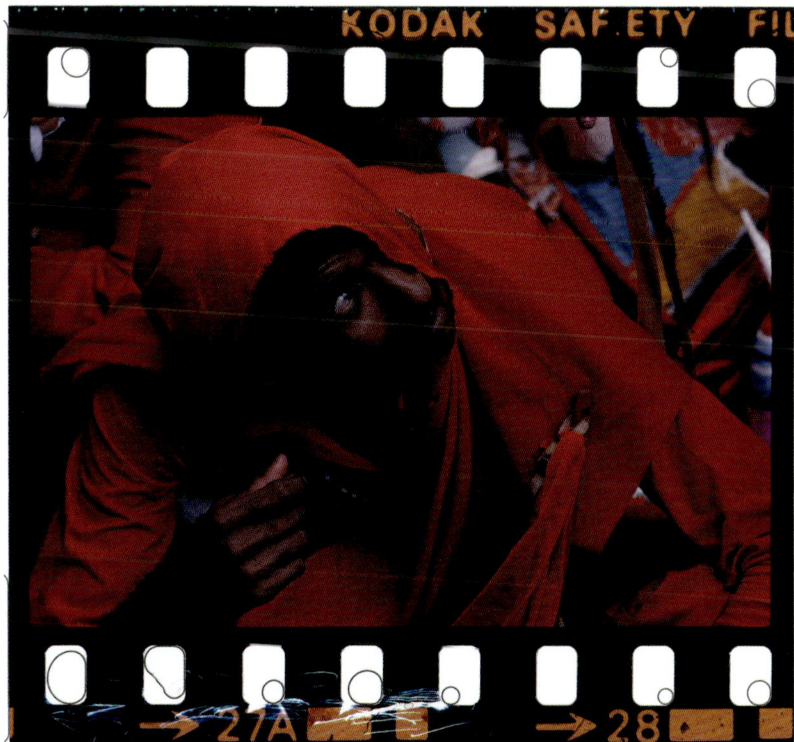

This picture was underexposed, and at the time I considered it a mistake. However, drum scanned and with the whites raised in ACR, it still works.

HIGHLIGHT COMPRESSION

So far, I have focused on shadows, but let's look at the opposite end of the scale – the highlights. Arguably, the bright end of the exposure scale is where film can still be more pleasing than digital. I should qualify this, because with the right exposure and certain processing, digital can be made to mimic film almost perfectly, but it takes more work, whereas film does it naturally.

The 'it' in question is a seamless gradation from bright to white, which you can see in the picture below. The reason is similar to the behaviour of deep shadows: film reacts less and less at either end of the scale. It's that characteristic curve

A clear summer sunset in northwest Scotland, photographed on Kodak Ektachrome 120 roll film using a 6x17cm Linhof camera. The panoramic sweep takes in a broad area of sky and a long, smooth gradient. The key area for compression is marked with the rectangle on the toe of the characteristic curve.

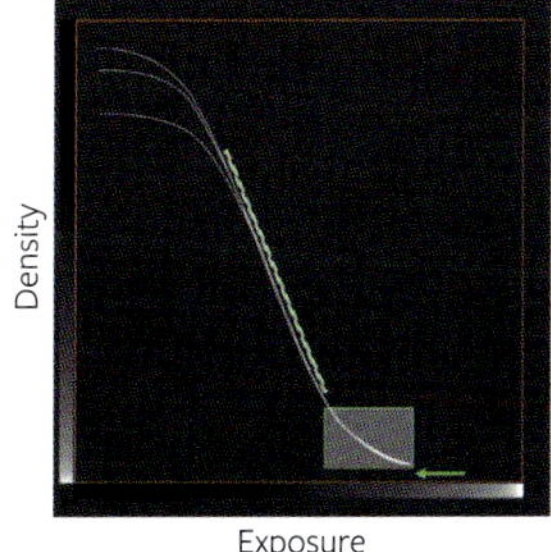

again, only now we're looking at the toe with colour slide film (with a negative, it's reversed and highlights lie on the shoulder).

The classic situation where it all happens in the space of a single picture is shooting towards the sun with a smooth and possibly slightly hazy sky. There's a natural ramp that goes across the sky towards the sun from bright to white, and if we follow this on the characteristic curve, the film's response to increasing light gets more 'sluggish'. That's not a film chemist's word, but I think it gets across the idea of slowing down. The result is that it looks natural and above all smooth, as there's no point at which the film suddenly fails; the brighter tones simply drift gently to overexposed white. Now, 'overexpose' is a term that I'm generally reluctant to use much, because it supposes there is actually an okay exposure somewhere. So, there's usually confusion over whether it means more exposure than the scene *ought* to have, or more than most people would like. With film, however, we used it to mean either a mistake (there were more of those because it was impossible to check exposures immediately) or that the photographer chose to go very light. Either way, you could defend it on the grounds of taste or looking interesting.

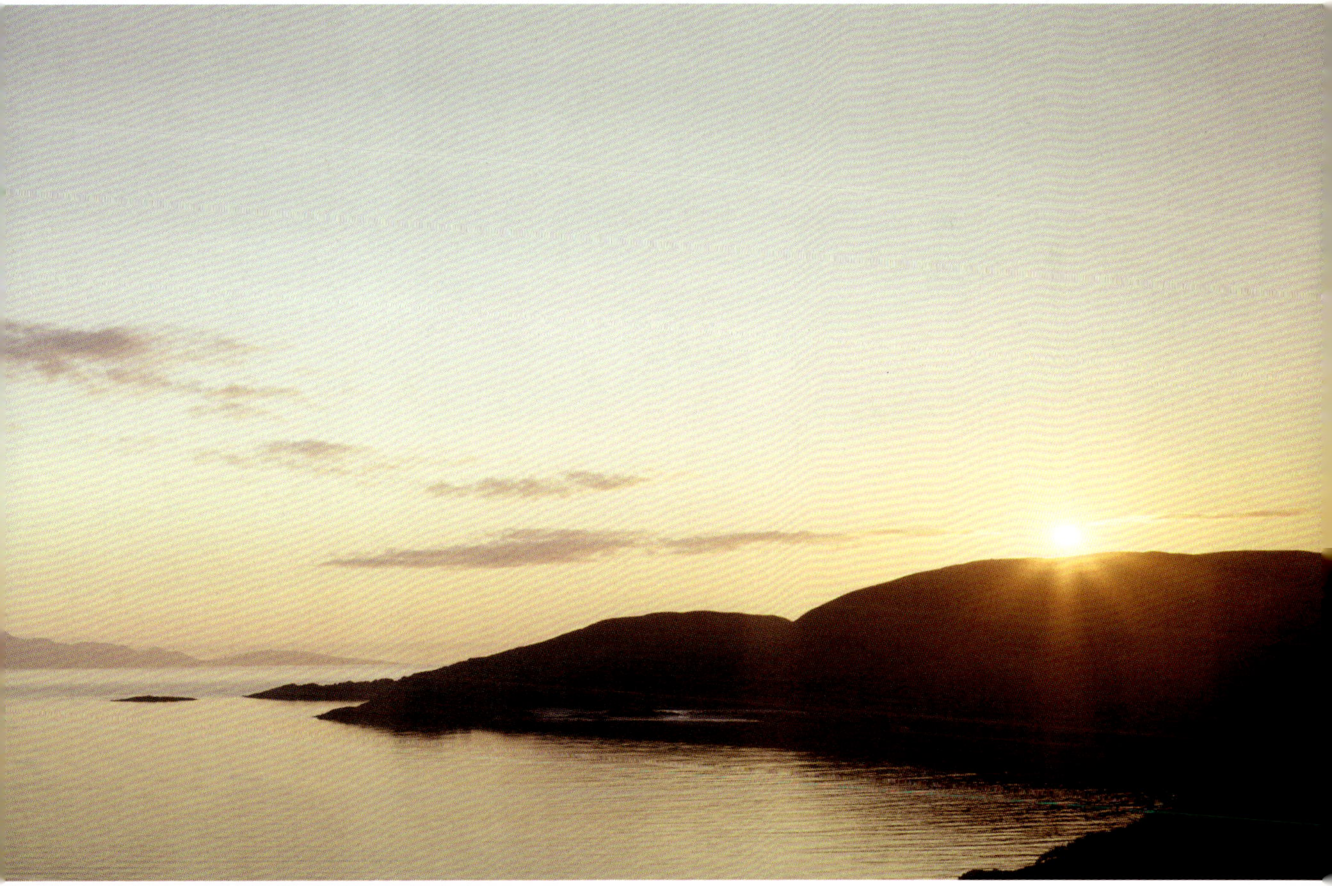

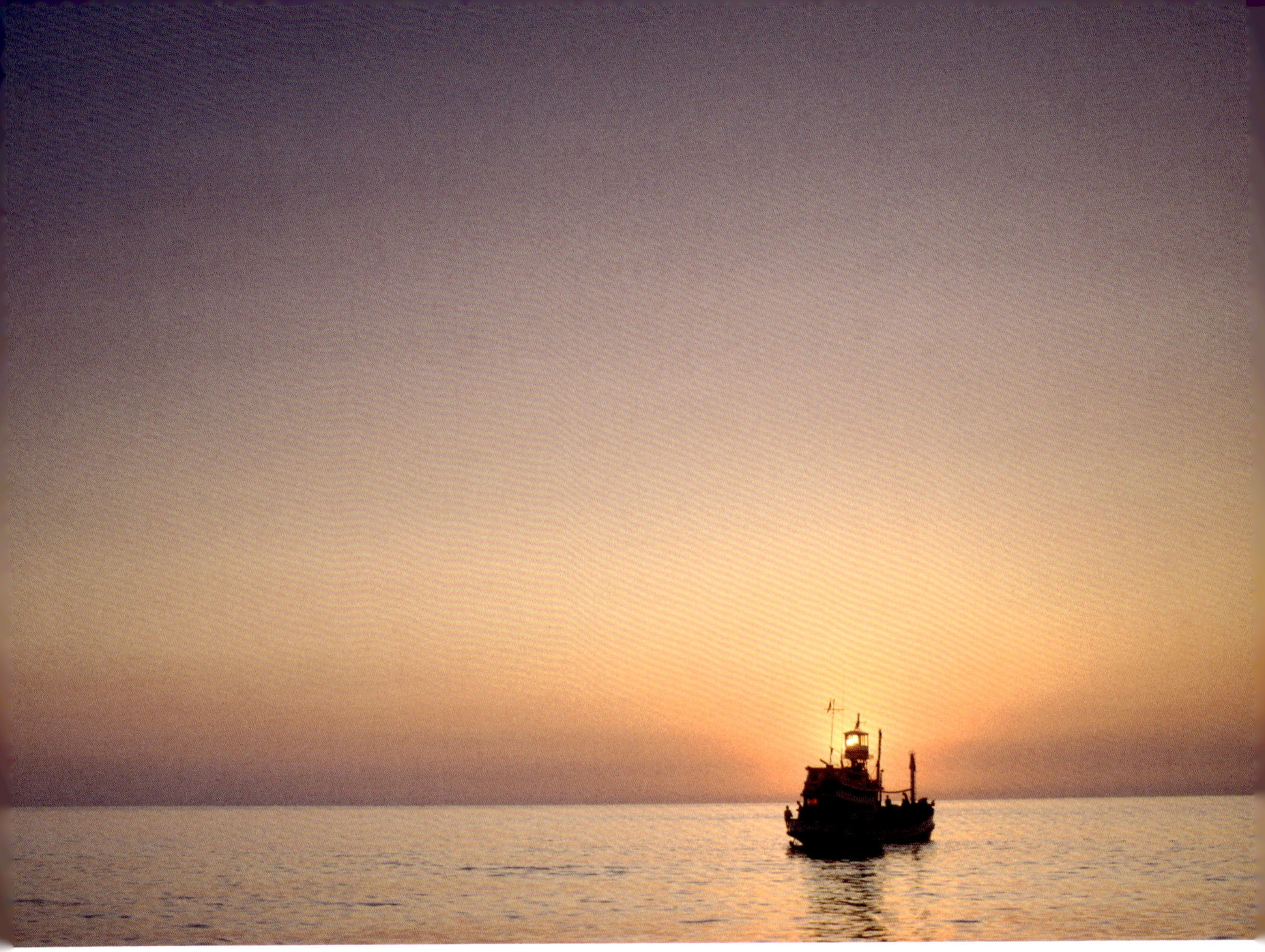

Another sky gradient, this time shot with a 20mm lens on Kodachrome, in the Gulf of Thailand.

An older model of smartphone camera struggled with this bright sunrise.

This isn't the case with digital sensors, as they cannot overexpose smoothly. The pixels get brighter in a linear fashion until, at a certain point, the photosites fill up and record nothing. With the same kind of scene I described previously, shooting towards the sun, there's an exact point at which the image becomes featureless white, hence the word clipping. Worse than that, the three colour channels (red, green and blue) clip at different points, so there's often a sharp change in colour.

You can see this at its worst when you are photographing a colourful sunrise or sunset with an average digital camera, as in the example at left (also on page 125). The shift from orange to yellow close to the sun is false. In reality, the hue stayed the same, but channel clipping from an older smartphone camera shifted the brighter areas to an unpleasant-looking yellow. Although it can be corrected during processing, it is annoying nonetheless.

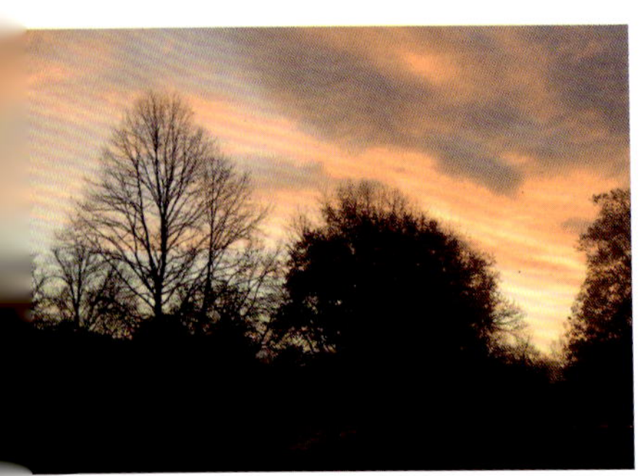

Film's organic-looking response to strong exposure is called 'highlight compression', and it has its good and bad points. The good is the smoothing, which is aided a little by the thickness of the emulsion and the film base, which themselves have a slight tone and prevent colour reversal film from reaching absolute white. Technically, the limit of brightness is called the Dmin (minimum density) or 'film base plus fog' because in addition to the clear film base absorbing a little light, there is always a small amount of unexposed silver halide that receives some development. The bad is loss of detail at the top end of the highlights. In between the good and the bad of highlight compression is the inevitable loss of contrast in the brighter half of the image, but this is very much a matter of taste.

All of this goes towards giving film its special look when it's strongly or fully exposed. This undoubtedly has its admirers, but more than that, the naturally smooth transition in the highlights towards white simply looks more acceptable than the harsh clipping of digital. All on-board digital camera software tries to apply something similar (with varying degrees of success), while apps such as Dehancer are dedicated to simulating highlight compression in a controlled way.

A meeting hall at the Shaker village in Hancock, Massachusetts (left), and the cabinet room at Monticello, the estate of Thomas Jefferson, in Virginia (right). In both of these interiors, 4x5in Ektachrome sheet film comfortably handled the high range, from patches of shadow to direct sunlight.

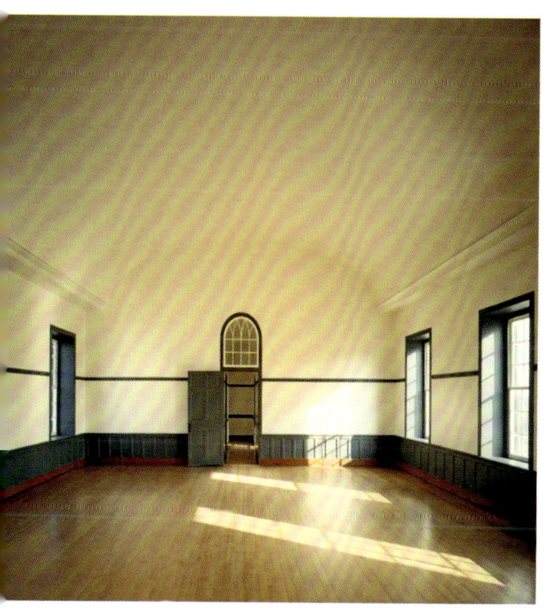

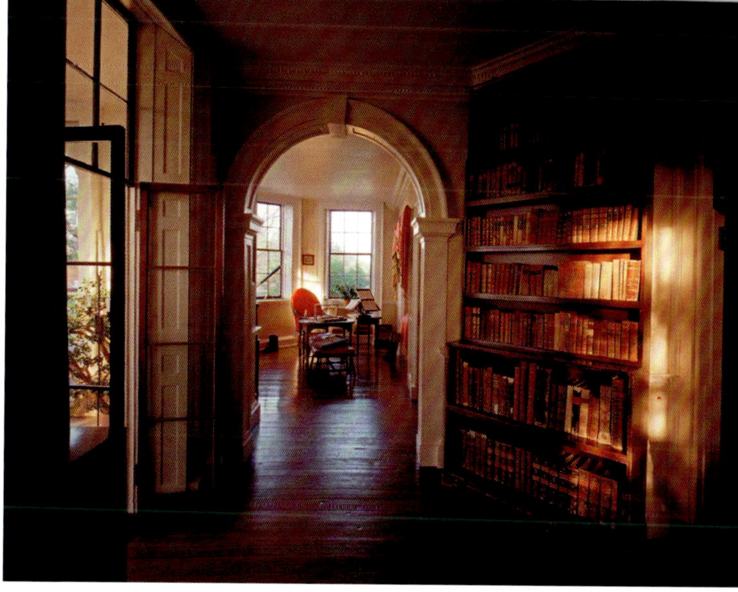

HALATION

F ilm has yet another highlight trait that can be seen as a 'desirable fault' – at least in small doses. Halation comes from stray light bouncing around the interior of the camera and back into the film, and appears as a coloured glow around extreme highlights.

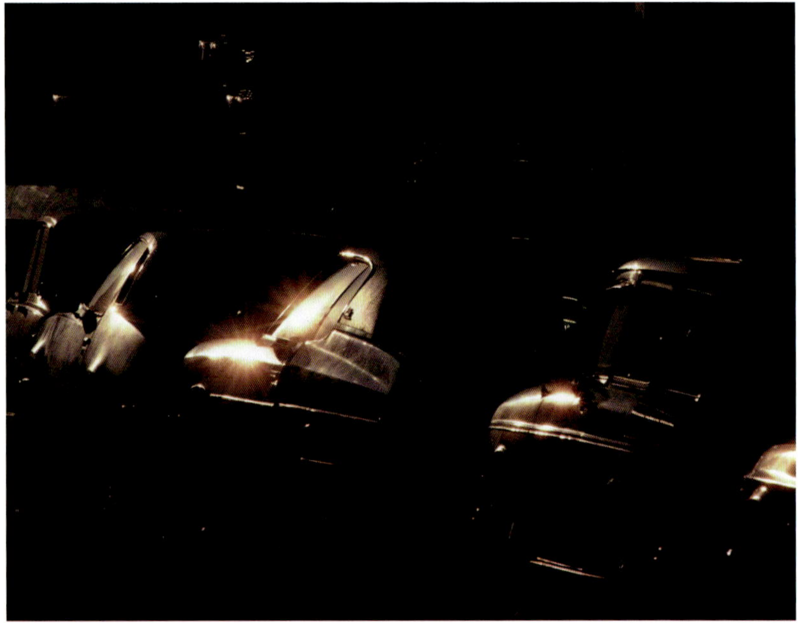

Halation around reflections of the sun in a wing mirror and bodywork of a parked automobile in New Orleans.

Although the interior surfaces of a camera are treated with a matt black coating to prevent this, some light still gets through, most of it entering through the back of the film base. To counter this, film utilizes an anti-halation layer, but even then a little stray light can get through, and the more light there is, the more obvious the effect, which is why it appears around very bright highlights.

Paradoxically, this effect is very much liked by most people, although it's absent in digital capture. One of the reasons that some degree of halation gets a thumbs up from viewers in colour is that it has a red or orange tint. This is because the red-sensitive layer in film is typically closest to the film base, behind the green- and blue-sensitive layers, so it's the red layer that absorbs the stray light. When there are very bright highlights, the stray light penetrates not just the film base and red-sensitive layer, but reaches the green-sensitive layer as well. When this happens, the halation appears orange, which is again not unpleasant.

It's worth mentioning here bloom, which also adds a glow around the highlights in an image. However, bloom comes from optical imperfections and is prominent in very old lenses (and in optical filters designed to give a soft-focus effect). This hazy effect became popular among the Pictorialists of the late 19th century and is now partially back in fashion on social media. While it naturally works on digital cameras, film enhances it by scattering the diffuse glow among the emulsion layers. As with highlight compression, both halation and bloom can be simulated digitally.

The setting sun just hits the edge of the sweeping roof line of a northern Thai temple in Chiang Mai.

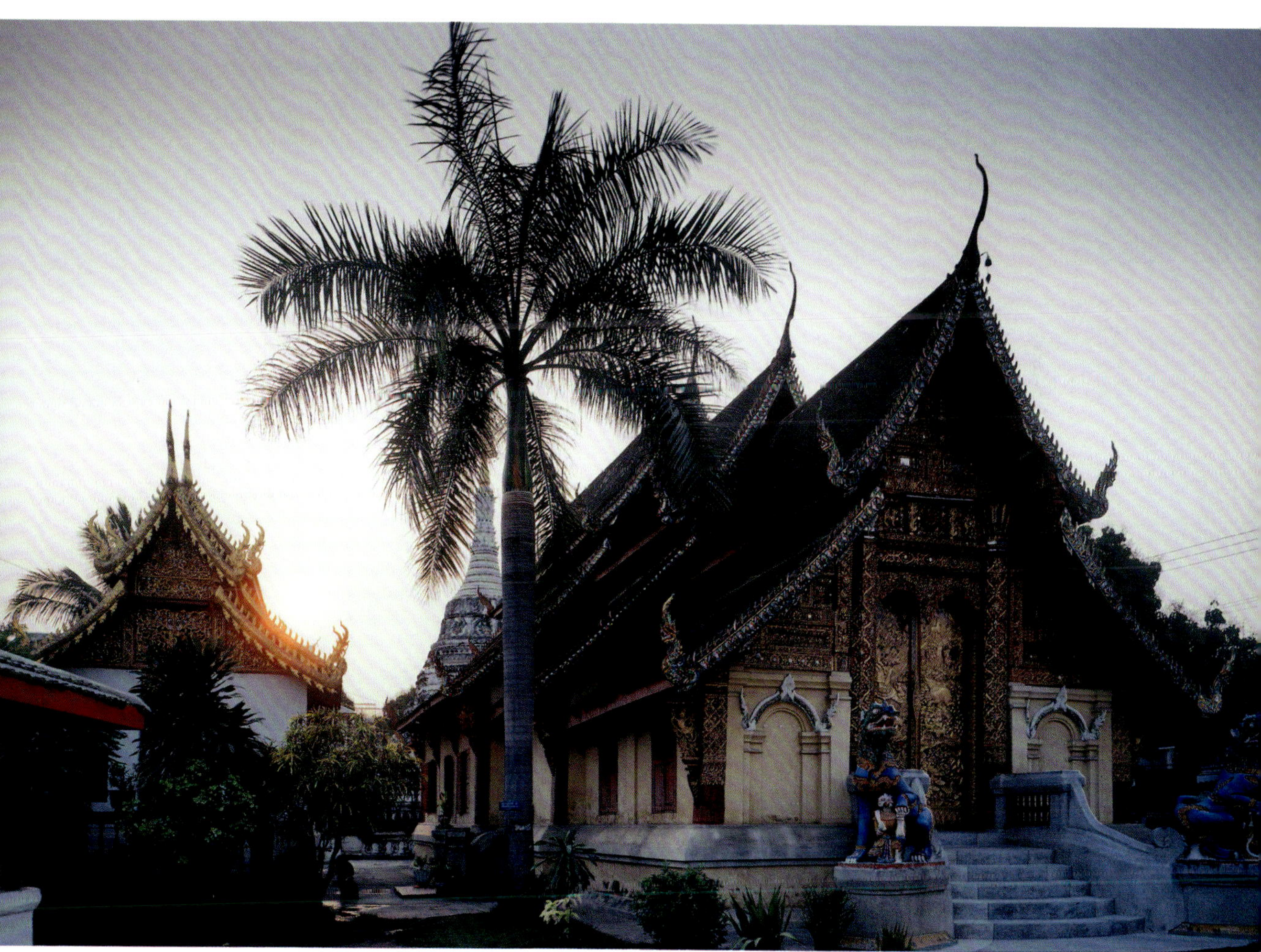

4

DARKER

The fundamental choice in exposure is to go darker or brighter; to limit the light reaching the sensor or film, or to open up. There are infinite nuances, depending on what the subject and scene suggest, and your interpretation of them, but the basic appeal of each is still quite different. We will start with the darker group, and you will soon see there are many different kinds of dark – and degrees of darkness.

As you'd expect, the sense comes from a first glance, or impression of a picture. Three things go into making this happen, the first of which is the subject or scene itself; a black cat, for example, rather than a polar bear.

Then there's the lighting, or rather what we expect from the lighting. If we're photographing at dusk, we will be aware of impending darkness, so ordinarily that would be something we'd like to preserve, by taking the exposure down by a stop or more. If we're the viewer, there are clues in the picture that the sun has already set, so we'd probably expect a sense of darkness.

The third component is the processing. That's a personal decision, which could follow the trajectory of the above elements – a dark subject and low light – or it could be a complete creative fiction, as in Magnum photographer Alex Majoli's series, *SKENE*. Here, studio flash overwhelms daylight, and the photographer's tableaux are printed to appear as hard-to-make-out underexposed images, leading the viewer into a different, uncertain place.

If you put these three components together – dark subject, dark lighting and a dark intention – you have the perfect mixture for a very dark picture.
So, let's step into the darkness.

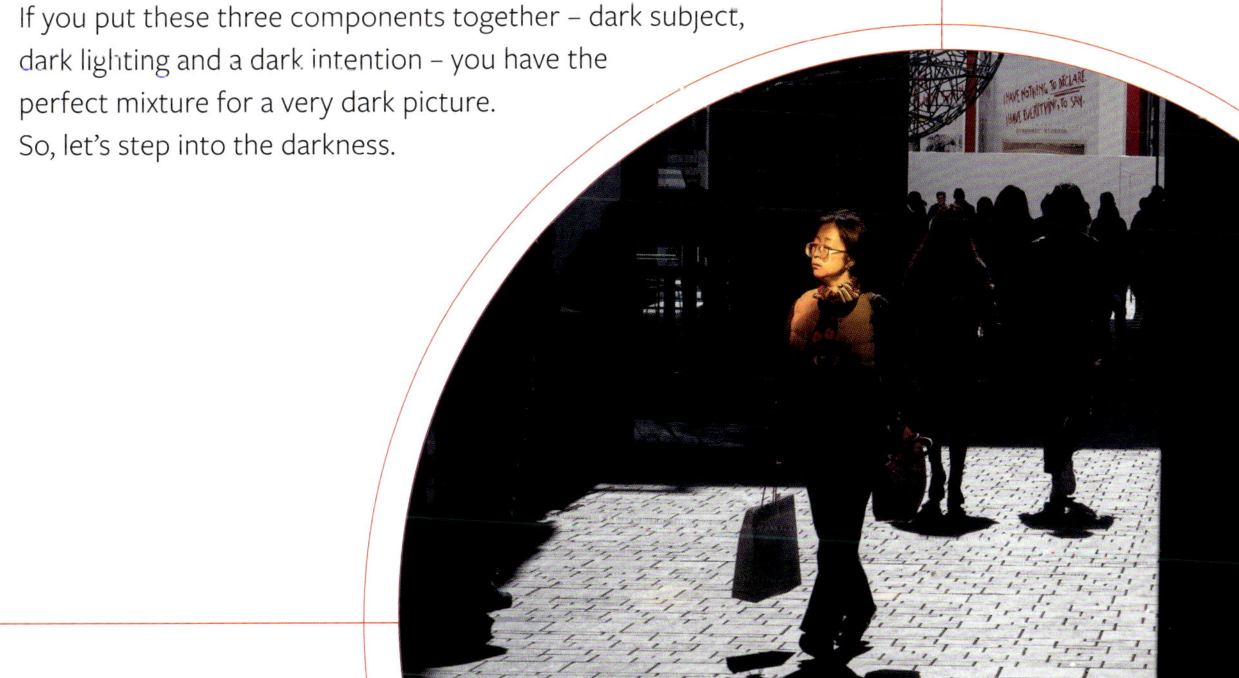

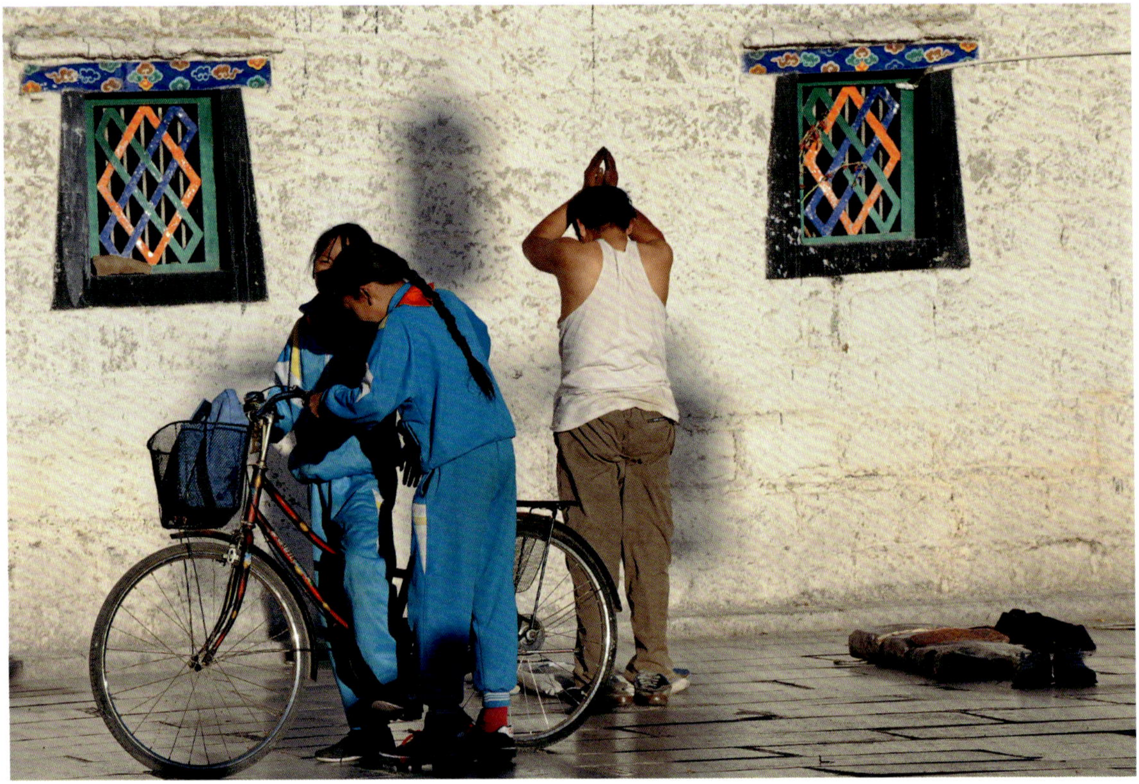

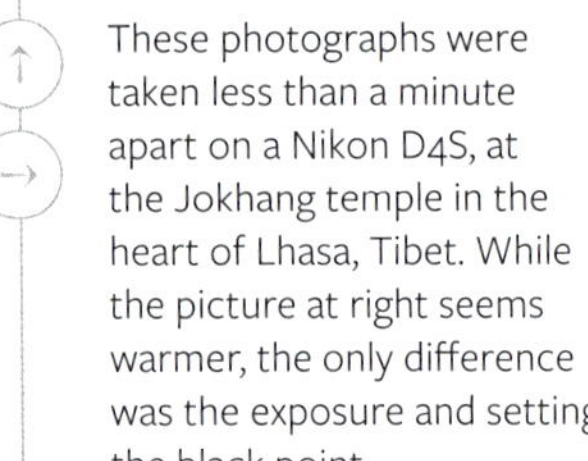

COLOUR RICHNESS

Continuing on from Kodachrome's reputation for rich reds, the digital equivalent doesn't always come naturally. In fact, modern default in-camera processing – especially in phone cameras – tends to go in a different direction, by automatically brightening dark scenes and opening up shadow areas.

This may be what most consumers want, but it is less subtle and more obviously saturated in colour. Depending on the sensor and the conversion that the camera manufacturer chooses to apply, digital reds can sometimes oversaturate badly, to the point where they need targeting and taking down in the processing. This happens more when shooting JPEGs or HEICs, which is another argument for shooting Raw whenever possible – the sensor and in-camera conversion determine the overall handling of the saturation, but at least with a Raw file you have the opportunity to change this according to what you want.

These photographs were taken less than a minute apart on a Nikon D4S, at the Jokhang temple in the heart of Lhasa, Tibet. While the picture at right seems warmer, the only difference was the exposure and setting the black point.

Returning to Kodachrome, much of its reputation for rich reds came from the film chemistry, which heightened the saturation when the reds were darker than average. In other words, underexposing made reds richer, and underexposing a little (even half a stop) was fairly common practice among professionals. Digitally, there are ways to imitate this, but it's important to really understand how the sensor in your own camera performs for colour. I don't mean a deep technical understanding (all camera manufacturers keep their colour conversion procedures secret anyway), but rather being familiar with the way the overall colour looks to you.

We all have our own interpretations of colour, and for this reason there are few, if any, widely agreed descriptions. The word 'richness' is certainly open to a range of interpretation, so to be clear, I'm using it in the sense of a colour that is in the darker half of the brightness range, which has presence and depth (unfortunately, two more terms that aren't precise). More often than not, this is about a principal colour rather than a kaleidoscope of hues, for the reason that one dominant colour has a better chance of engaging the viewer's attention.

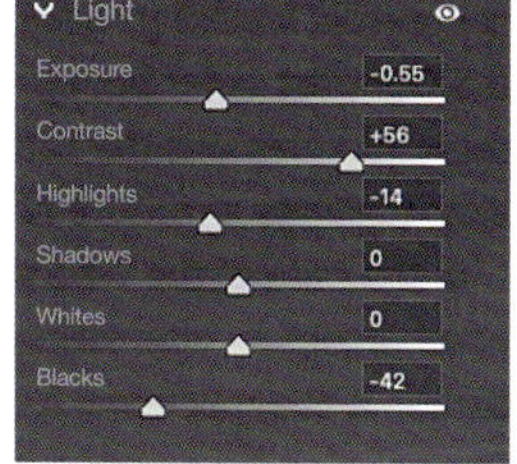

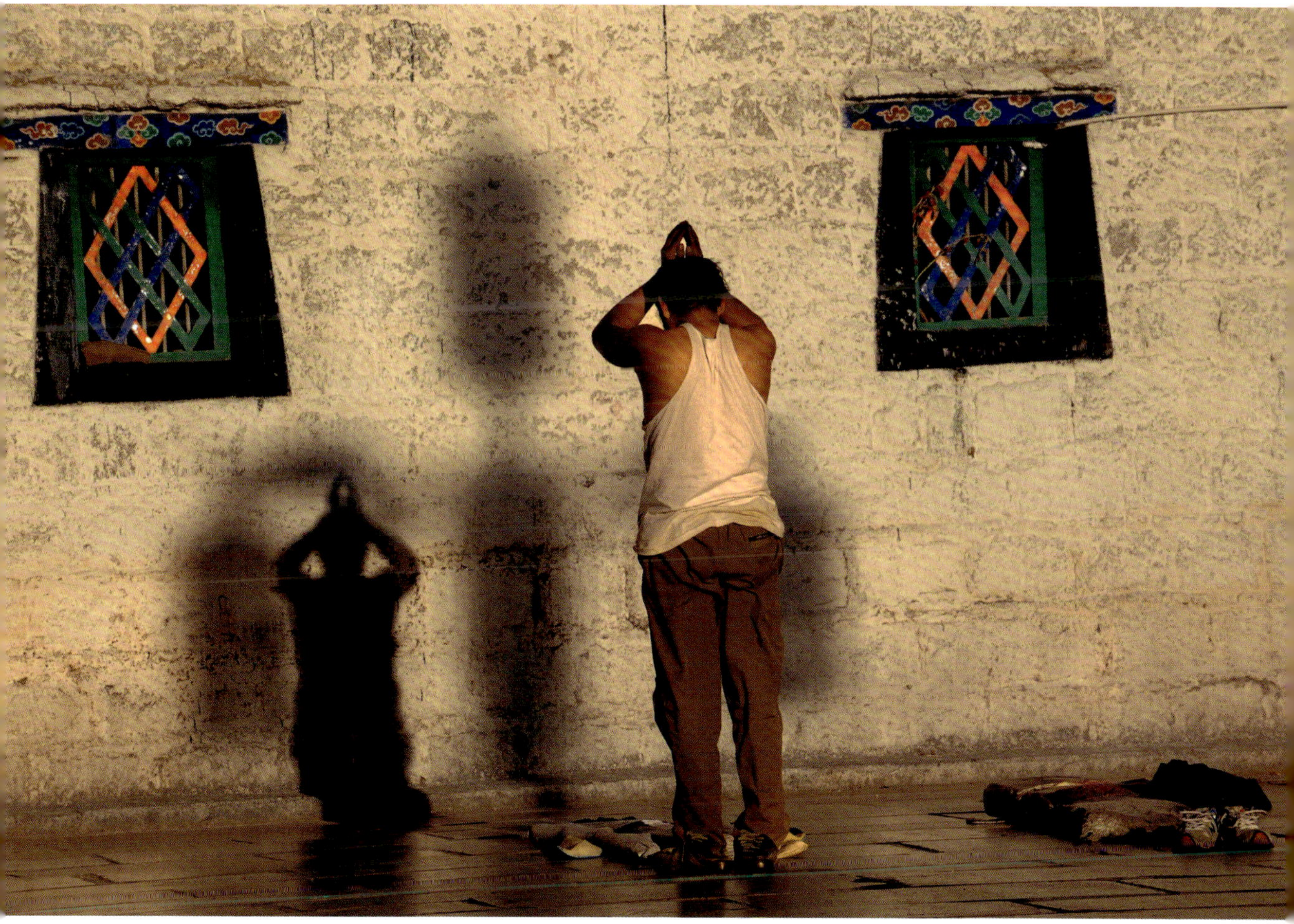

This is not just about saturation, but also about brightness and contrast, and these three combine to give the impression of richness or, at the opposite end of the scale, paleness and pastel. In processing, it might seem an easy step to reach for the saturation slider, but this rarely works. Compare the main picture of Tower Bridge (opposite, top) with the other two versions: one a more normal rendering close to what was captured, and the other with a 40-percent increase in saturation applied. The saturated version isn't convincing, and looks simply over-vivid.

The settings show that the main 'rich' version was made by lowering Exposure half a stop, lowering Highlights considerably, and increasing contrast, not by using the Contrast slider but by stretching the Blacks and Whites. In fact, in none of these pictures was the Saturation increased directly; the most effective approach is almost always a mixture of darkening and retaining contrast, sometimes selectively.

In the case of the Tibetan prayer room (below), the strong colour is yellow, which poses an interesting problem. Yellow exists *only* above a certain brightness; darken it too much and it becomes ochre, or even brown – another colour entirely. The solution here was to emphasize the contrast, in combination with lowering the colour temperature considerably, which shifted the yellow to a warmer and therefore more intense version.

A Tibetan prayer room in a house in northern Yunnan. Shown here is the Raw file, shot on a Hasselblad SWC with a digital back (1), and the final, processed image (2).

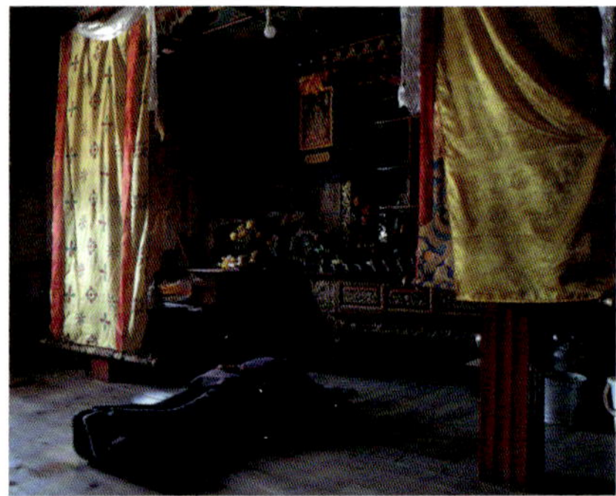

1.

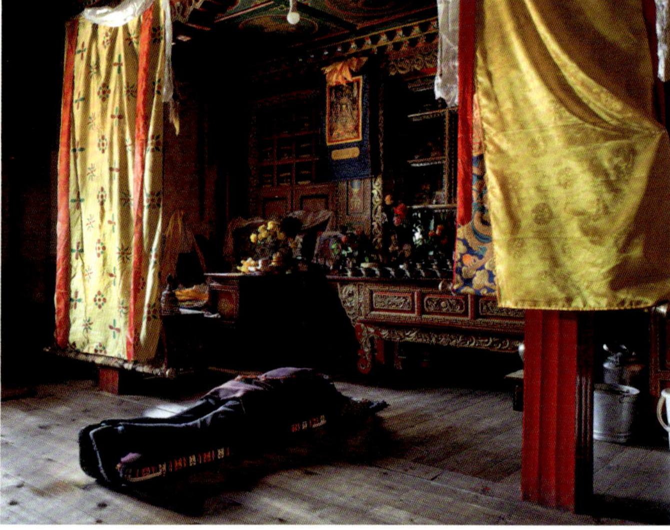

2.

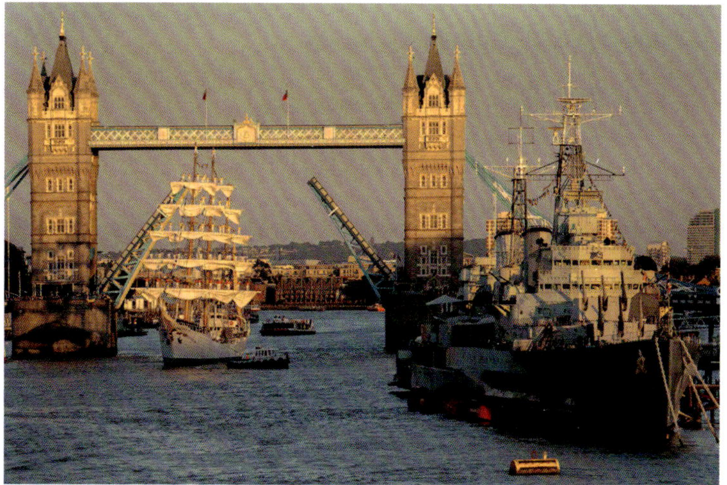

1.

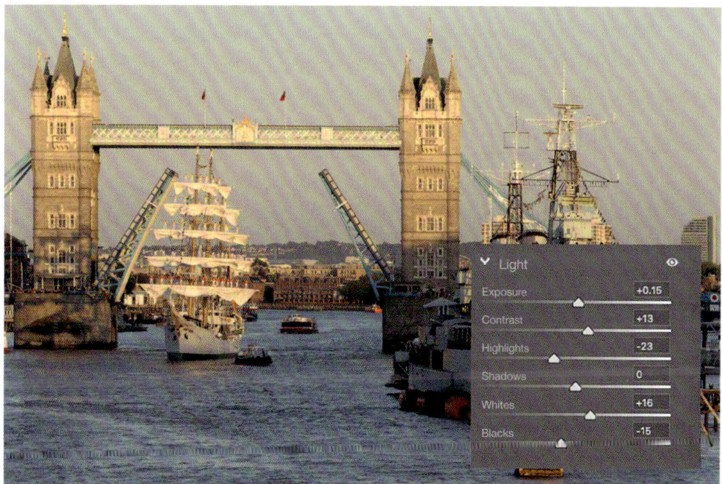

2.

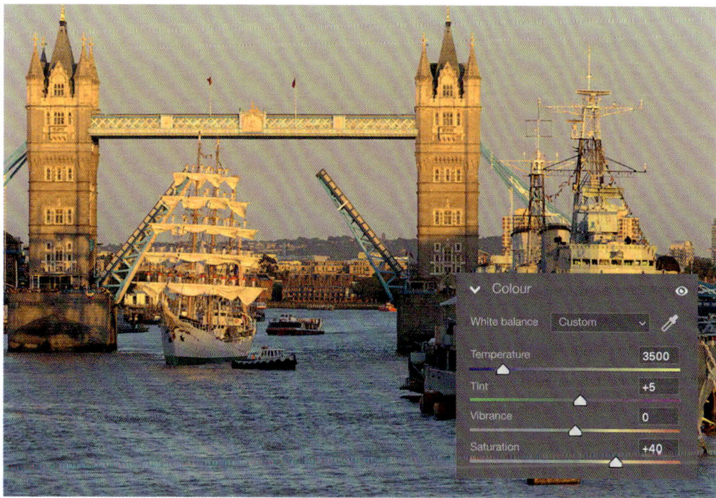

3.

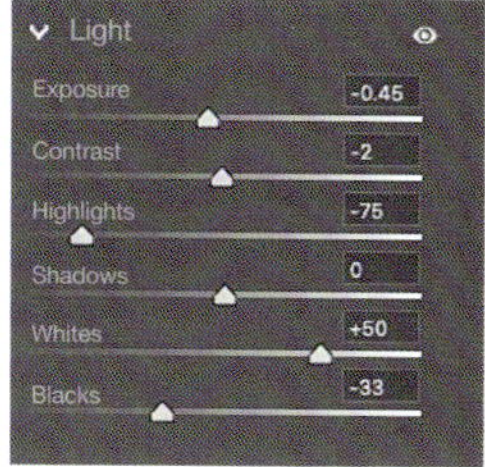

The Colombian naval tall ship, El Gloria, passing London's Tower Bridge. These three processed versions show, from top to bottom:

1. Enriched processing using Blacks, Whites and Highlights sliders

2. Conventional processing

3. Saturation increased by 40 percent

GRAPHIC SHADOW BLOCKS

In the previous chapter, we looked at a powerful way to use the shadow 'crushing' that Kodachrome was famous for, by using blocks of shadows as distinct shapes in a composition.

Translating this style for a digital file is not at all complicated; it simply calls for a firm view of how the image should look and a willingness to crush the blacks. Or perhaps that should be a *determination* to crush the blacks, as this is counter-intuitive to many people. However, it is guaranteed to produce interesting results.

An obvious candidate for this Kodachrome treatment would be any scene in which there are shadows that make distinct shapes, such as the example below, which was taken at an archaeological dig in Kerma, northern Sudan, in 2004. The date is significant, because this was my first reportage assignment where I mixed film and digital (in this case, using a Nikon D100), and I was essentially learning on the job. It was a minor miracle that the book – *Sudan: The Land and the People* – came out so well, and on the page opposite you can see how this picture appeared: very standard, unexceptional processing. In defence of this lighter treatment, I was trying to keep something of the sense of dust hanging in the air as the digging work proceeded.

Now, however, with all the improvements that have taken place in Adobe Camera Raw, and knowing how Kodachrome worked in some detail, I can produce the image as if it had been shot on film. As you can see, it's totally different in appearance and sensation: it's rich, dramatic and the shadows have become main actors in the scene as a result of exposing down with strong contrast. But remember that this is all a matter of taste and not everyone will like the Kodachrome-style version.

An archaeological dig at Kerma in northern Sudan. This is a more recently processed version, in which the shadows become definite shapes that contrast strongly with the white-robed figures.

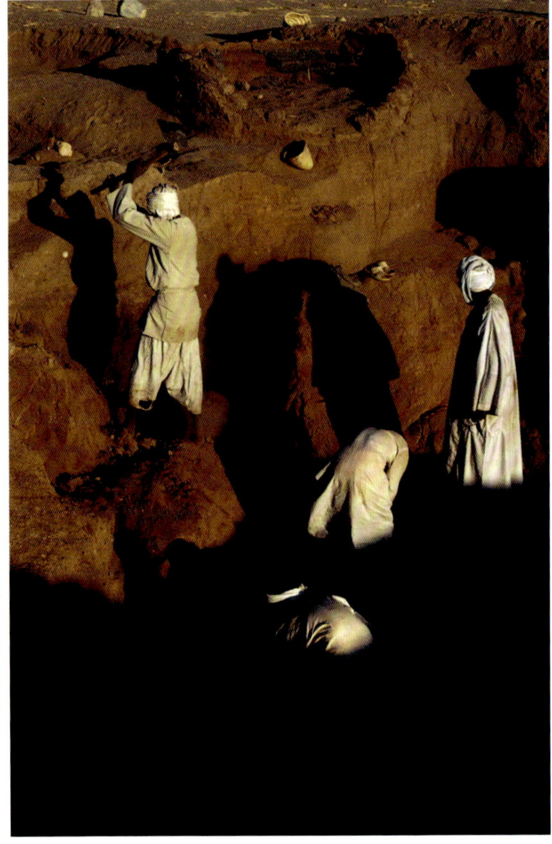

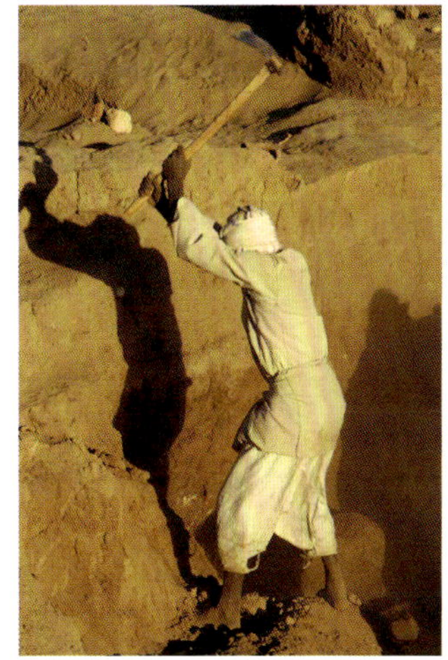

1. A detail from the picture shown opposite, processed as it appeared published in the book, nearly 20 years ago.

2. This is how I would process the same image now, according to the 'shadow block' method.

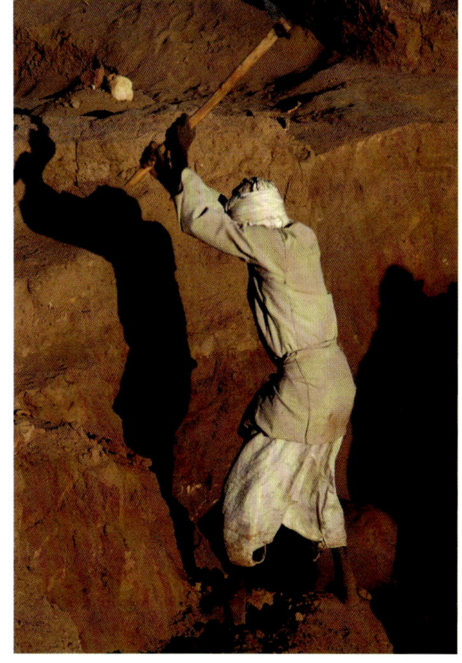

1.

2.

From the same story in northern Sudan is the shot looking out into the courtyard of a house from one of the rooms (below). There was a choice of two different ways to go here. The first, as processed and published at the time, held some sense of the shadow detail inside the room, which emphasized the sliver of weak sunlight filtering through at the top left. Without any local adjustment, this gave the scene beyond a pale, sandy look, which in memory seemed fine. More recently, I reprocessed the image to crush the shadows and treat the entire shadow area as a black frame for the outside view. Simply taking down the exposure deepened and enriched the colours, without requiring any saturation adjustment.

1. Another pair of pictures from the same Sudan book. This version is as it appeared in print.

2. A recent version of the same image. There was no adjustment to the Saturation on processing, just the Exposure and Blacks.

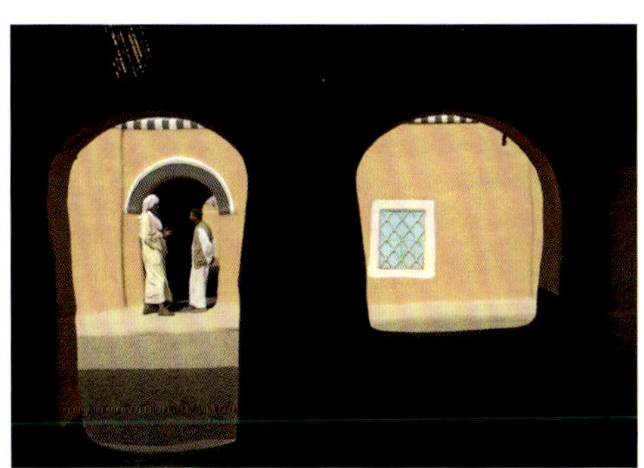

1.

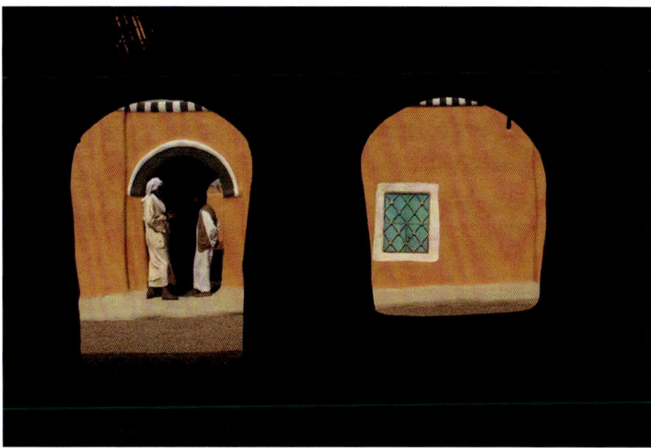

2.

FILM-LIKE SILHOUETTES

Shooting for a silhouette on transparency film – particularly Kodachrome – encouraged exposing down, as opposed to 'underexposing', which sounds like some kind of mistake.

This wasn't universal, but a large number of professionals took the Ernst Haas approach of concentrating on the texture and detail in the background. After all, once you've reduced the exposure to the point where the silhouette is more or less solid and featureless, it doesn't matter if you go down further– the silhouette isn't going to change.

Maybe it sounds strange to identify this kind of dense image solely with film, but because the early days of digital capture enabled photographers to open up the shadows in processing, the trend towards dark backgrounds and solid silhouettes, niche though it may have been, didn't continue. However, it is so different to what we now consider 'normal' that it's perhaps worth investigating afresh.

The lighter version of the handsome tree overlooking the Pacific on Mount Tam, near San Francisco (below), was the originally processed one, and it probably remains the more sensible. I was interested to see what would happen if the tones of the sky and ocean were made more important, though. Reducing the Exposure setting in ACR renders the tree solid black and draws more attention to the sunstar, which is also given more colour.

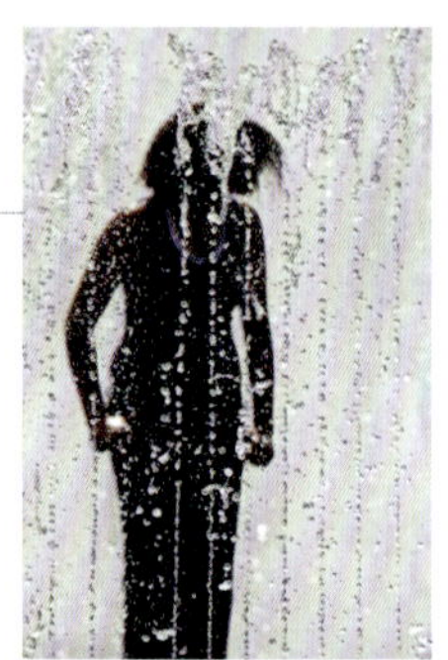

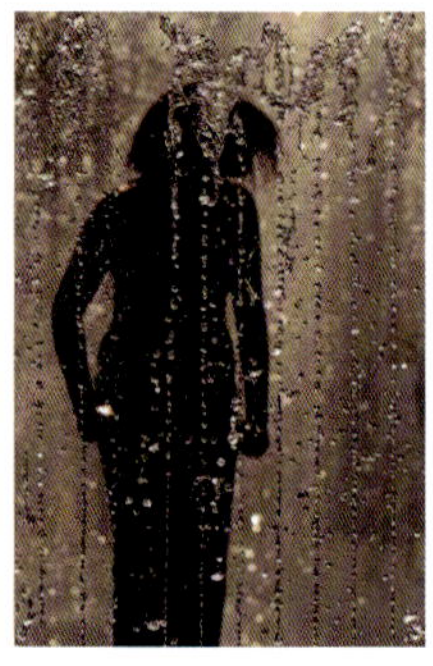

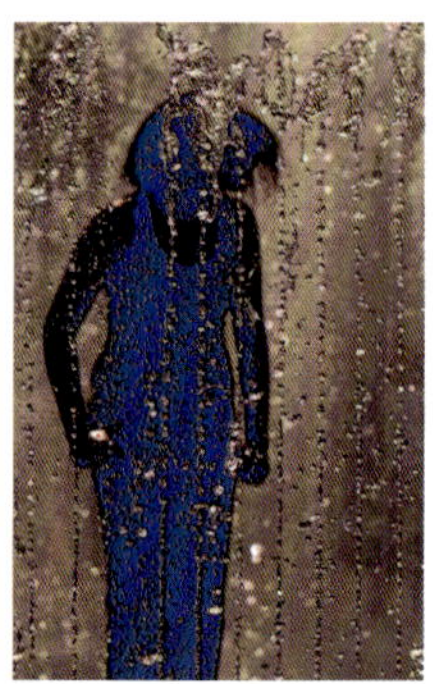

Girl in a city fountain. The top version is 'normal', while the middle version has been reduced by 2½ stops using Exposure during processing. This gives body to the water, but the figure is completely clipped to black, as the blue mask screenshot shows.

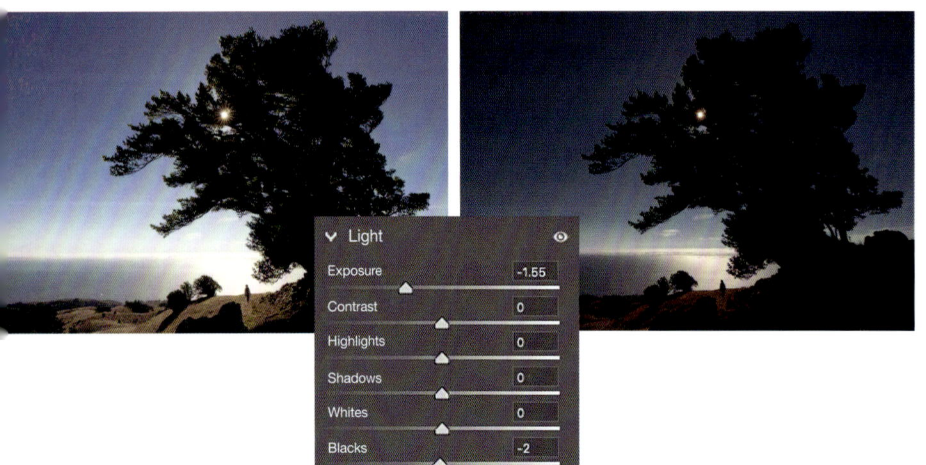

The tree on the Pacific coastline, as described in the text. Shown originally and 'normally' processed (1), and with the Exposure reduced by just over 1½ stops (2).

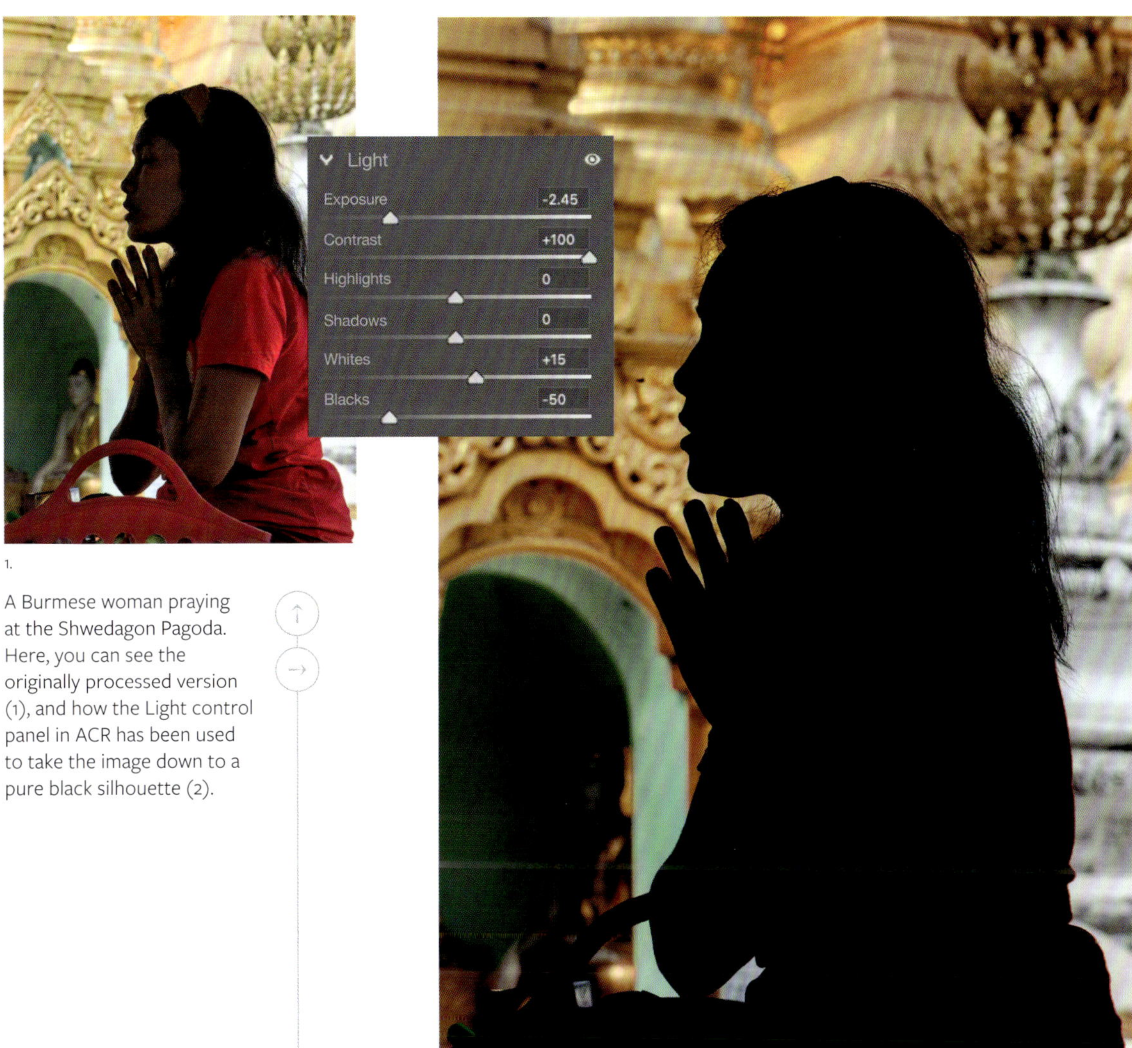

1.

A Burmese woman praying at the Shwedagon Pagoda. Here, you can see the originally processed version (1), and how the Light control panel in ACR has been used to take the image down to a pure black silhouette (2).

2.

The picture above, of a Burmese woman praying at the Shwedagon Pagoda, needed more careful, localized processing to handle the background of gilded decorations and stupas. I didn't shoot it with a silhouette in mind, and the lighting was softer, but all that gold had the potential to be treated richly, as outlined on pages 86–9. As with the tree picture, this had the Exposure slider taken down by 1½ stops, but also required ten retouching masks to even out the illumination on the background and ensure that all of the edges of the silhouette, especially the hands, stood out clearly.

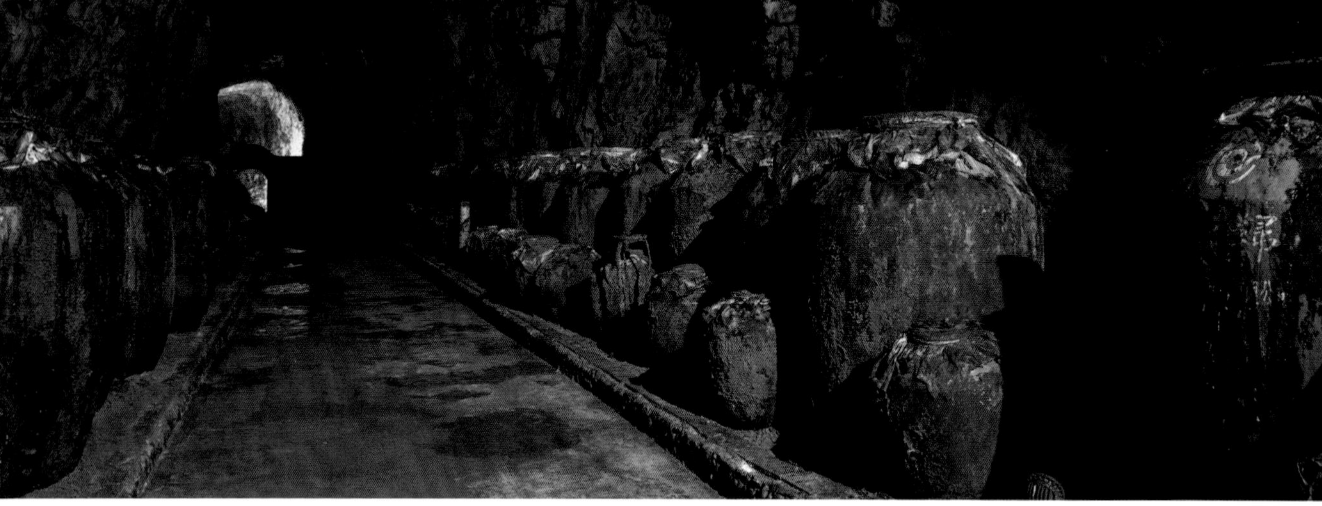

LOW REGISTER

T here are two different styles when it comes to changing the overall level of brightness. They vary most obviously by brightness, but also in a more nuanced way by the way the content of the picture is organized, and by atmosphere.

The first and more straightforward approach is what I call low register, which means lowering the brightness across the board, either at the moment of capture by reducing the exposure, or later when processing to achieve approximately the same result. I say 'approximately' because if you use Lightroom or ACR, you might think the Exposure slider is exactly the same as actual in-camera exposure: it isn't, but comes close in result, basically by moving around the extra 'headroom' given by a typical Raw file.

What interests me more than the techniques for darkening is the range of reasons for wanting what most people would consider an 'underexposed' image. There's a history behind this, and one of the first notable photographers to work deliberately in an extremely low register was Roy DeCarava. He was a self-taught New York photographer who shot almost exclusively in Harlem, starting in the

A cave in Yunnan, China, used for ageing white alcohol in earthenware jars at a constant temperature and humidity. As the available lighting was harsh, I chose a black-and-white treatment, keeping everything dark so the row of jars would emerge from blackness.

late 1940s. Trained as an artist, he was never part of the New York editorial and commercial photographic scene, and developed a distinctive style of printing of 'a world shaped by blackness'. This was no doubt part of his aim to counter what he described as 'black people ... not being portrayed in a serious and artistic way'.

Since DeCarava, other photographers have produced projects that involve an unexpected darkness, including Alex Majoli, Dawoud Bey and Jeffrey Conley. Bey's series, *Night Coming Tenderly*, portrays landscapes from the Underground Railroad, a network of secret routes used by escaped African American slaves.

The main picture shown opposite is a section of a partly finished, abandoned railway tunnel in China, which has been repurposed as a cellar for ageing jars of white alcohol. The smaller colour picture (right) is the scene as shot, under uninspiring lighting from a single arc lamp – the only light that was available.

The cave as originally shot (this is the JPEG that accompanied the Raw file).

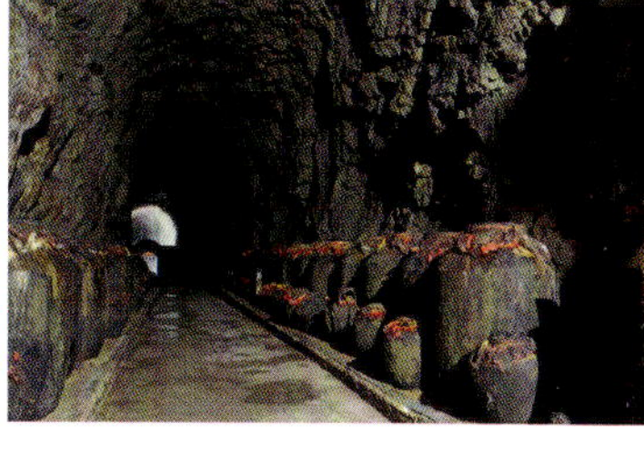

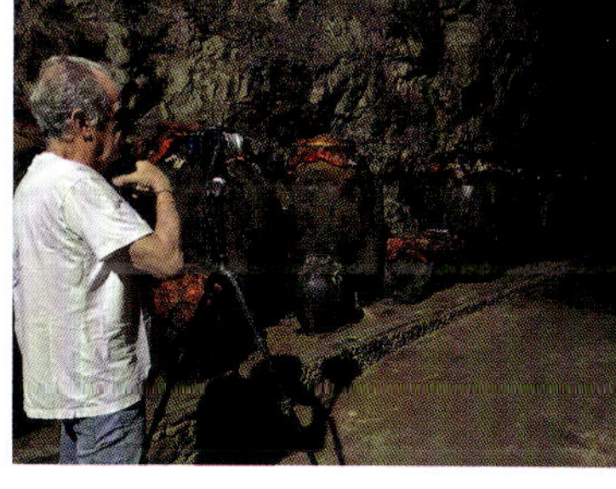

A deep gorge in the Scottish Highlands, shot on Polaroid SX-70 instant print film. I had actually misjudged the setting and was aiming for something lighter, but the Polaroid emulsion gave a strange and mysterious depth that I preferred to the 35mm film version.

LOW KEY

L ow key differs from low register in that while most of the frame is dark, there are bright accents that make for high contrast. This inevitably makes for a chiaroscuro effect, and there is a long history of this type of low-key lighting in cinema, which reached its height in the film noir movies of the 1940s.

As with low register, the motivation usually has to do with withholding information from the viewer. Typically, this is not because the shadowed areas lack interest, but more as a way of inviting the viewer to peer into the darkness. That at least was my intention with this interior of a traditional Tibetan house in northern Yunnan (below). For as long as I have been travelling in this region, I've been fascinated by the atmosphere of these dwellings. Tibetan houses are large and sturdy, with the living quarters on the upper floor, above storage and animals at ground level. Thick walls, relatively small windows and ample space make for a natural low-key light for daily living, with large pools of darkness and a bright pool around the (usually single) window. For this reason, there is an upholstered bench set into the window frame, where here the grandmother of the family is repairing a garment with needlework.

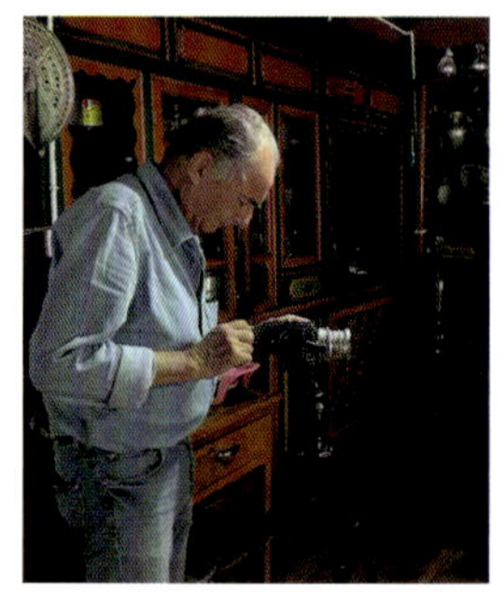

The living room of a traditional Tibetan house in northern Yunnan, near the town of Benzilan.

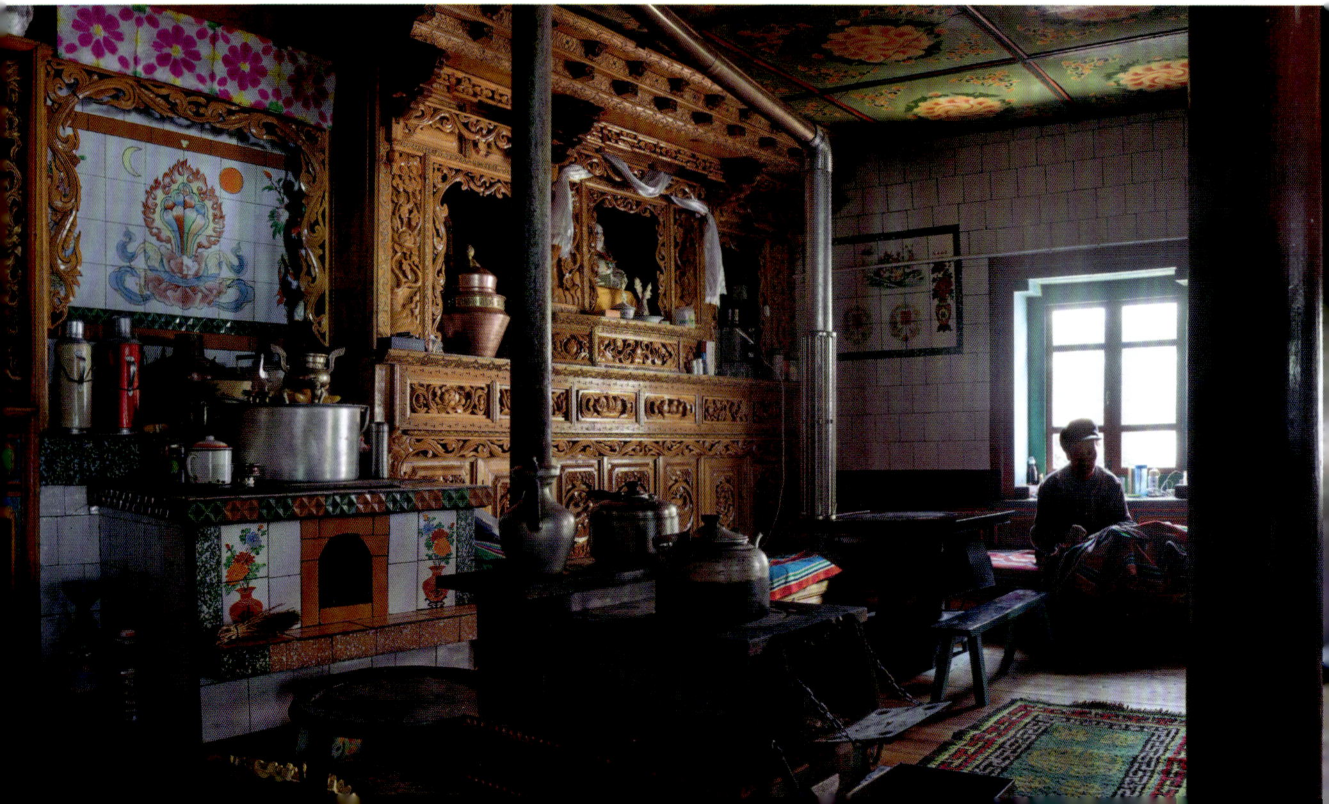

Interiors like these present themselves very differently according to your viewpoint. I chose this angle for my low-key treatment, looking towards the window from the doorway on the other side of the large room and favouring the dark walls and shelves, as you would see when entering the space. I was using a larger sensor on my old Hasselblad SWC, and panned slightly for a wider view to be stitched. The sensor and colour conversion are particularly good with this camera, and it would have been easy to open up all the shadow detail, but that would have destroyed the atmosphere, as shown below.

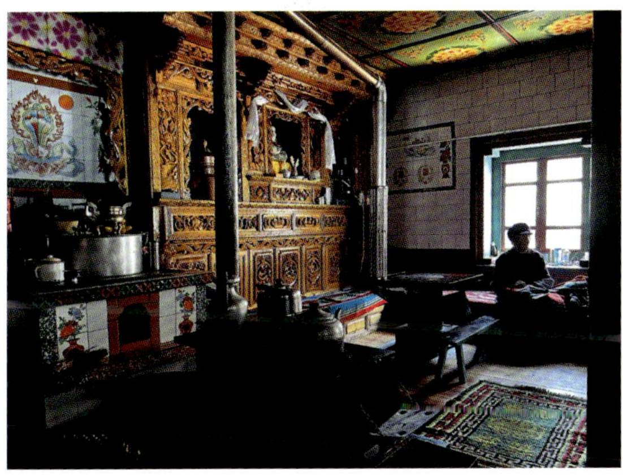

1.

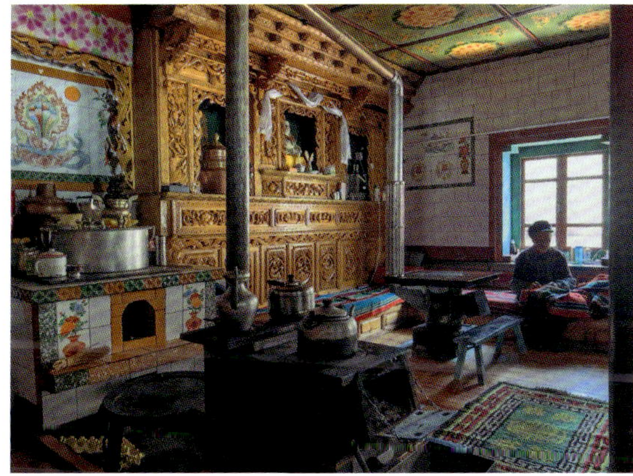

2.

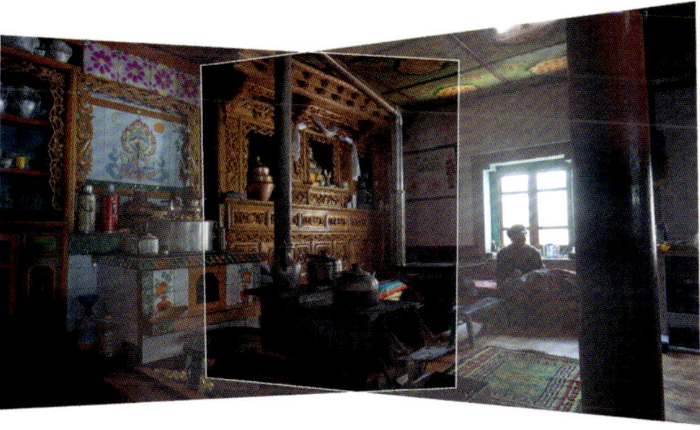

3.

1. The same scene shot on an iPhone using its in-camera computational processing

2. The same iPhone DNG file with shadows fully opened up

3. The stitching process for combining two horizontally overlapping frames

DENSE & RICH

T he subject here is a fairly well-known Tibetan temple and prayer wheel in the town of Shangri-La in southwest China. At an elevation of 3,000 metres (almost 10,000 feet), the air is crystal clear, and a couple of hours after sunrise there is this classic lighting, facing into the morning sun.

The sunlight catches the edges of the temple buildings, and what gives the scene interesting possibilities is the backdrop of mountains, in shadow. This is an example of edge lighting, and a scenario I've always been drawn to, whether in the street or a landscape. Depending on how you to choose to expose, it delivers very different results. Unless the subject itself is strongly coloured, the effect is always close to monochrome, which makes it tempting to treat it as black and white, in which extreme processing is perfectly acceptable. The one technical precaution is to shield the lens against flare, as the sun is shining straight onto the front element. In the two small colour versions overleaf, which I took later with an iPhone for reference, you can see the typical loss of contrast this can cause – it's nothing too serious, and straightforward enough to fix in processing.

The scene itself was conveniently how it appeared from my hotel balcony, but it wasn't quite special enough to be worth shooting until I heard shouts in the distance and saw smoke beginning to rise from behind the temple. I should have realized there would be Tibetan worshippers around this time burning incense for prayer, and this was suddenly a picture with some purpose. The smoke plumes appeared briefly, one at a time, and drifted around the building, beautifully backlit. By good fortune, one rose clear and straight, and that was the moment. Fortunately, having had several minutes to think idly about the view over my morning coffee, I was prepared to expose quite a way down so as to hold the highlights in the column of smoke, as those were the critical tones. The highlights on the tiled roof were much brighter, but they didn't matter – they were specular and could happily blow out with no loss.

That exposure safety precaution had already pushed my interpretation of the scene towards dark, but I had the idea while I was taking the picture that it might be interesting to see just how far I could go towards actual black. I had two reasons for this. The more obvious was to make the column of incense smoke really stand out dramatically, as it was, after all, the point of the picture. The other reason is harder to explain, but I didn't want the scene to read clearly and instantly. That might sound perverse, but I wanted to ask viewers to wonder what was going on for just a second or two. I didn't see this as a piece of reportage, but as an opportunity to make an unusual image that would require a little effort to work out. It wasn't a case of 'that's what Dafo Temple looks like in the morning', but rather how it could be the start of a strange image.

1. Reference shot on an iPhone (cropped to same proportions)

2. The same iPhone shot optimized to remove the haziness from light flare

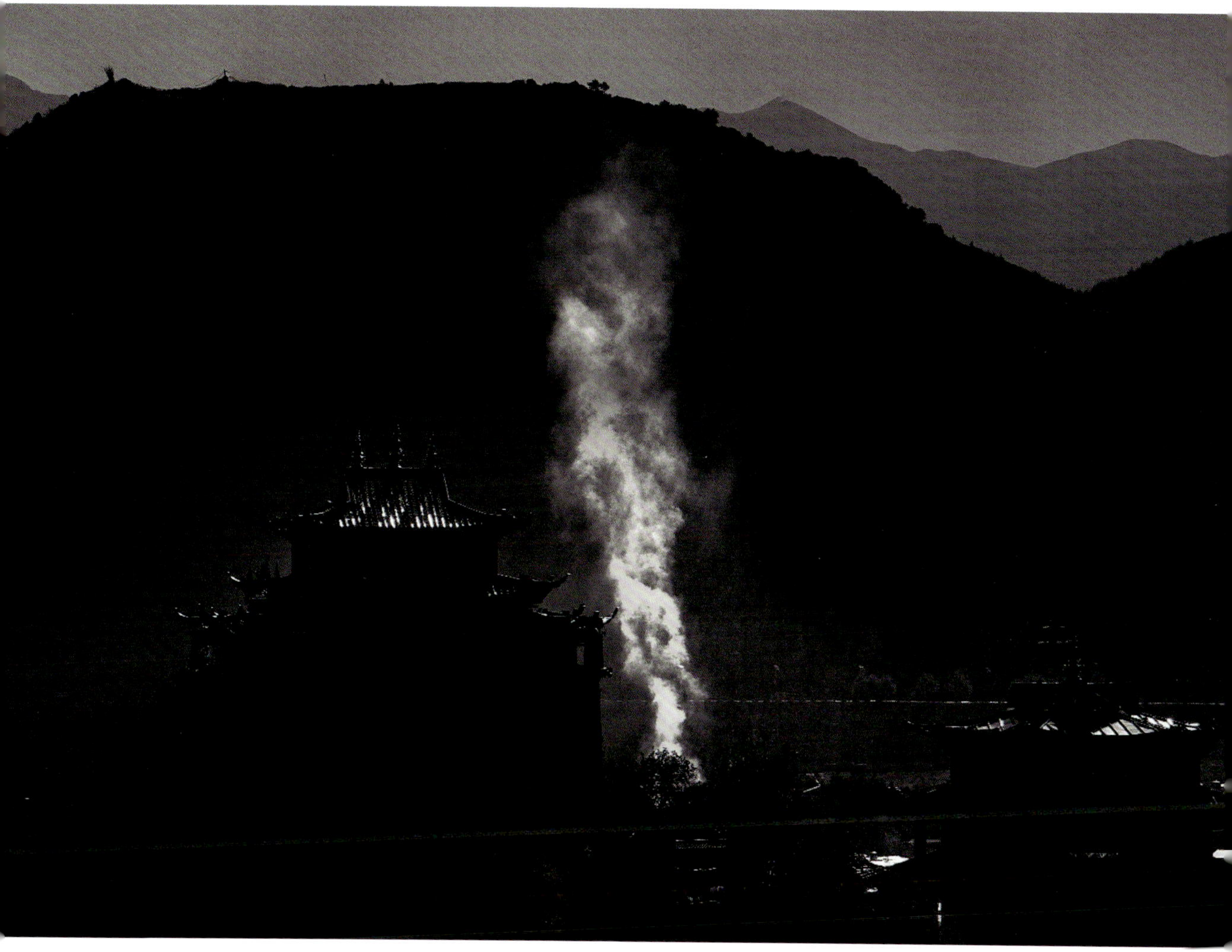

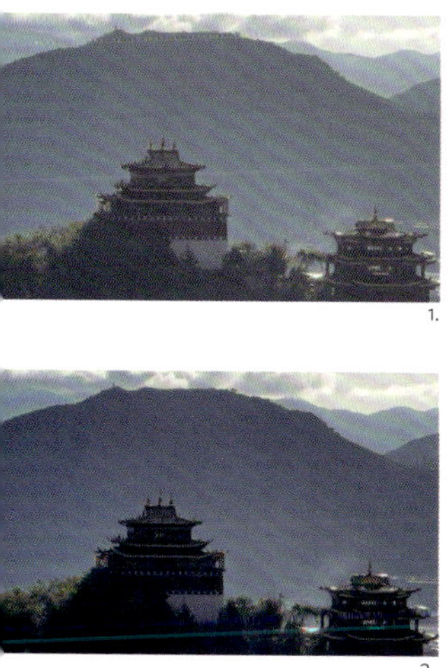

1.

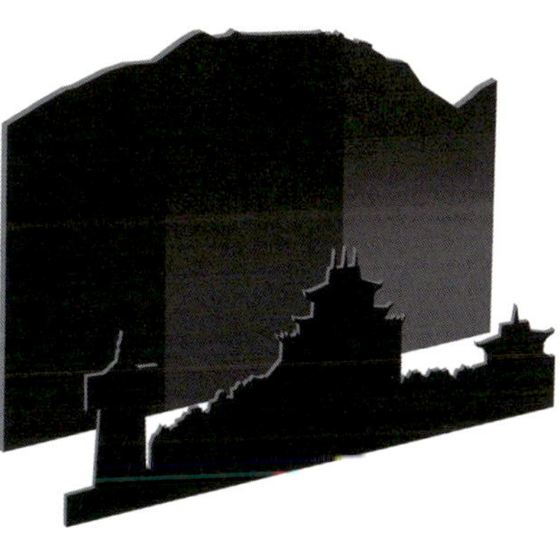

2.

Morning incense burning at Dafo Temple in the town of Shangri-La, Yunnan.

There needs to be a just-noticeable tonal separation between the temple and the hills behind. Of the three basic choices shown here – very dark, dark and medium – I opted for between dark and very dark.

Processing the image took much longer than I expected, and any thoughts I might have had about the tones and the different elements simply falling into place to match my slightly vague intentions quickly went out of the window. One obvious priority was to maximize the contrast between the delicate curls of smoke and the dark background without allowing any of the smoke to blow out to white. That required delicacy, working with a soft-edged radial filter, but there was a limit to how dark the background could go – it had to remain constant and smoothly graded across the entire mountainside.

This was where the real problem lay, as the key to this image is the separation between the outline of the temple buildings and the shaded mountains. The temple is one plane, the mountainside another. I had no problem with the darkest parts of the temple going to black, but how dark should the mountainside go? And to keep the contrast in the upper half of the frame good and strong, I needed it to shade smoothly from very dark on the skyline down to a grey that just allowed the temple to stand out clearly. Too light and the mystery of the scene would evaporate. Too dark and the temple wouldn't stand out.

Aldermen of the City of London at the annual Lord Mayor's Show. Taking the background down to black and their robes almost as dark allows the gold braiding to dominate the picture.

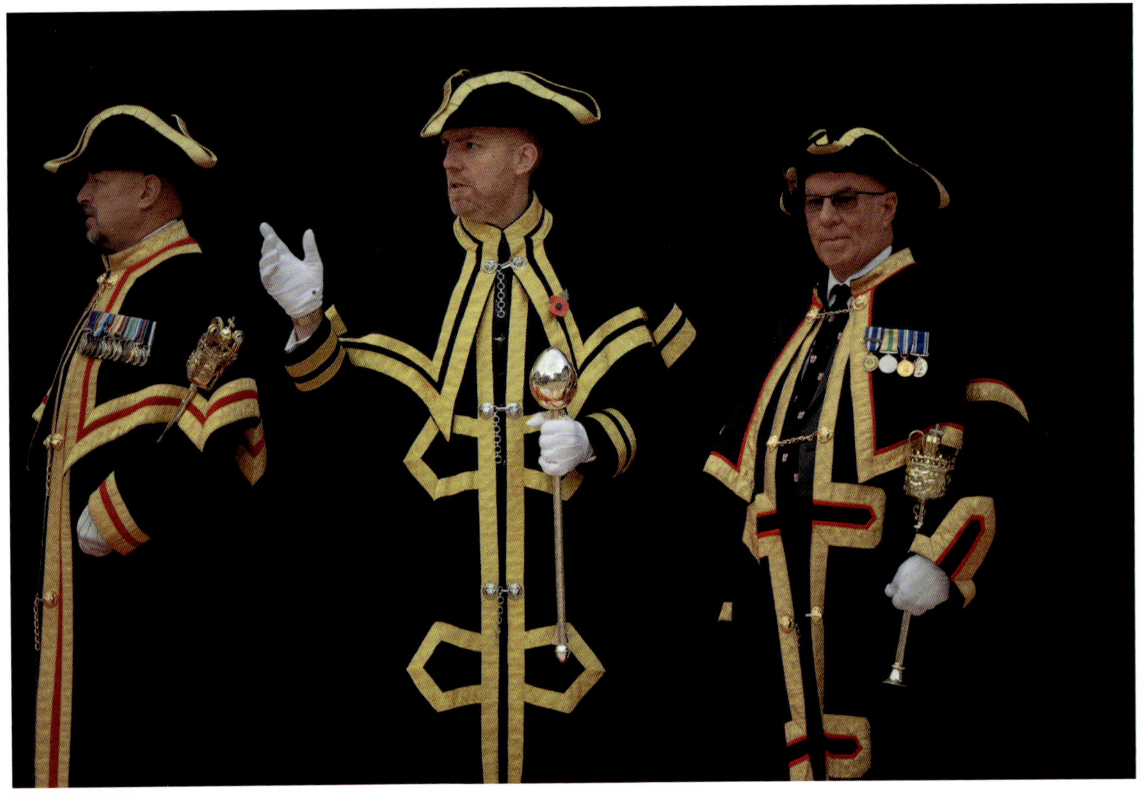

At the same Lord Mayor's Show, underexposing slightly and increasing contrast slightly during processing ensures a rich red in the coachman's cape and no highlight clipping in the traffic light.

There's no objective best treatment, only judgment and personal taste (my ambition to hover on the edge of black). To this day, I'm not completely sure, and have to admit to making two versions: one for the printed page (here) and another, slightly brighter and higher contrast for a phone screen (which you can see on my Instagram account). The two displays work differently, and the tricky one to predict is the printed page, because of the variables of paper coating and inking. In the end, the publisher's production department have had to keep an eye on it.

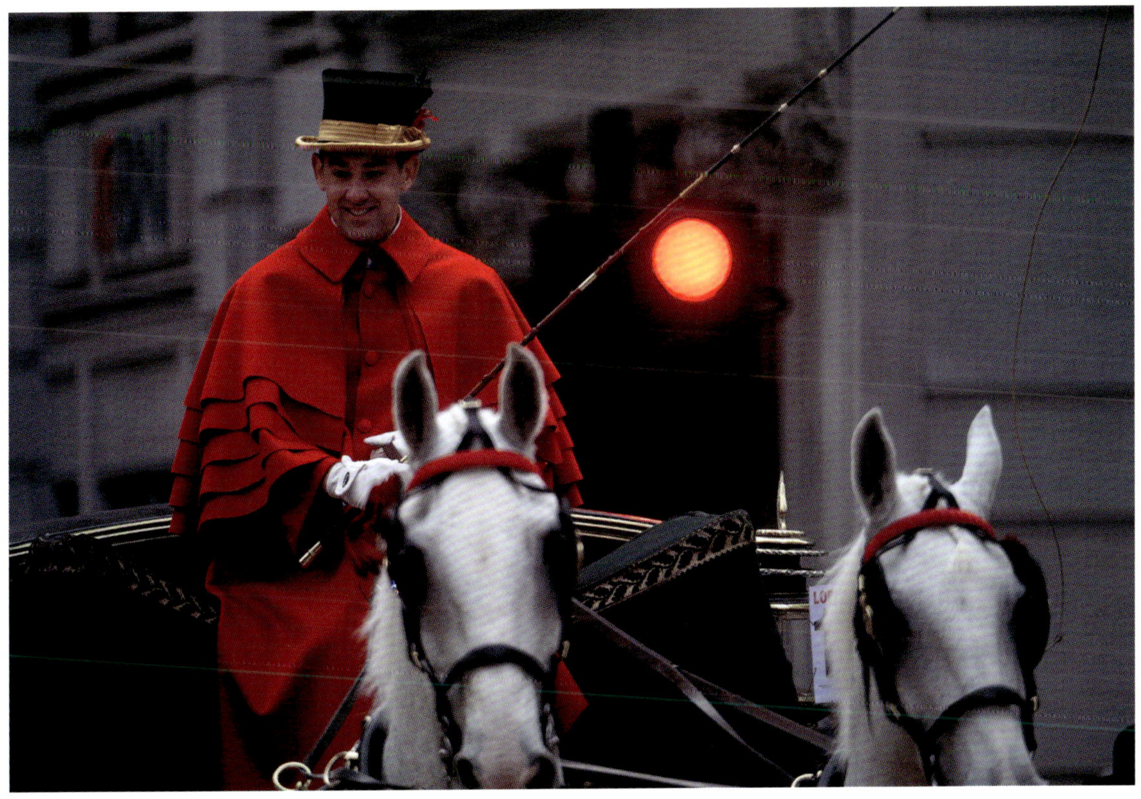

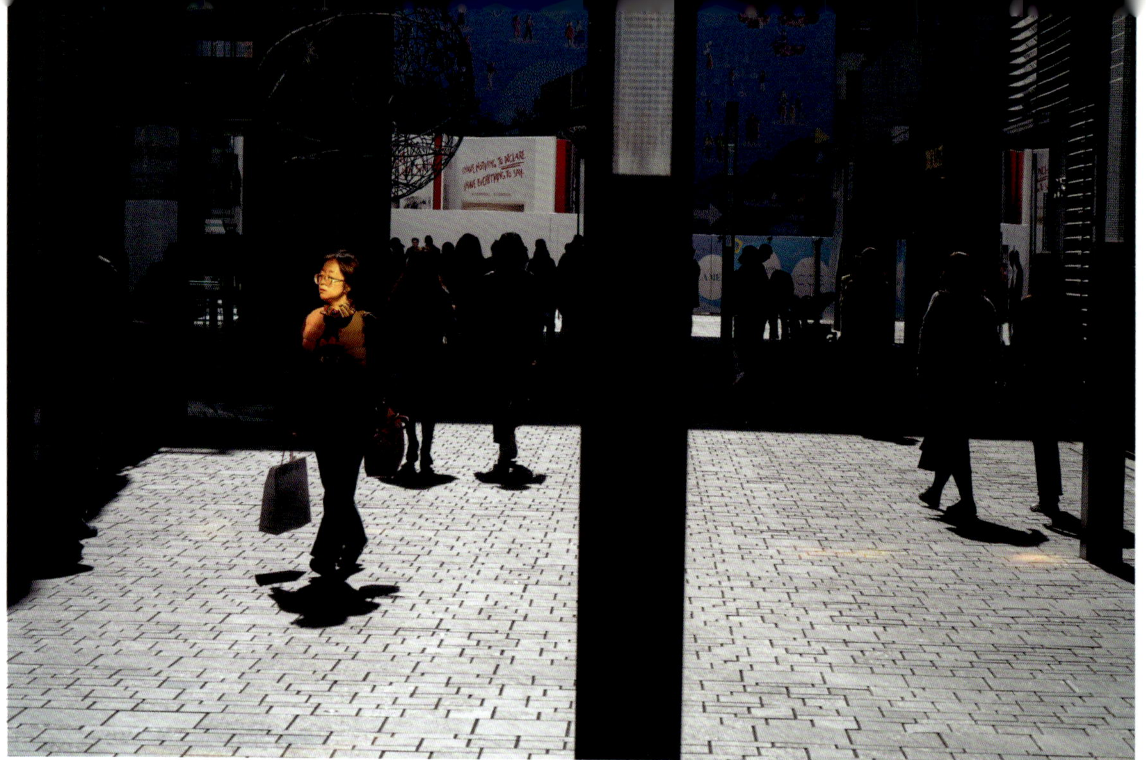

EXPOSING FOR SPECULAR HIGHLIGHTS

Traditional exposure and processing wisdom has it that specular highlights – defined as the small, bright reflections of the sun and other lights – don't count in the calculations. You simply let them blow out and because they're tiny, nobody minds. This extends to actual light sources, as long as they're little more than points, such as street lighting in a broad urban night-time view.

For most photography, this works – scintillating dots of light have their own place in a picture and don't need to have tone. But what about larger reflecting surfaces, such as those shown here? As you saw on pages 68–69, exposing down so the reflections have texture, a tonal range and colour will change the image radically. Realism goes out of the window, because the exposure needed is so great that most surroundings become unrecognizable. With transparency film, this was always experimental – it was almost impossible to predict how the picture would come out, although depressing the depth-of-field preview button at a small aperture setting gave a few clues.

Reflected sunlight from a gold-coated window in Beijing's Sanlitun district gives a strange spotlighting effect on shoppers.

With digital capture, there's more control in some ways, because of the range of processing methods, but the problem of clipping is ever-present. Holding large specular details digitally means paying close attention to whatever clipping warning you use on the camera, and shooting a range of exposures if there's enough time. Some recovery is often possible at the processing stage (using the Highlights slider in ACR, for instance), but by making specular highlights the focus of attention, any loss of detail becomes all the more obvious.

In the case of the oil storage tank in Sudan (below), I exposed for the paler, more 'normal' version, and that's how it appeared in the book: open in feeling, a slightly hazy desert sunset, and even lighting across the frame with the exception of a few highlights reflecting the sun. I still have no problems with this interpretation, but out of curiosity tried to reinterpret it with a more film-like, richer exposure. This version makes more of colour, and the attention is drawn inwards and downwards by the tonal gradient.

1. One of the main oil storage tanks at the central processing facility in Heglig, south of the Nuba Mountains in Sudan. This paler version is how the image appeared in the book it was shot for.

2. An image taken a moment later given a richer exposure through processing. I'm not sure which I prefer.

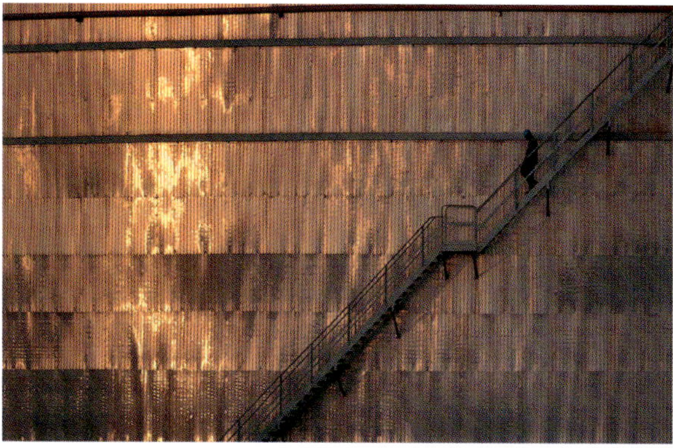

1.

2.

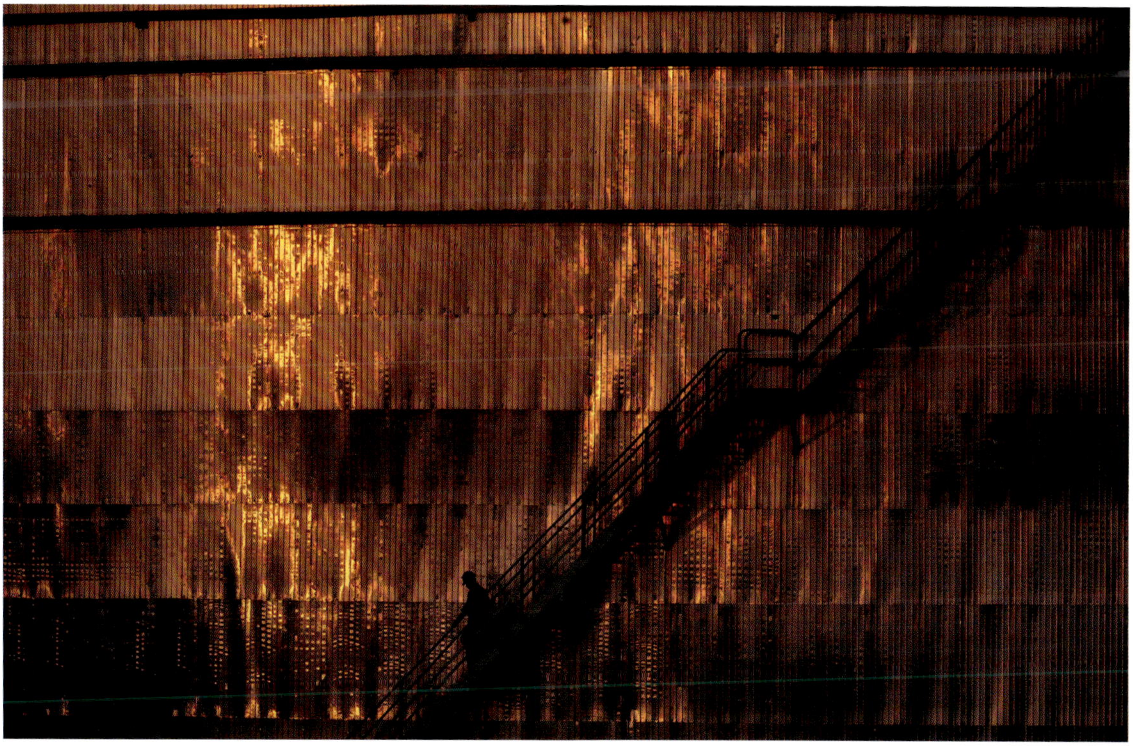

SULTRY LIGHT

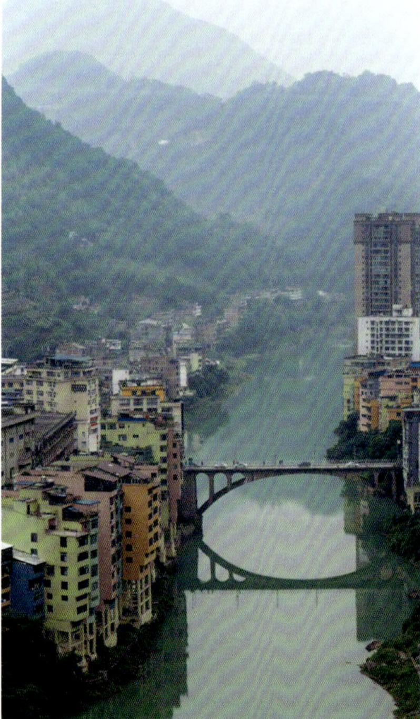

’m always quietly surprised, even after all this time, at how seemingly unrelated things in a scene make me wonder how bright or dark it should be. In this case, it was the weather. The town here, in the northeast of Yunnan Province, has something of a TikTok reputation as the narrowest town in the world – just 30 metres (100 feet) across in places.

That normally wouldn’t encourage me to hunt down a location like this, but I happened to be nearby and the TikTok views are all from drones high above the narrow, steep-sided valley. I was more interested in a view from Yanjin’s only bridge.

There usually isn’t much choice in lighting when you’re on the road, unless you’re very determined and the scene is important enough to fixate on and keep returning to, as dedicated landscape photographers tend to do. That wasn’t the case here. I was passing through, but happy for this quiet, flat daylight; there were no sharp shadows to interfere with the details of the scene, of which there were plenty. On both sides of the Guan River, a tributary of the Yangtze, the thin slabs of apartment blocks are raised on concrete pillars, partly to cope with the uneven rocky slopes, and also to protect from rises in the water level. In fact, there’s a dam downstream that keeps this steady, and the ribbon of still water is an important part of the scene.

It was hot, still and oppressive, as summers across much of China can be, and to me this added to the sense of closed-in crowding, which I wanted to make part of the picture. That meant exposing just a little darker than usual. With transparency film, this would be critical, but these days, I do this kind of photography with a medium-format digital back, and fine-tuning can happen later.

The setting and viewpoint on the town’s only bridge.

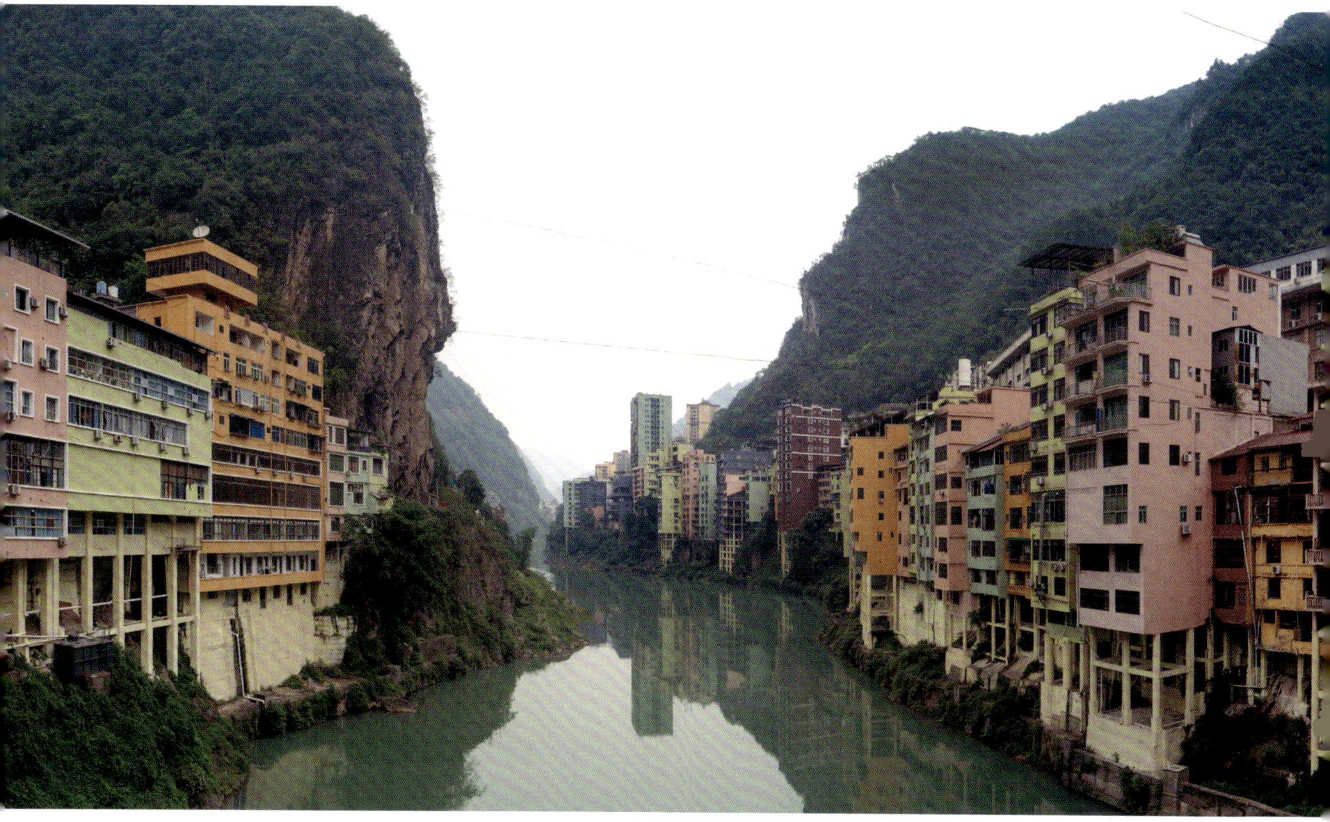

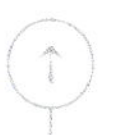

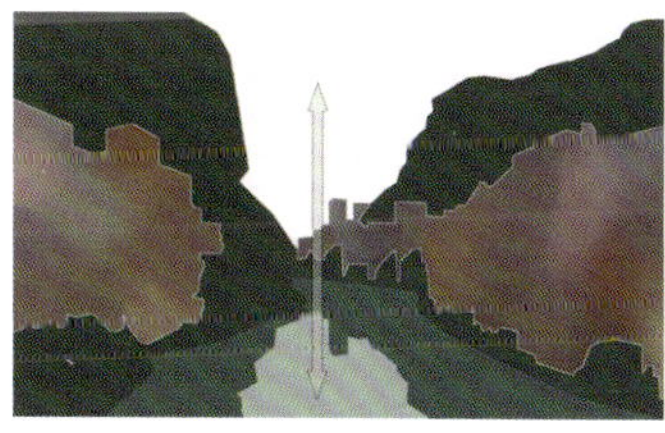

1.

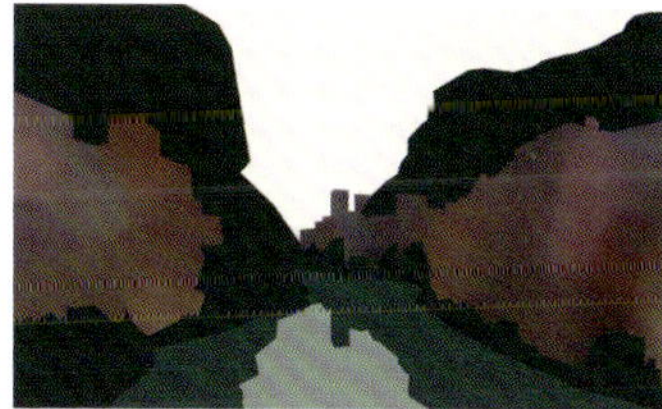

2.

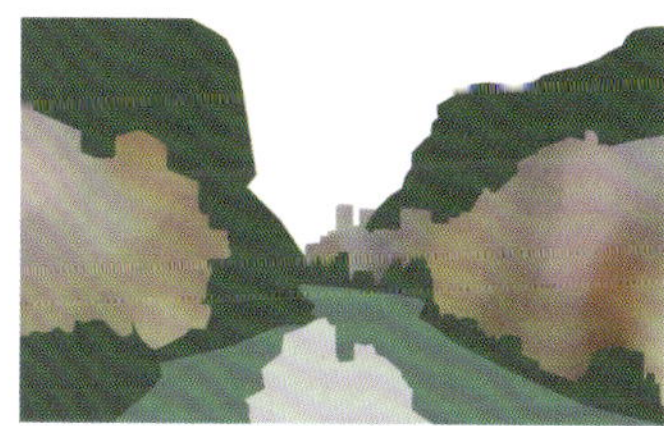

3.

   With completely even light like this, the measurement of choice is an incident light reading that ignores differences between surfaces (such as the coloured buildings and dark forested hillside). I use an old Weston Master IV with a plastic dome, which is perfectly accurate and needs no power, and adjusted half a stop down from the exposure reading it gave me.

   If you work with in-camera light readings, they will measure the light reflected off whatever you're shooting, which calls for a little more careful judgment. What's important in the frame? In other words, what's the key subject? Here, it's the mass of differently painted buildings. The forested hillsides are tonally just a backdrop, while the cloudy sky needs to be just short of absolute white (and its reflection a realistic couple of f/stops darker). My interpretation is an average 45-percent brightness for the buildings *en masse*.

The final image was a two-frame, horizontal pan-and-stitch. The schematics show the scene reduced to simple graphic blocks, with the three basic brightness choices:

1. Final choice (note the two-stop difference between the sky and its reflection)
2. Very dark
3. Conventionally bright

BRIGHTER

5

I mages that are bright overall are almost universally seen as upbeat and positive. Our eyes are naturally attracted to the light, and without getting too deep into it, this has come from our evolution; as a species, we have learned to welcome the light.

In the history of photography, it was around the 1860s when some photographers began to see themselves as artists rather than camera operators, making a visual record of people and places. Consequently, the idea of shooting into the light took hold – not just accepting the flare that lens optics created, but enjoying it for its glowing, feel-good effect.

This has never gone away, and the most popular style in contemporary wedding photography is actually called 'light and airy'. It combines a number of techniques that include shooting towards the light (a low sun or a large window), exposing fully so that parts of the image go towards white, and embracing flare that adds even more bright tones.

As with darker images, there are three possible components. First is a naturally light-toned subject or scene, with winter snowscapes leading by a long way. Second is the light, of which the classic scenario is shooting into the sun (we expect such a view to make us squint, and a sense of brightness is inescapable). The third component is the personal decision to shift the image to a higher register by either overexposing at the time of capture or raising the brightness during processing, or both together. This doesn't have to be logical; it can simply be creative expression.

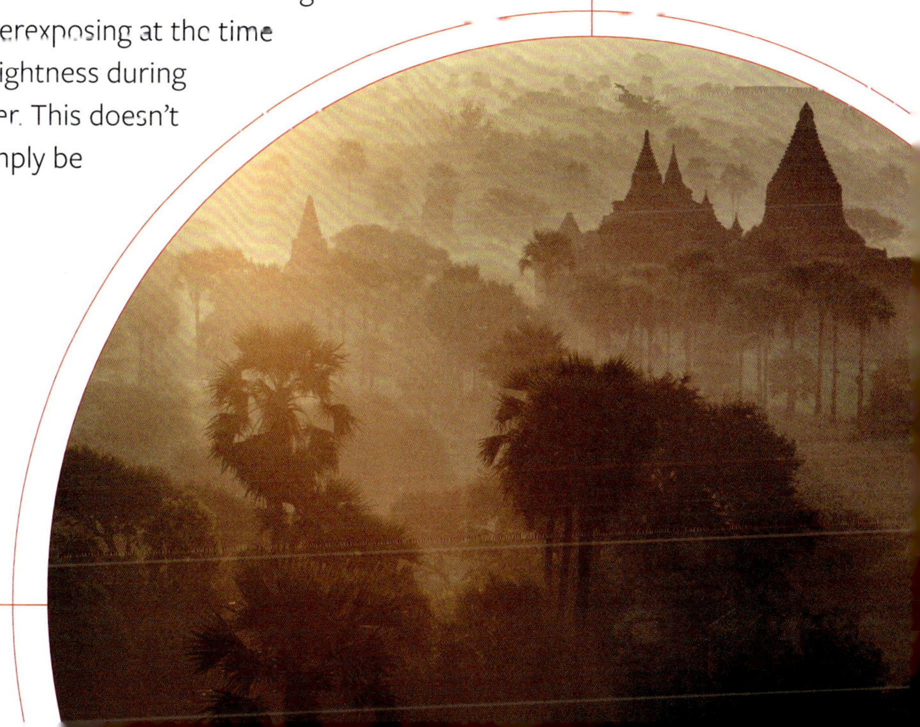

HIGH REGISTER

There are two related ways of achieving a significantly brighter look to a photograph. The first is to raise the amount of light through exposure or processing, and this is what I call high register. The other is a more specific style – high key – in which most of the frame is in the highlights, but punctuated by small, significant, dark features.

A simplistic difference is that high-register pictures have low contrast and no dark shadow areas, while high-key pictures have small black elements that give them a high contrast. With high-register images, the idea of moving all the tones up the brightness scale is firmly a personal choice linked to taste. It can be applied to just about any scene or subject, and the general result is a more open, airy feeling.

There's already a latitude in what most viewers accept as a normal, average brightness without much questioning, and while there's no way to measure this tolerance, from experience I would say it is almost one stop in either direction, brighter or darker. The high register style pushes the exposure further – above one stop at least – and as you might expect, it's not going to be acceptable to every viewer. Some people, maybe many, will see it as overexposed, particularly if they have some knowledge of photography. Others will more willingly accept it as a stylistic statement.

White Sands, New Mexico, exposed very fully on Ektachrome film. A more 'standard' exposure would be between one and two stops lower, which would have favoured richer colours in the sky. However, it would lose the ethereal atmosphere of this treatment.

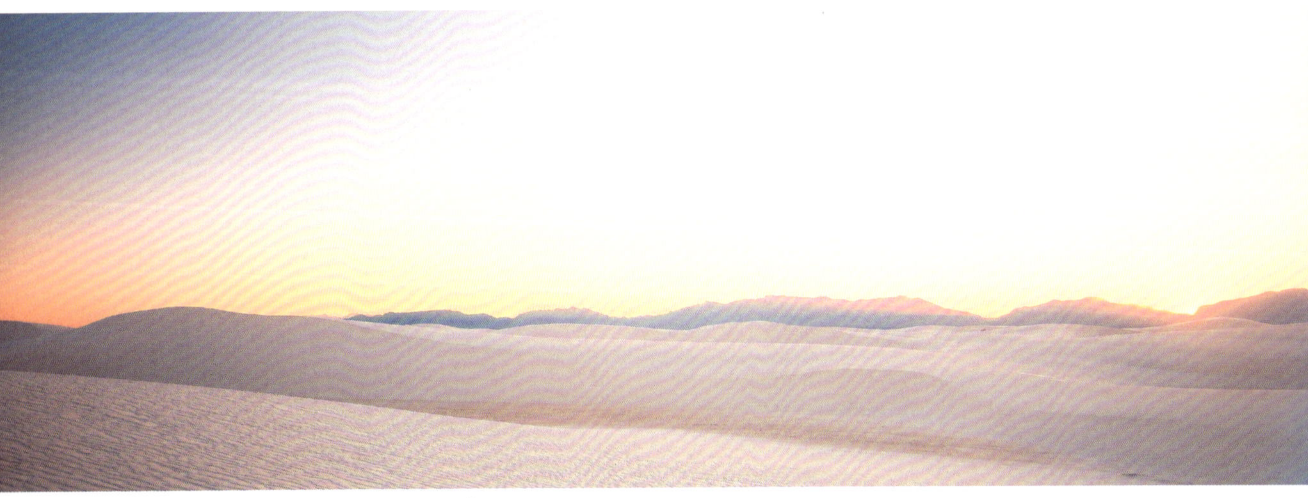

Exposure is, naturally, the obvious one-step control for giving a light, bright and open mood to a picture, but processing and printing can do more or less the same, and offer more control – and importantly the time to reflect and experiment. As with all matters of adjustment, colour transparency film stands apart as being the least adjustable. 'Pushing' means increasing development time or temperature or both for a brighter result, but also more contrast. Negative film, both black-and-white and colour, can also be pushed, but the darkroom stage of making the print is the usual place for making brightness decisions. The digital equivalent in Lightroom, Adobe Camera Raw or any other processing app offers more controls, with the basic Exposure slider, as Adobe calls it, doing most of the work.

I'm showing two examples here, from both the film and digital worlds. The panorama of White Sands, New Mexico (opposite), was shot on Ektachrome, and is a good example of film's tolerance for overexposure, without clipping. Landscapes such as this, with a light subject and the sun in the frame, can benefit from a high-register treatment, which helps them look expansive and open.

The second example (below) was a commercial shoot of yoga at a resort in China. Shot digitally, the colour version was standard, but I wanted to see how far up the brightness register I could take the image, without it becoming unrecognizable. This is about as far as it could go.

A yoga shoot at the luxury resort of Bei Bei, near Chongqing, China. With this flat light, there are multiple choices for how bright or dark you could go; this is a 'standard' rendering.

This black-and-white version is at the upper limit of exposure, and maybe even a bit beyond.

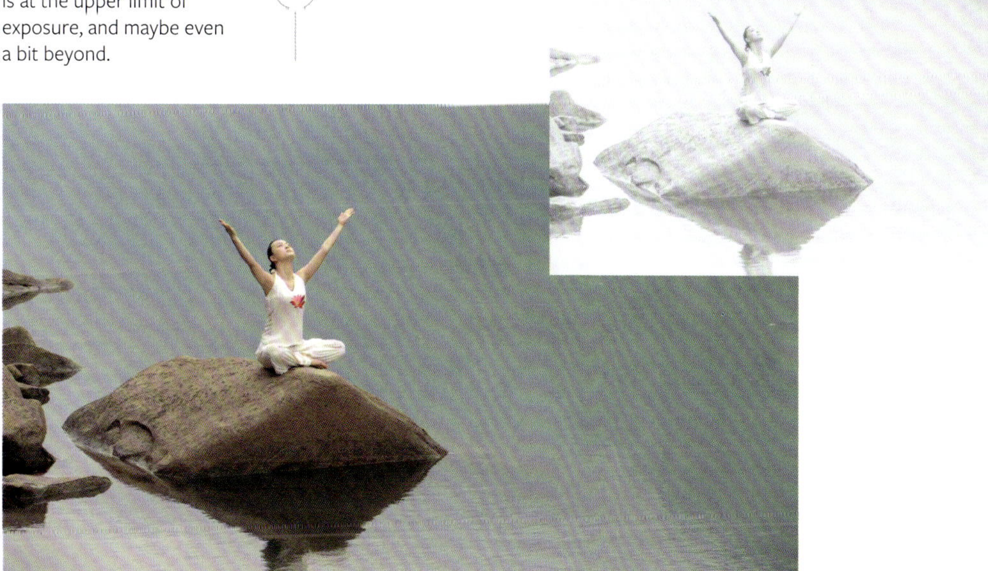

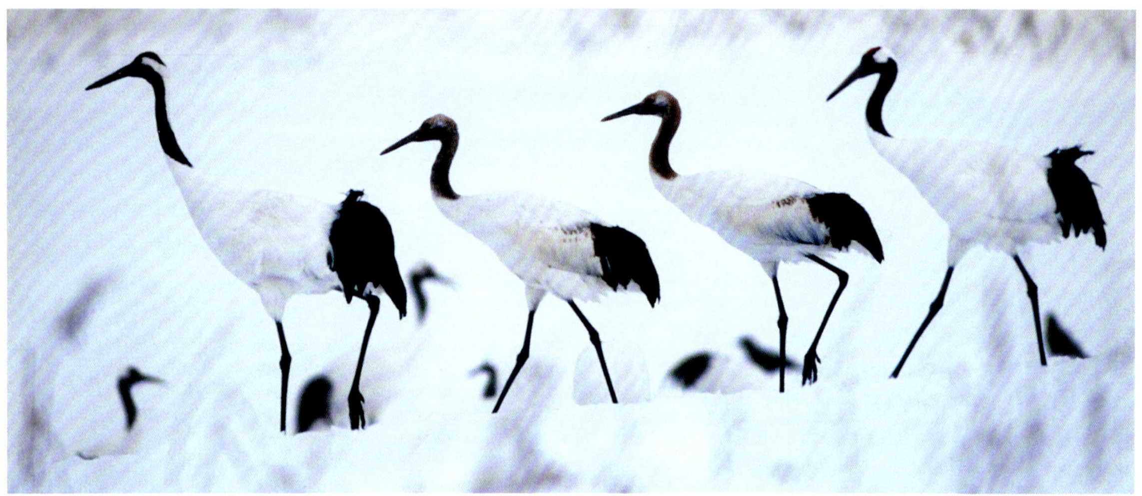

HIGH KEY

W hile high-key images still rely on a full exposure and an overall very bright (often white) appearance, they differ from high-register photographs, as they also require small, dark – even black – features. That might sound like a minor difference, but pictures in this style are conceived differently, work on contrast and are far more dependent on the subject and scene.

Crudely put, high-key images depend on a small, dark subject set against a very pale, ideally featureless setting or background. The result is always graphic and simple, and this alone is usually enough to justify the picture. The circumstances that allow this are not that common, which perhaps explains why high-key imagery is well-liked by most viewers.

An obvious example is snowscapes with features, and in the photography art world, Michael Kenna, Tim Rudman and Chuck Kimmerle are known for their high-key snow pictures. My picture above follows the same path: Japanese cranes in the winter snow on the northern island of Hokkaido. The exposure and processing for high-key images are a little more demanding than they are for high register, because they depend on separating the background and subject very strongly. Exposing for a near-white setting such as snow means increasing by about two stops, but the dark features need a black point. In processing, setting the Blacks and Whites (using Adobe's terminology) to their limits is a useful starting point.

Siberian cranes in winter on the northern Japanese island of Hokkaido. Their plumage almost blends with the snow.

To be honest, I'm a little reluctant to use the term high key, or at least cautious, and the reason is that its meaning has changed over the years to the point where it means different things to different people. My definition is what most photographers think of, but the original term came from early television studios in the 1950s and was very specific. On the traditional three-point lighting scheme used in Hollywood, it meant using two or three key lights across the set, with a bright background, so that the general appearance was bright and shadow-free. It made production faster, though lacking atmosphere. The modern meaning inherits only a little of this.

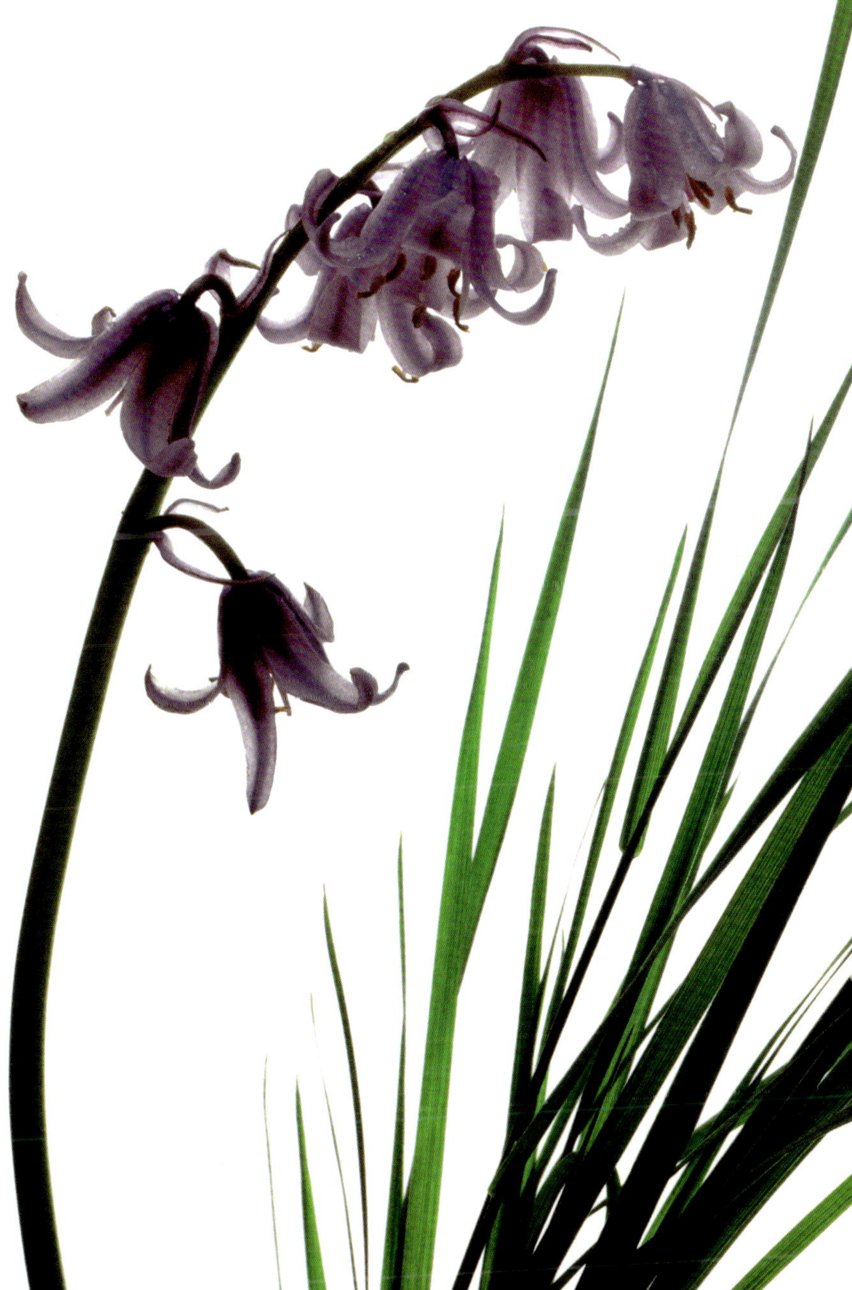

A backlit shot of bluebells, taken in the studio. A single light was positioned behind the subject and diffused through a large sheet of translucent Perspex.

TWO-WAY CHOICE

S ome shooting situations offer two perfectly valid ways
to go with the exposure, such as darker and richer,
or lighter and more glowing. This scene is just such an
example, and it's a reasonably famous location, the interior
of Saint Peter's Basilica in Rome.

We were actually on an assignment, the filming of the 2023 movie *Samsara* on
70mm film, but I was taking time off to shoot stills. As you can see, the space is
enormous and has a lot going for it photographically. The architecture soars, there's
a rich interplay between marble and gilding, the sculptures are exquisite and
the light that streams in from the cupola is, to put it mildly, atmospheric.

Just from these few words of description, it's clear that there could be
competing interpretations for the camera. Gold, for example, generally looks most
impressive when it's a little underexposed, and that means taking the exposure
down and raising contrast. The light beams, on the other hand, are hard to ignore,
and special enough for me to want to make them prominent.

Now, there are two ways of handling them. One is to have them much lighter
than their surroundings. As they are already high on the tonal scale, approaching
white, that suggests darkening the surroundings, which means going richer (in the
same direction as the gilding I just mentioned) and more contrasty.

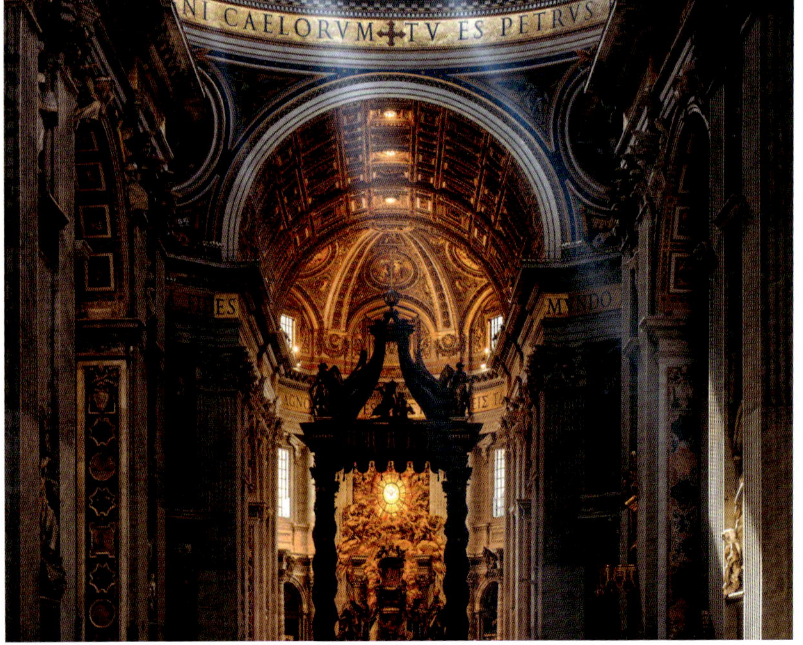

The darker choice in the Vatican aimed for a dense and rich look. There was no increase in saturation.

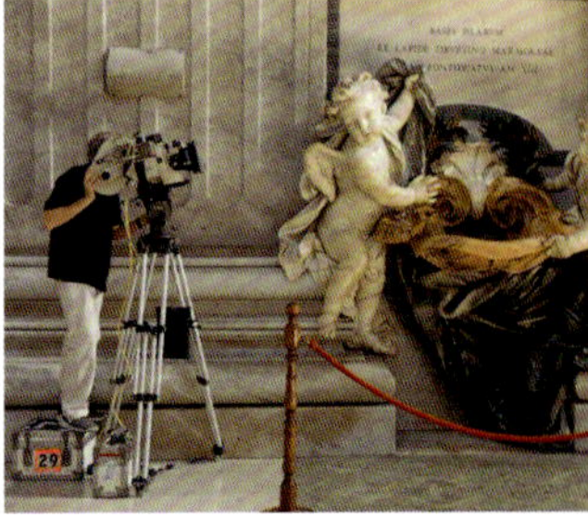

The 70mm camera set-up for the view on the page opposite.

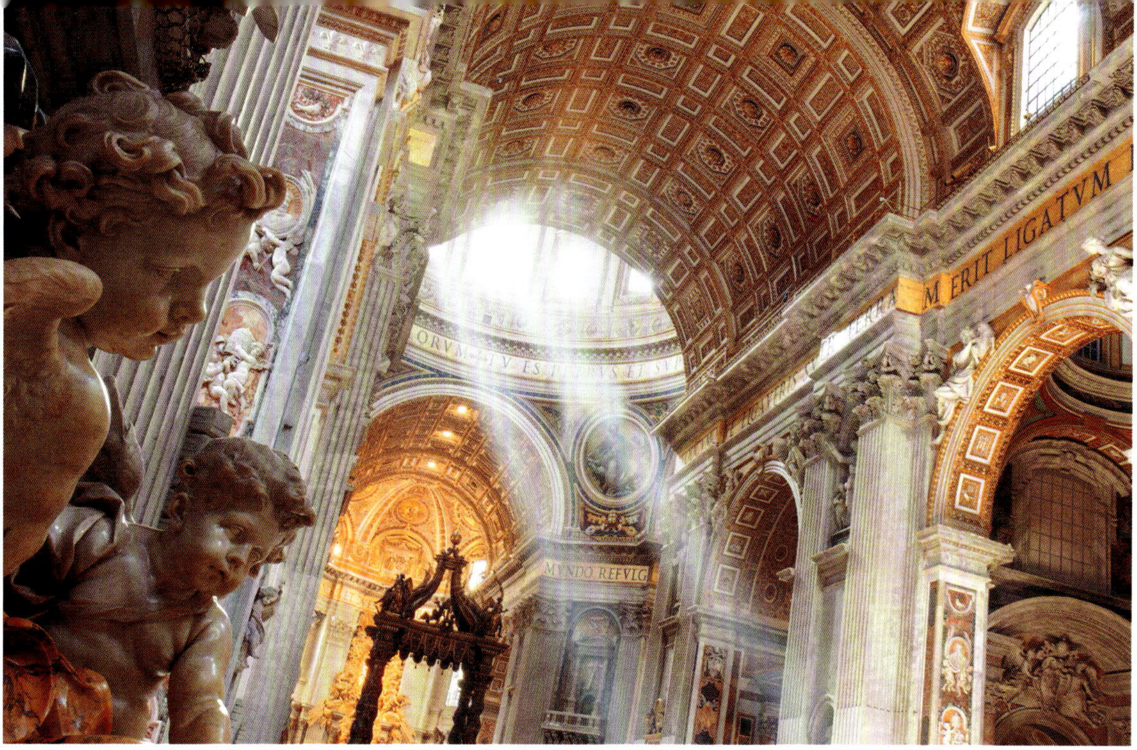

The second way of dealing with the beams is to make sure
they have a moderate contrast along most of their length, but
spread out from their source – the windows of the cupola –
with a lot of glow, or luminosity. The idea here would be to
give the viewer the impression that the light is almost blinding
and hard to look at, which is quite a reasonable idea for a
place of worship.

For the image opposite, I opted for a tighter, head-on view
of the end of the aisle, and a deeper and richer treatment
to emphasize the richness of the colour and focus attention
inwards. The main picture (top) is at a more powerful angle,
taken from a position right next to a pair of putti, looking
upwards, and tilted. This gives the image a near-far construction, with a strong
impression of depth that is exaggerated by the diverging light beams streaming
down towards us. The smaller version (above right) was my original processing,
which is a little brighter than the end-of-aisle picture, but I reworked it for the main
image to make it more luminous. This meant sacrificing detail and colour richness,
in return for a feeling of spreading, glowing light. Ultimately, both are
valid choices, and depend on taste.

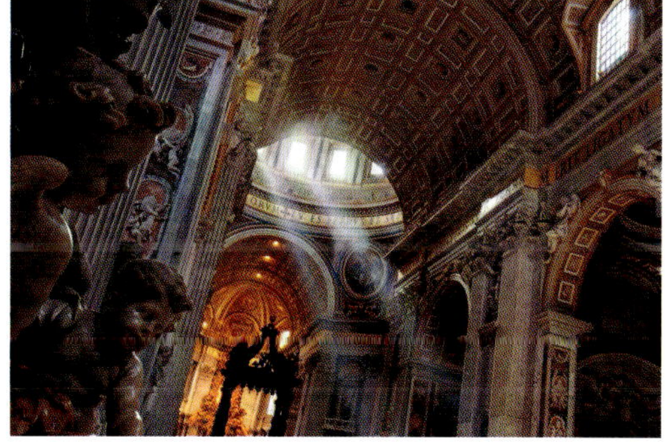

2.

1. The main shot makes the
two putti at the left far more
prominent, and creates a
bright glow to the shafts
and windows.

2 A darker choice that
heightens the contrast
between the interior and
the light shafts.

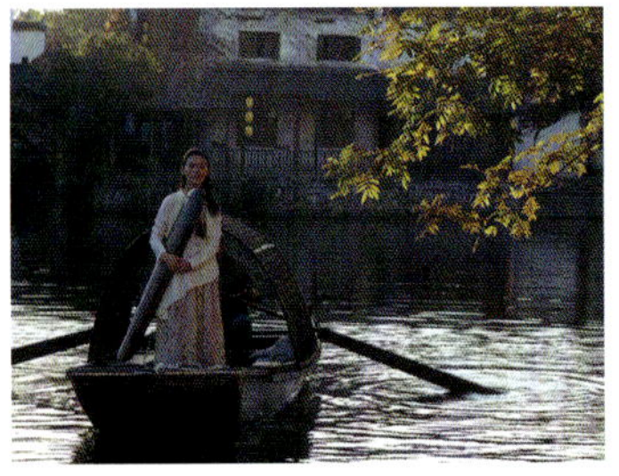

1.

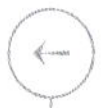

1. The original JPEG image, saved alongside the Raw file.

2. This darker, richer version aims to project the musician forward and add richness to the rippling water.

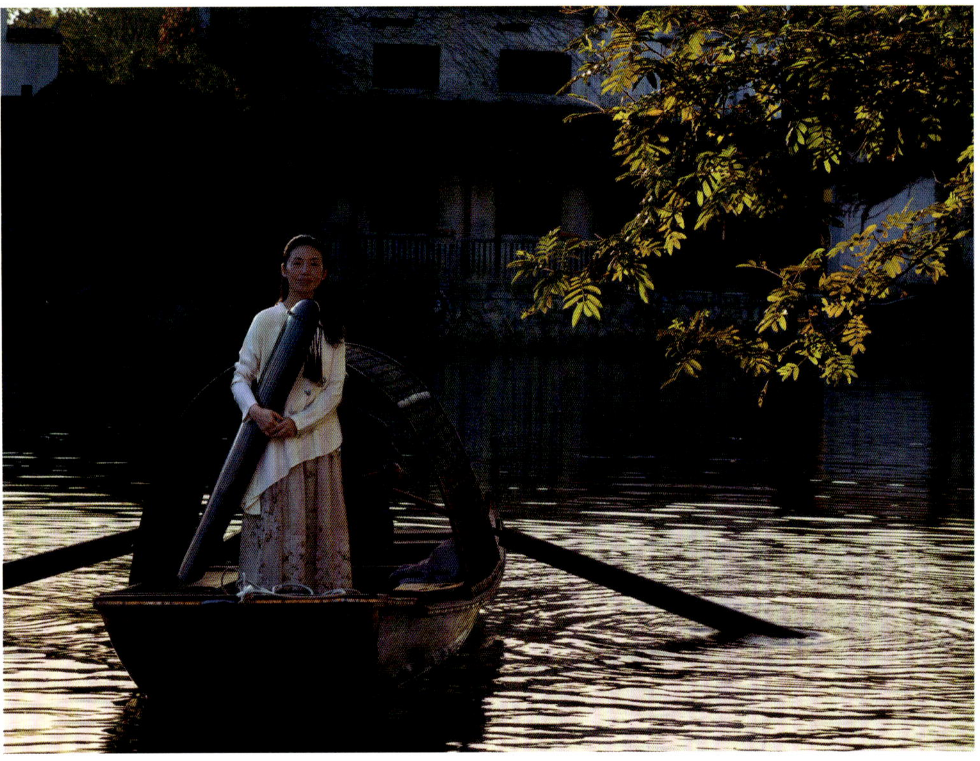

2.

Another two-way choice, which will segue into the following pages on a deliberate luminous effect, is this water-borne portrait of a guqin player in an old village in China (the guqin is a classical stringed instrument). I timed the shot for late afternoon so that I could shoot towards the sun for an edge-lit effect. With no change in the shooting, only in the processing, there were two obvious ways to go, as always in this kind of lighting.

One is towards contrast and density, keeping the background on the other side of the river dark so that the lit parts project forwards (above). The other way is towards a lighter, airy, luminous look, so the viewer has the feeling of backlighting with the sunlight flooding into the scene. A very slight shift of position and flare enters the frame in the form of a polygon streak, which results from reflections from the aperture inside the lens (opposite).

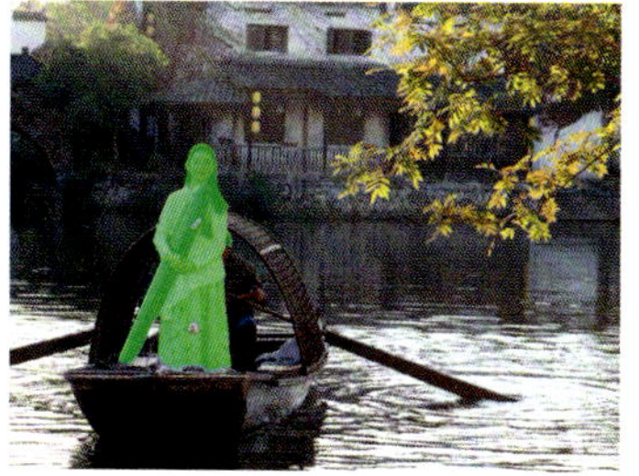

3.

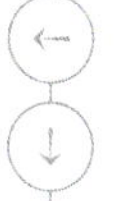

3. The mask for the main figure, which was used to make local adjustments in both versions.

4 A 'light and airy' render that aims for glow and flare.

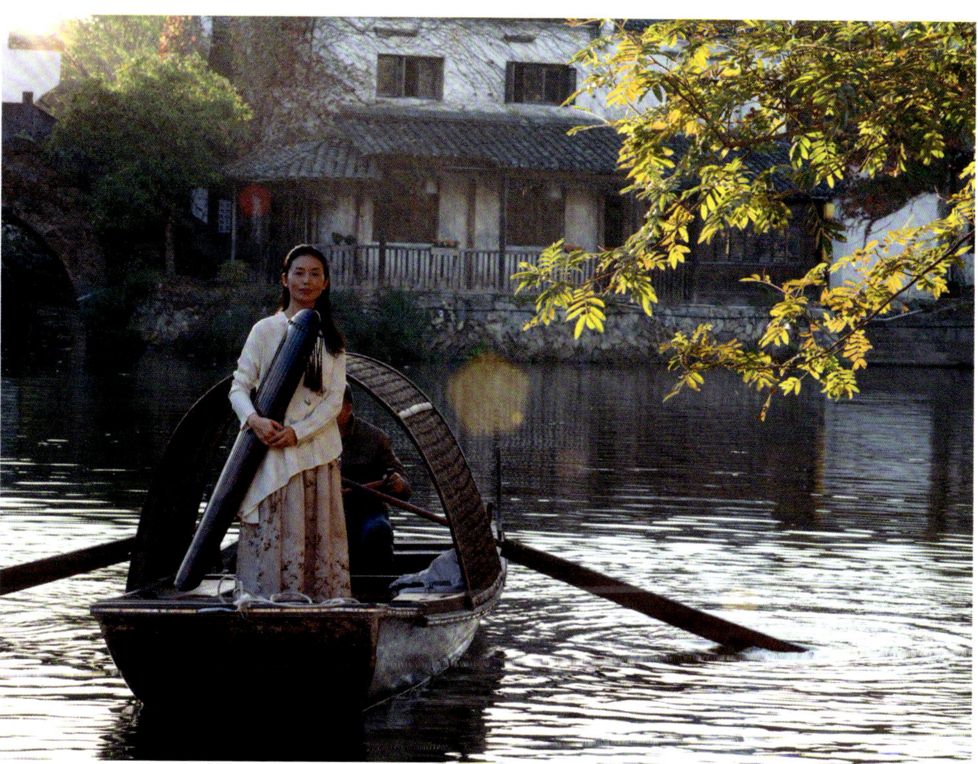

4.

In terms of density and contrast, the unprocessed file is perfectly up to the job of producing both of these very different versions, although they both called for several localized masks to balance the various elements of background, figure, boat, water reflections and leaves on the overhanging branch. In each instance, the musician and her instrument were individually masked using Subject in ACR (top). For the luminous version, this area was lightened, with a slight increase in contrast, while for the darker, richer version, the black and white points of the masked area were set, along with an increase in contrast.

AIRY, LUMINOUS

I used the word luminous quite a lot on the previous pages. It perhaps gets used more than it should, but it's a positive term for a currently popular look in photography. Like many descriptions in the world of imagery, it creates expectations and adds 'value' to pictures, even when it is undeserved (rather like real estate jargon).

What it actually describes is open to discussion, but I think most people would agree that it involves some sort of glowing, flaring light spreading out and towards the camera. It's especially popular in wedding photography, particularly in the USA, for the predictable reasons of being uplifting, romantic and vague.

In fact, it has a long history that dates back to the Pictorialists of the late 19th century, and continued until the First World War. However, Modernism put paid to the generally dreamy and light-hearted ethos, and reality intervened.

A field in eastern England at sunrise in summer, shot on Kodachrome. Note the smoothing effect in the highlights around the sun.

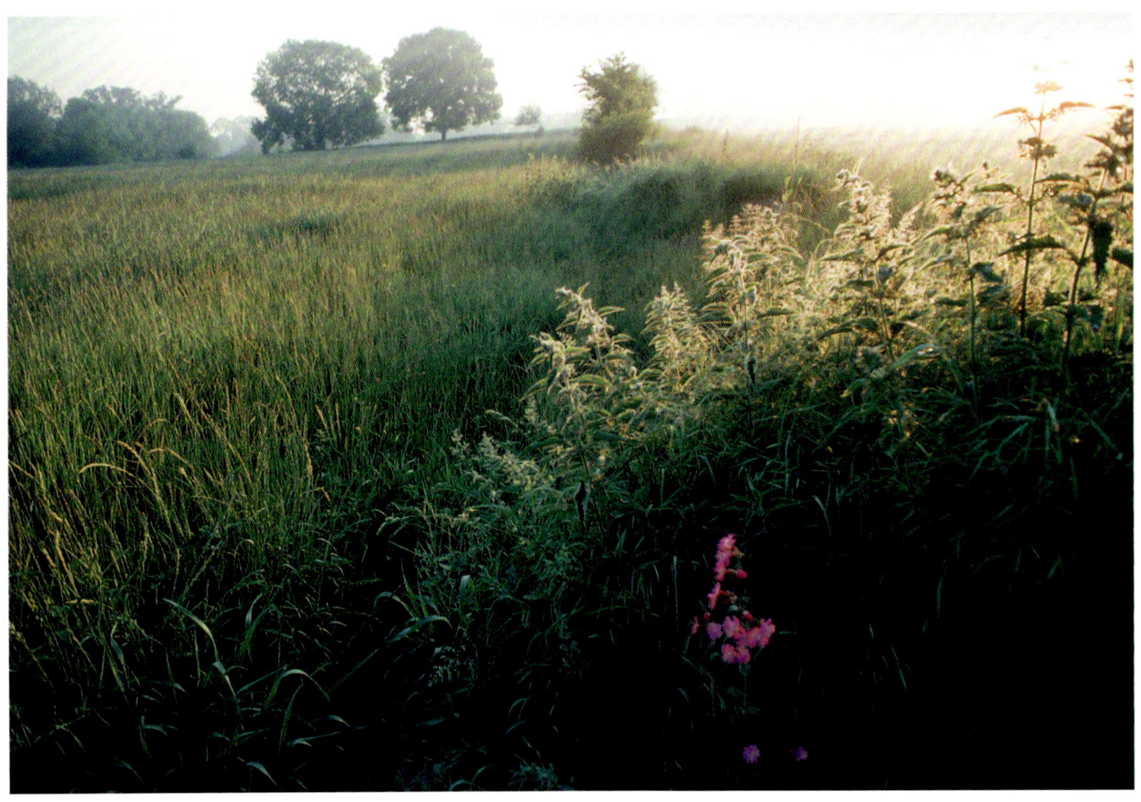

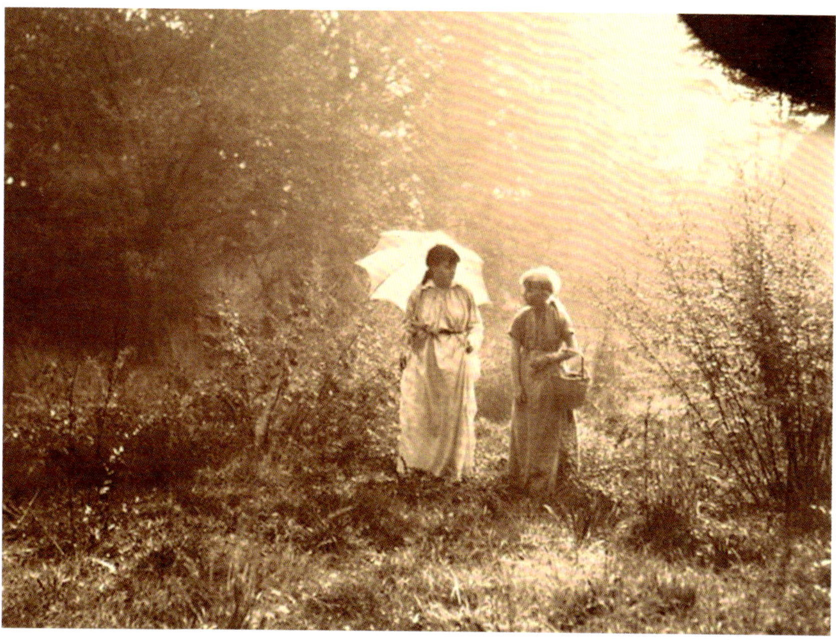

The interesting thing is that while it was obviously exploited by Pictorialists such as Léonard Misonne and Robert Demachy for its backlit, flooding-light effect that romanticized a scene, it was also a technical feature of the emulsions and lenses of the time. This is something of a recurring theme in this book – how the look created by exposure choices usually starts from the technology of the moment. Time and again, photographers adapt to what's available at the time, do the best they can with it and quickly come to like the result.

This particular luminous look was a natural feature of film that was exposed fully. It came baked into the emulsion, if you like, and the Pictorialists learned that they could go brighter with a fuller exposure than most people would have expected or tried and still have an acceptable image.

Of course, there were many other photographers, critics and commentators who actively disliked or despised this luminous, fairyland look, particularly in the way that photographers such as Misonne and Demachy created idyllic scenes with actors, but generally it was successful and popular with the public. You could charge it with lazily exploiting cheap and undemanding emotions (it was so criticized at the time), but that's been a successful strategy in every art form. Tellingly, luminous exposure, and the techniques of viewpoint and lighting that go to support it, has resurfaced in the century since, and is alive and well in Western wedding photography.

In a slightly more restrained way, luminous exposure that relied on the crushed-highlight response of film became a popular approach for photographing architectural interiors. Again, this can be traced to the end of the 19th century and simple necessity. Film, and collodion wet-plate glass emulsions of the time, couldn't possibly cope with an interior that included a window with daylight streaming through it. The range was far too high, and if it was a grand public space, such as a cathedral or a public library, photographic lights to fill the shadows were out of the question. If the exposure favoured the details of the interior, as it almost always had to, the windows or doorways just flared massively. Added to that was halation, which created even more glow around the overexposed highlights.

One solution to the problem was to find a camera angle that hid the offending window from view, as can be seen in the photographs of cathedral interiors by Frederick H. Evans. The other solution was simply to accept the effect and let it romanticize the scene. Evans did this too, and like others found that a misty, dusty or smoky atmosphere in a tall interior space produced God-like shafts of light, which everyone liked – and they still do.

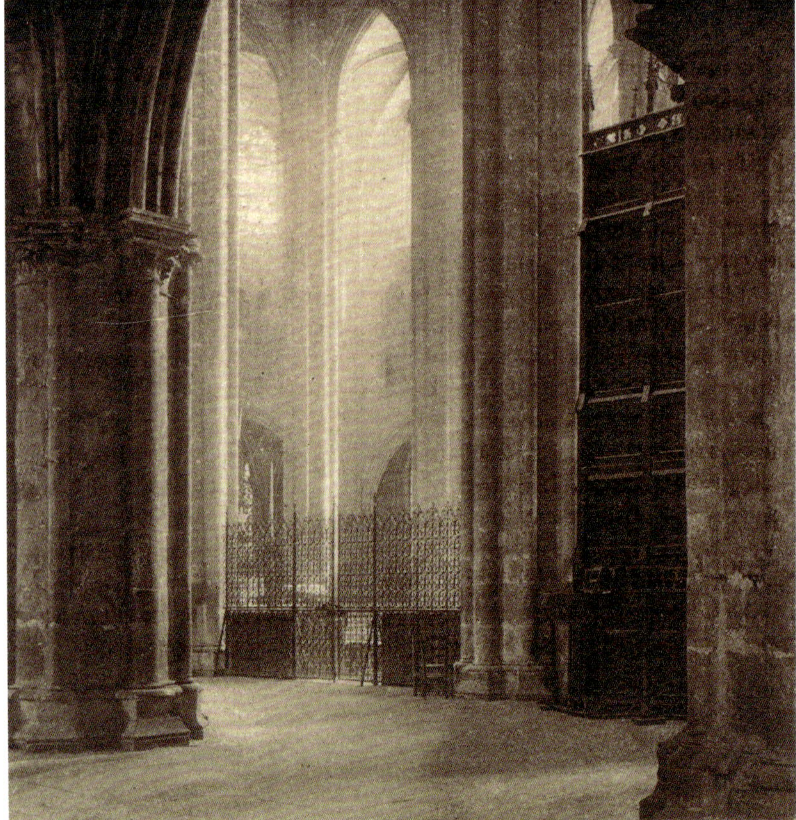

Frederick Evans, *Height and Light in Bourges Cathedral*, 1903.

In another instance of the technology of the time helping to create an exposure look, until well into the 1920s emulsions were blue-sensitive (orthochromatic). With a normal exposure, this meant that anything blue – such as a clear sky – would appear lighter, and that included shafts of daylight in large interiors.

In fact, interiors with the potential to be given a luminous exposure make an excellent test bed for exploring the whole question of interpretation and creative expression. Digital HDR photography seemed tailor-made for interiors with day-lit windows, and in early testing church interiors figured prominently. This is perhaps because HDR came from the world of CGI in the movies, where there was a need to capture the entire lighting range in a scene so that computer images can be made to blend realistically with live action.

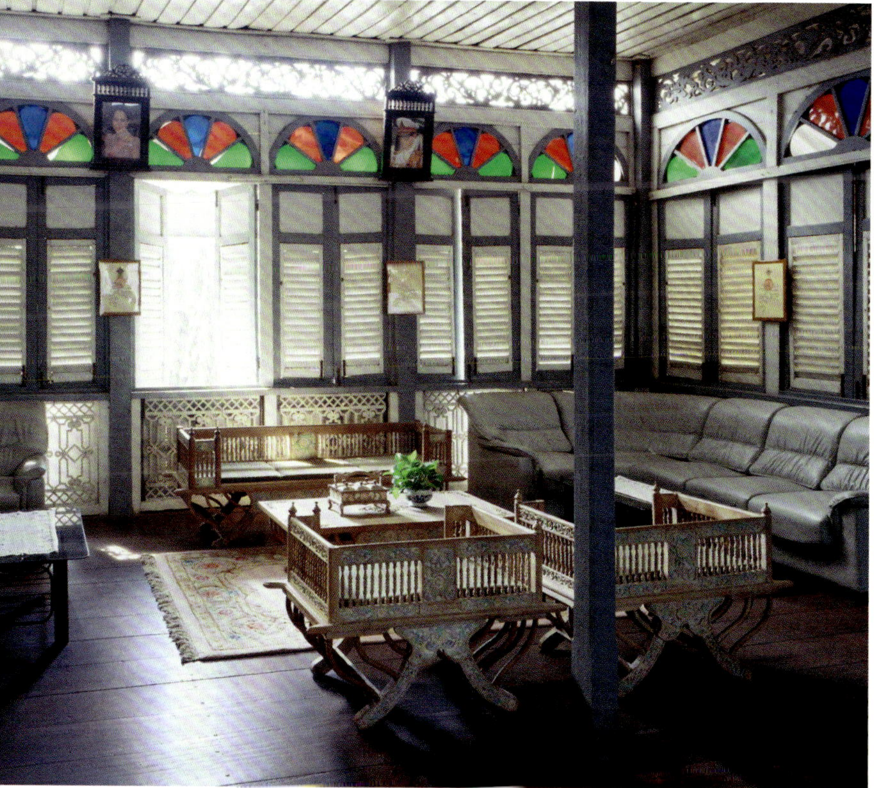

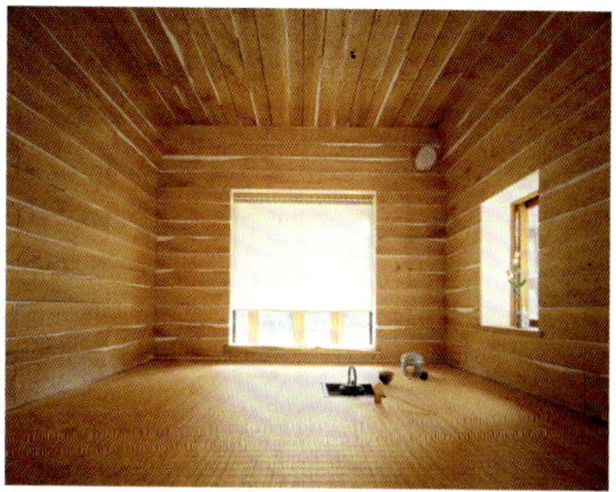

Two Asian interiors – Thai colonial style (left) and modern tea ceremony room in Tokyo (below). Both were photographed on Ektachrome transparency film with no additional lighting. They were simply exposed fully to reveal all of the interior detail, while letting the windows 'blow out' with a glowing effect.

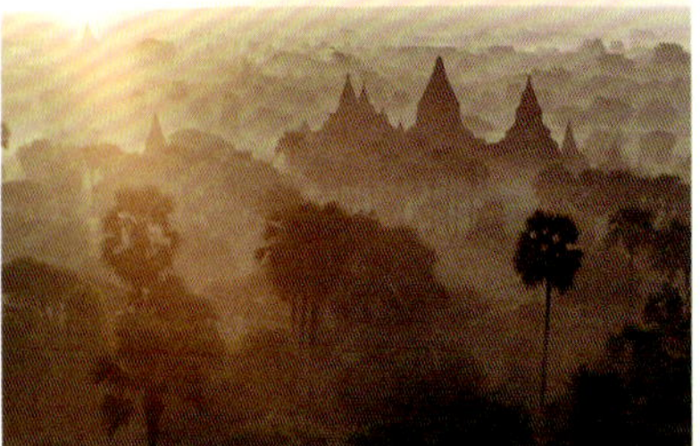

Original

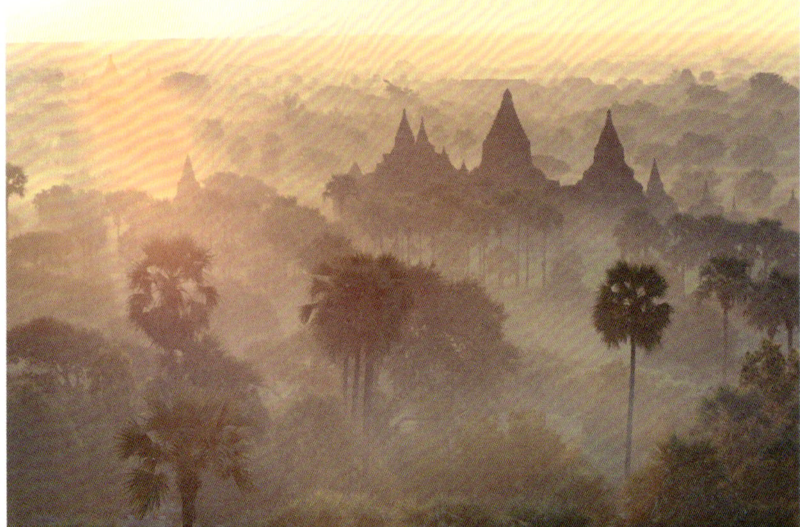

Light

This is a classic luminous landscape scene, with all the necessary ingredients. It was shot from a balloon over the Bagan plain in Myanmar, an area of thousands of ancient brick and stone temples. A light ground mist covered everything and the sun had just risen. I was shooting into the sun and this combination meant that the scene was simplified in tone, colour and detail.

The tones were resolved into a few simple planes and shapes, presenting some wonderful opportunities to outline silhouettes against paler misty mini-backgrounds, such as the small complex of temples in the middle distance and the palm tree at the lower right. This kind of separation within a scene can make for a satisfyingly graphic composition. Colours at this angle to the sun are heavily desaturated, and recede even further because of the shrouding light mist. Detail is in the outlines, such as the palm fronds, rather than within the shapes – classic luminous territory for those who like their landscapes overwhelmed by atmosphere, which I sometimes do.

I increased the exposure slightly from average, knowing that this was the bright, light direction in which I was going, but not much, as highlight clipping would be a disaster. If I were shooting film, I could have gone brighter, but clipping is an important reality in digital and this is a good example of why it pays to know how your camera's meter reading will react, especially if it's set to smart metering.

I was taking full advantage of what backlighting can do by placing the sun just above the top-left corner of the frame, so that streaming light would help create diagonals downwards and to the right. Yet while this was what I was shooting for, there remained a surprising variety of interpretations, mainly because of the low saturation and low dynamic range. The histogram of the original capture shows that while the highlights are locked just below pure white, there's quite a bit of headroom at the shadow end. There are so many ways to process this image file

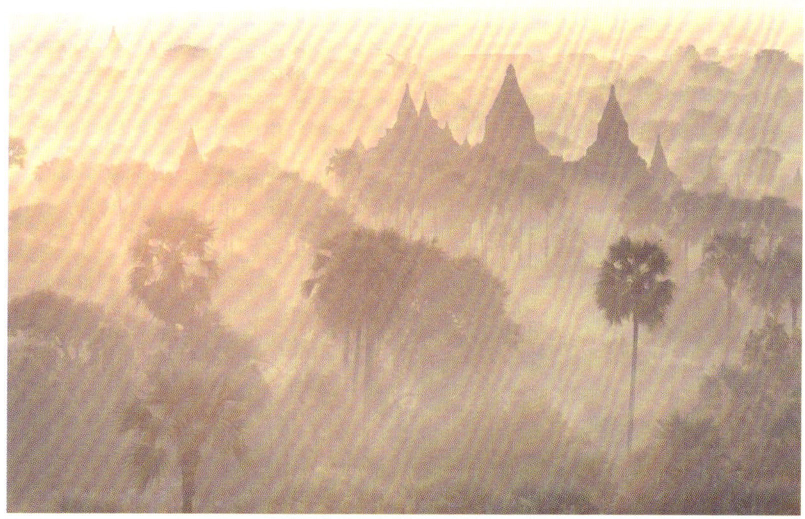

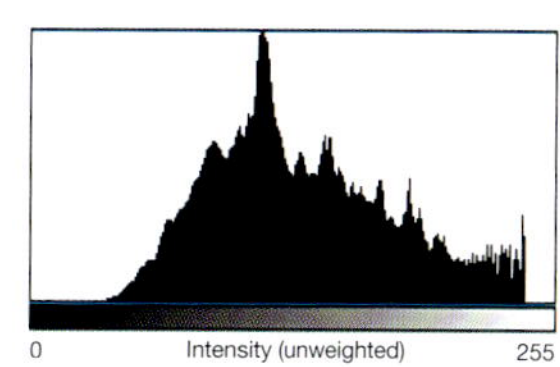

Very light

that it calls for some self-discipline. Brightness could go higher or lower, as could the contrast and colourfulness. It would also be perfect for a black-and-white treatment, as tonal extremes are then more acceptable.

Tonally, I wanted to even out the overall brightness on the diagonal ramp between the top left and lower right. I also wanted to make sure that the silhouetted temple tucked into the top-left corner stayed prominent, because it's a key to the composition, anchoring that end of the diagonal. In addition, there was a need to balance the generally warm colours that suffuse the scene, including a yellow flare cast at the left, which was a typical trait of the Nikon D3 (from 2007) that I was using.

These adjustments are what I considered 'practical essentials', and once done, I could follow my taste. I adjusted the overall colour a little towards red, and made a little separation between cool shadows and warm highlights. Tiny adjustments to the colour temperature and the red-green axis made big perceptual differences (many of them easy to dislike) and I took the cautious route of keeping the saturation well down. I'm torn between the generally light and very light rendering, and still haven't made up my mind, so I'm showing both.

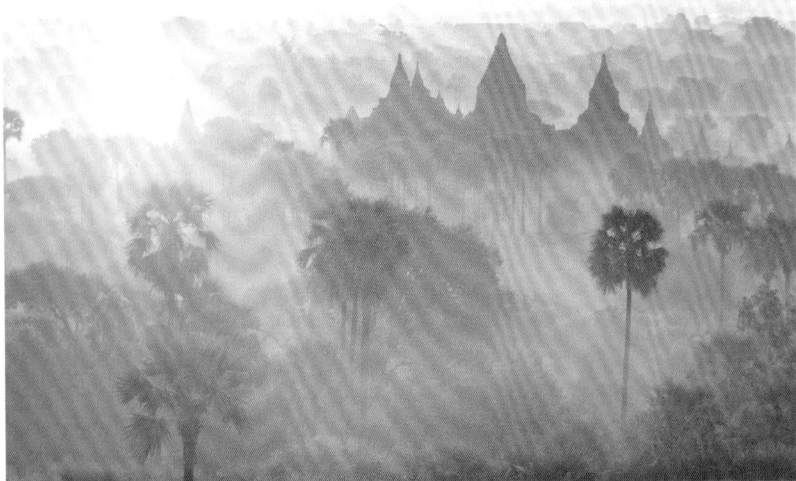

Black and white – light

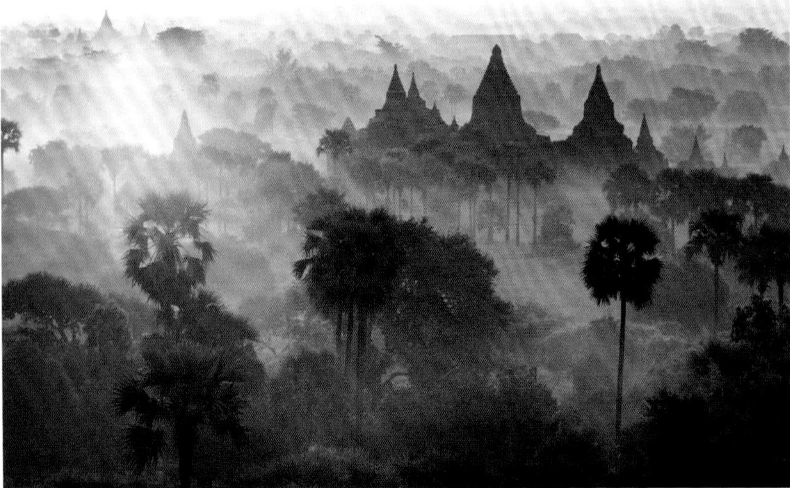

Black and white

Now let's move to black and white. I had this vaguely in my mind as a possibility when I took the picture, as it certainly removes all the tricky problems around colourfulness and colour casts. More than that, it provides more freedom in contrast. There are two routes that can be followed: one in the same low-contrast, pale direction as the colour image, and another that is much stronger in contrast. This would be impossible in colour, at least to my mind, because it would become unrealistically colourful. This is pure taste, of course, but there are limits as to how far into candy-coloured treatments I'll go.

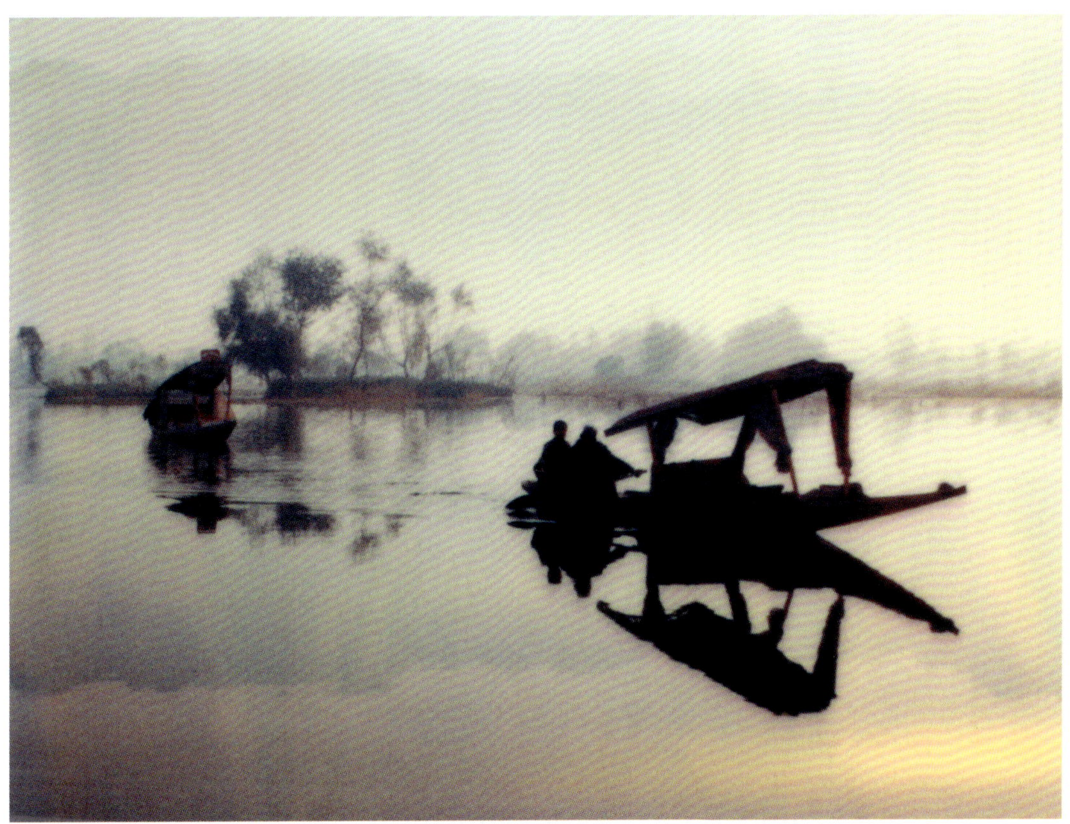

Small boats on Lake Dal in Kashmir, photographed on SX-70 colour film, which adds its own characteristic diffusion, as it develops in its sealed pod.

In common with the other exposure styles in this chapter, this treatment goes further than simply opening up the exposure to be brighter. It involves a combination of lighting, viewpoint, the subject and a variety of techniques, and while the name 'airy, luminous' quite clearly describes the impression, it really requires a commitment on the part of the photographer. It isn't, for example, a look that can be recreated just through the processing – and that's always a sign of a style with some substance.

Choosing to raise the exposure by about two stops or more is the easy part, but the key technique is shooting towards the light, as in the examples here. This naturally favours early or late sunlight for landscapes, or shooting downwards towards full reflections of sunlight, or towards a large window. These are exactly the same conditions for making silhouettes, so keeping the entire image luminous means avoiding these, or filling in the shadows. If silhouettes are an important part of the scene, as in the picture of boats on Lake Dal (above), strongly raising the exposure usually creates a glow around the outline, which helps, but even so, the luminous effect is restricted to the background.

Airy and luminous works particularly well with film, due to its highlight compression and halation characteristics. The panoramic landscape of White Sands on page 108 was shot on film and is a good example of highlight compression. You can also see the second film effect, halation, in the soft orange 'halo' around the setting sun and the mountain tops.

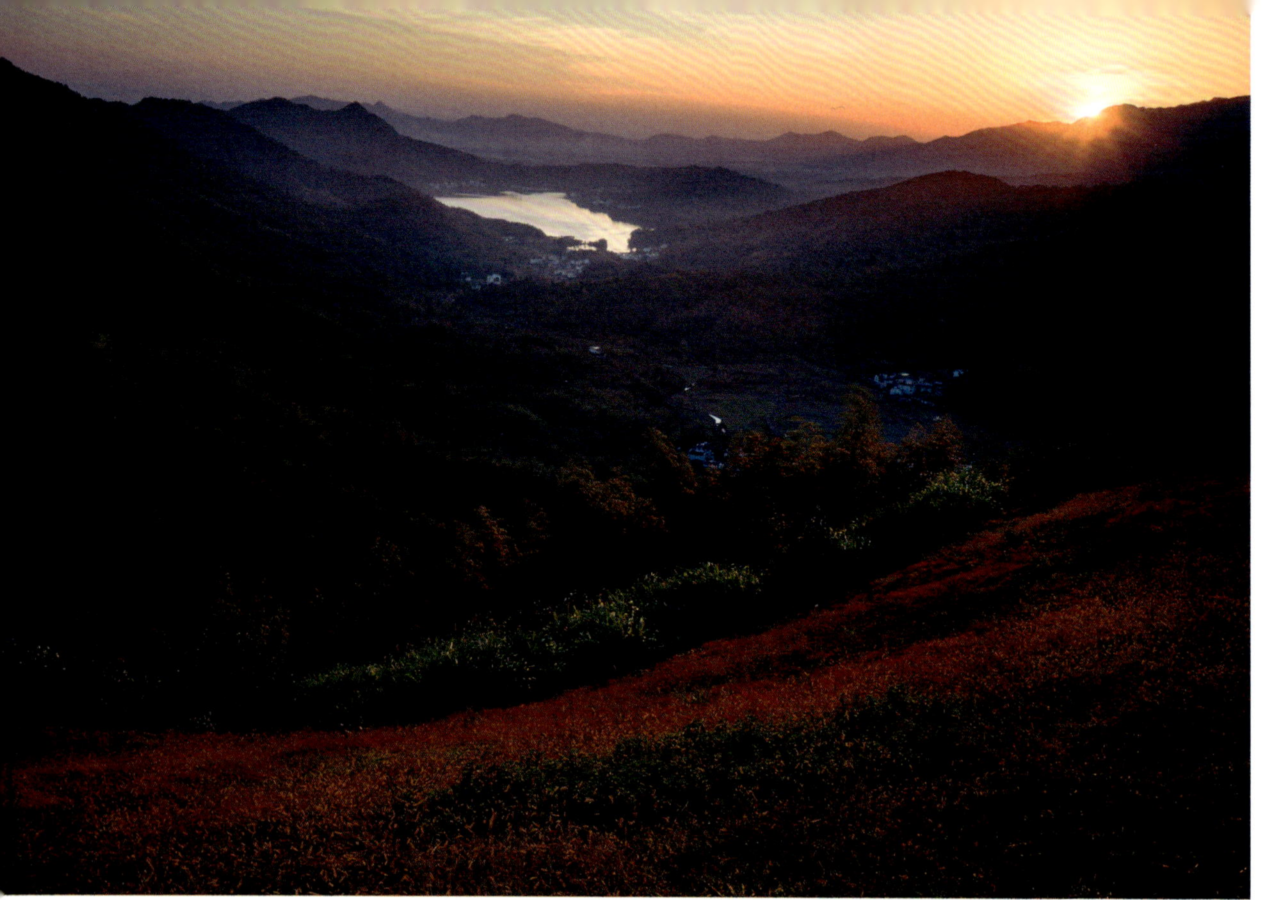

SUN IN FRAME

This is a typical end-of-day scenic landscape from an overlook; the kind where most people would wait until the sun just starts to touch the horizon, both for attractiveness (there's the opportunity to catch a radial sunstar effect with a wide-angle lens) and to keep the overall range of brightness under control.

That's exactly what I did here, with a Hasselblad SWC camera fitted with a medium-format digital sensor. In the days of film, the standard practice was to use a graduated neutral-density filter over the lens, sliding it up so that the transition zone between clear and grey aligned roughly with the horizon – a one-stop grad for a gentle darkening of the sky, or a two-stop grad for a more obvious effect. Digitally, this filtering is no longer necessary, as long as you have the camera on a tripod, as you can bracket a range of exposures and then blend them in one way or another. However, getting a good result from the sky around the sun is extremely difficult, even with a Hasselblad, which has large pixels, good colour depth and boasts good

A sunset view in Anhui province, China. The final image is a layered composite of different exposures, which gives a more realistic interpretation than a single HDR image, as there is no artificial tonemapping. Compare this with the sunset on page 127, which was shot on film with a graduated neutral-density filter.

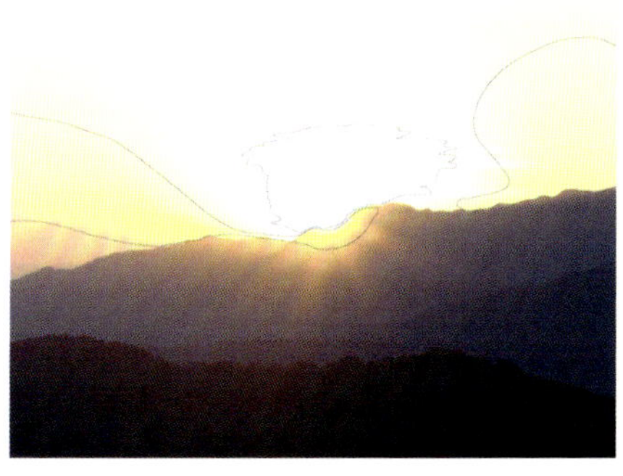

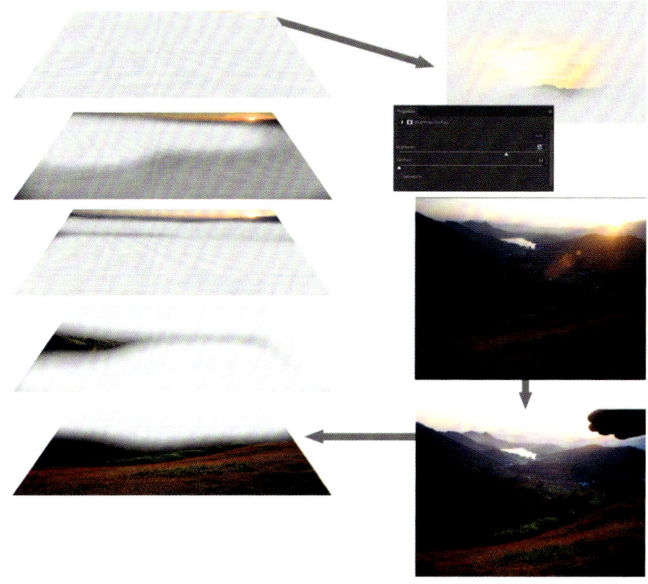

colour conversion. The problem is highlight clipping, especially as the sun's disc needs to be white, or close to it. If you look at the individual frames from dark to light, you can see there's clipping around the sun on every one, making a hard-edged white circle. Worse than that, there's a yellower ring around the white. That's caused by the blue channel clipping before the other two, and it looks ugly because as our eyes see it, the actual hue changes. We see that (correctly) as unrealistic.

So, there are three exposure issues in a scene like this. The first is deciding the balance (in terms of brightness and contrast) between land and sky; the second is deciding the balance between different parts of the landscape (foreground, middle ground, distance); and the third is solving the clipping problems around the sun. Bracketing the exposures provides plenty of dynamic range to play with, while shooting some frames up to half an hour earlier gives the choice of a more sunlit foreground for the lower half of the picture.

Creating an HDR image with the sequence of frames is less useful than you might think, because it won't solve the clipping problem close to the sun, and my plan for the picture is as you see it here – a sky with full texture, a bright and slightly contrasty distance around the lake, and a lightened foreground with sunlight glistening on the grass (from half an hour earlier than the actual sunset). Another small but solvable issue was the string of flare polygons coming diagonally into the picture from the sun. For this, the simple solution was to shade the sun with my hand. By far the easiest way to combine all of these was in a layer stack in Photoshop, using a broad, feathered eraser brush, as shown at the top right.

A detail of the exposed frame that best suited the landscape, before processing. The inner black outline shows the completely clipped area, while the other two outlines show the partially clipped areas that result in a hue shift to yellow.

The layered sequence used to create the main image.

In the picture below, of a canal in a beautifully preserved old village in China, I could easily have positioned the camera to just hide the sun, or waited until it had set behind the rooftops, but I wanted atmosphere from a prominent sunstar. As I was using a wide-angle lens stopped down, this was very much on the agenda. Conditions like this – shooting into the sun with a smooth sky – absolutely call for bracketing a series of frames and using HDR, but even HDR can't prevent clipping close to the sun. The solution was to get the best result I could with HDR processing, and then add the darkest frame in the series on top, 'lifting' it to match the brightness of this small part of the picture.

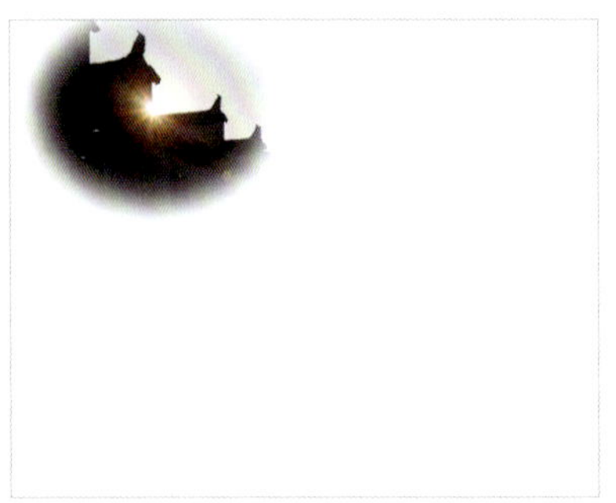

1.

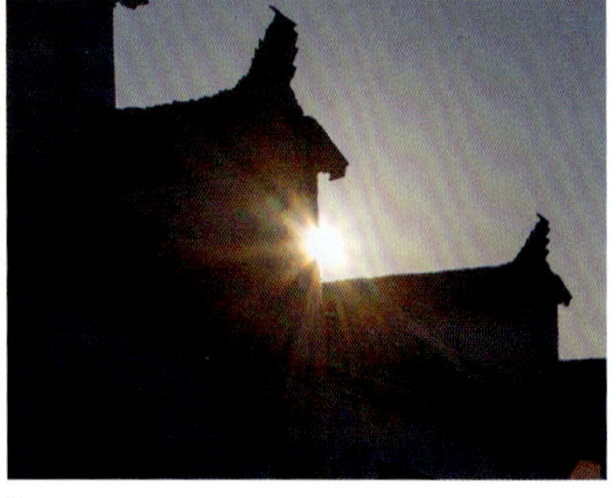

2.

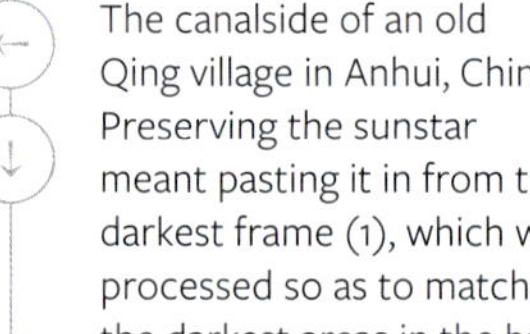

The canalside of an old Qing village in Anhui, China. Preserving the sunstar meant pasting it in from the darkest frame (1), which was processed so as to match the darkest areas in the base, HDR tone-mapped image (2).

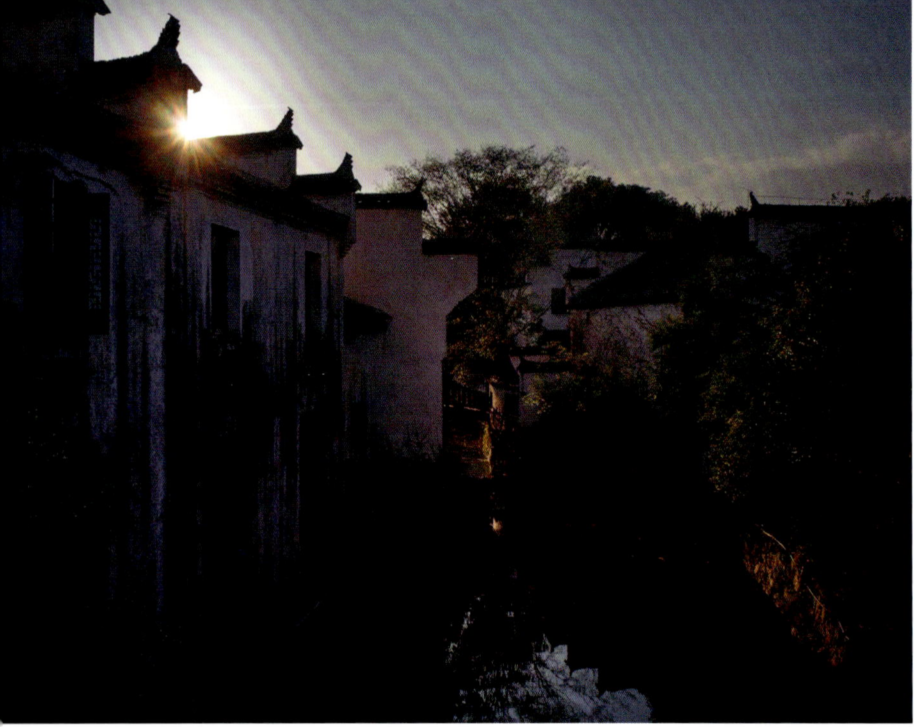

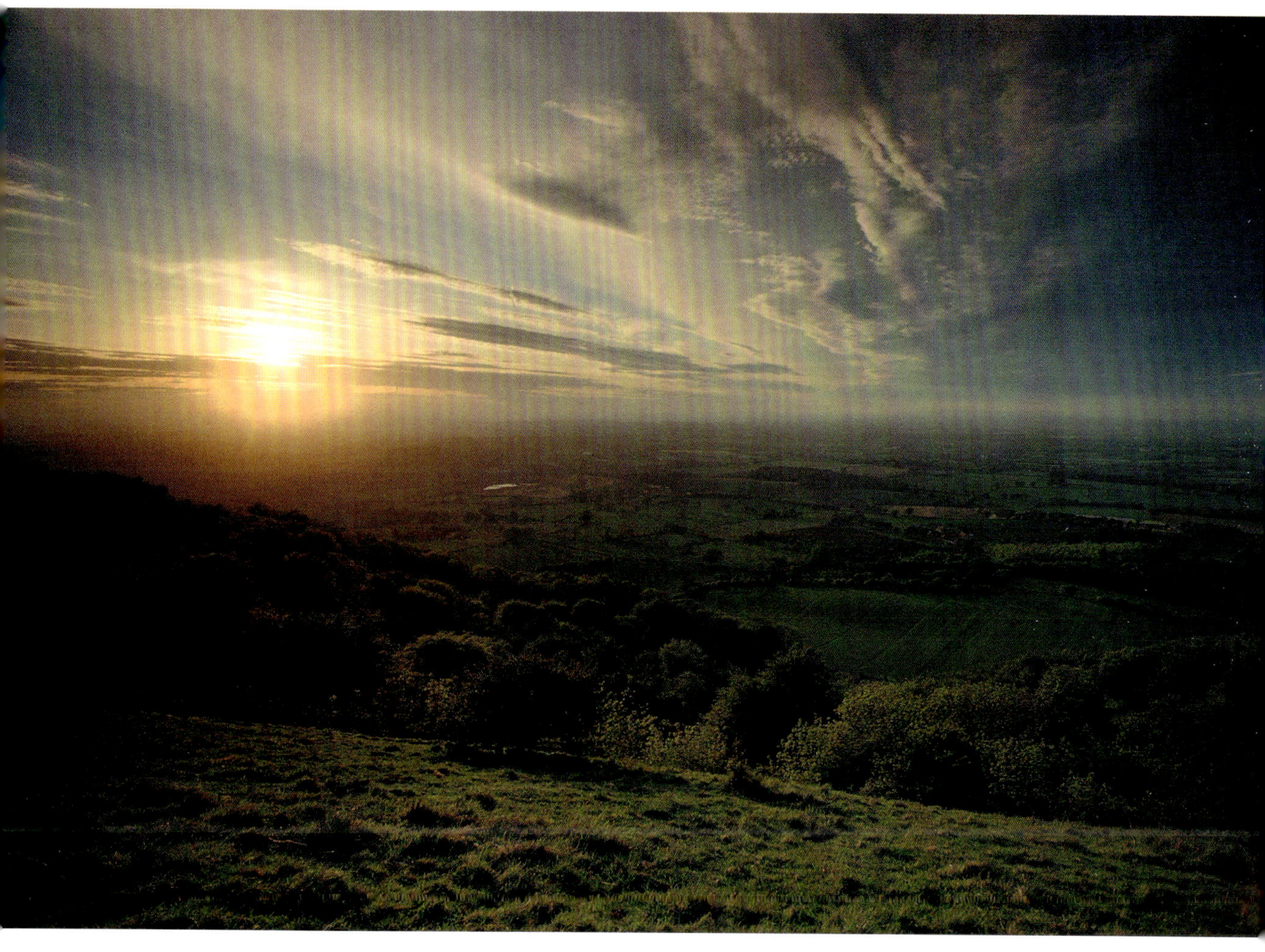

The sun and its immediate surroundings need special treatment, and the unfortunate truth is that if you crave perfection, it will take some kind of retouching. The solution is to take the least clipped frame – the least exposed, naturally – and drastically raise the brightness while lowering contrast. There's a small increase in noise when making this adjustment, but as you're working in the highlight zone, not much. This frame then sits at the top of the layer stack and is blended into the existing sky (I use a soft brush eraser for this). Even then, some finessing will be required, such as changing the blend mode to Soft Light, for example, and altering the density.

Sunset over the South Downs, England, shot on Kodachrome with a graduated neutral-density filter over the sky.

IN PRAISE OF FLARE

don't wholeheartedly subscribe to this myself (I prefer flare in small, accidental doses), but it's a fairly short step from the airy luminosity that we just looked at to making use of full-on flare artefacts.

That's a little redundant because all flare – and there are several kinds – is an artefact, meaning it's not a part of the image being captured. Rather, it's an overlay of things that are wrong in the optical system, or a simple misuse of the lens. As with so much in this book, there's a disconnect between engineers' and technicians' efforts to perfect the tools of photography and the ways in which photographers actually like to use them. Decades of lens development at Zeiss, Leitz, Nikon and other companies has gone into avoiding flare, but people continue to like it.

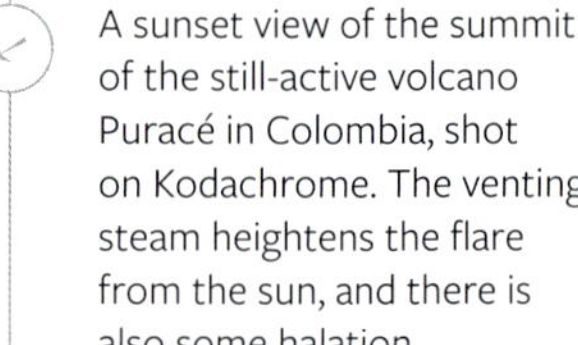

A sunset view of the summit of the still-active volcano Puracé in Colombia, shot on Kodachrome. The venting steam heightens the flare from the sun, and there is also some halation.

Flare enhanced by overexposure. An alligator on Florida's Myakka River, shot on Kodachrome.

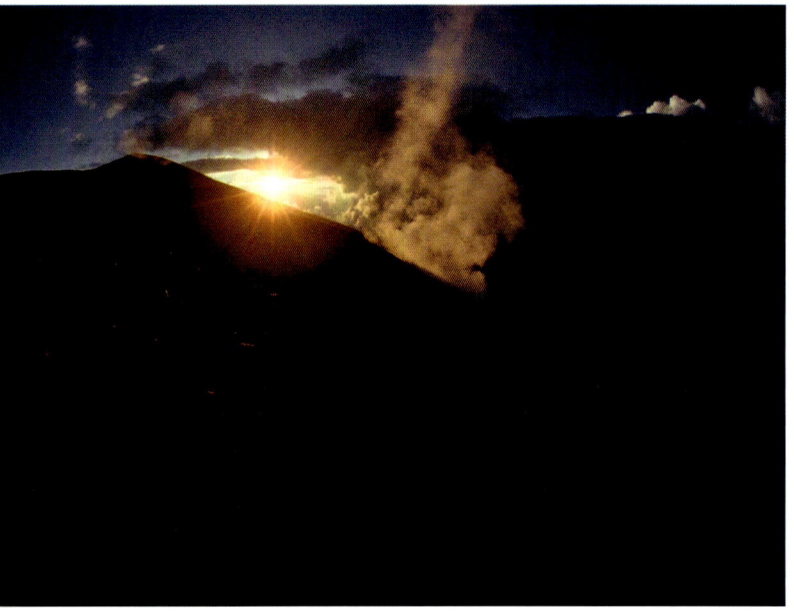

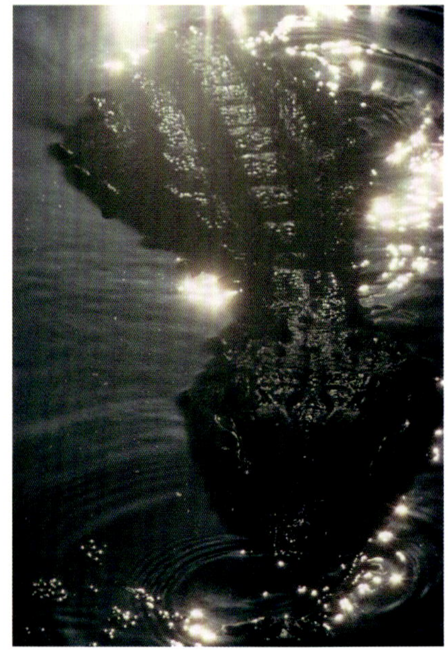

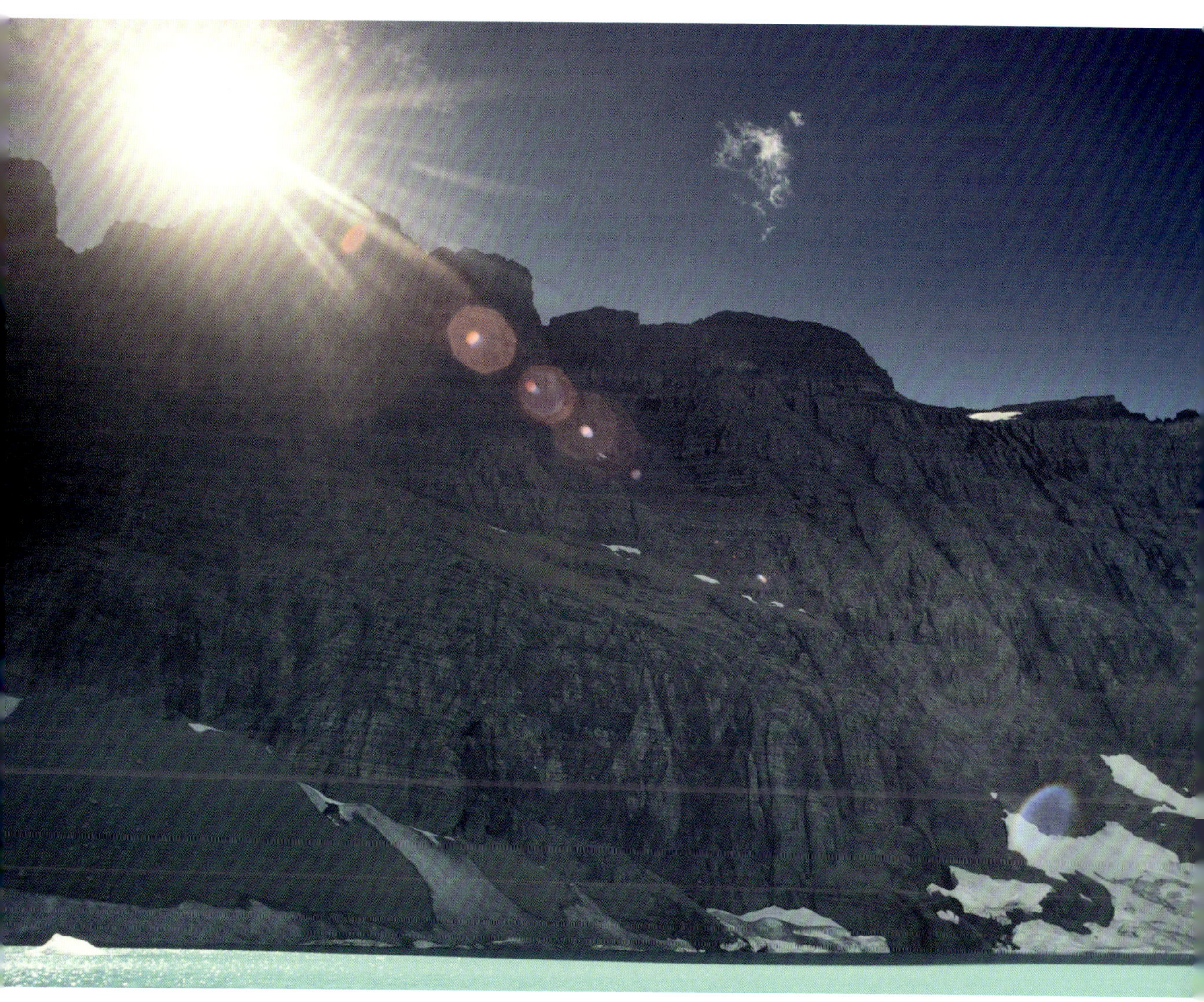

Iceberg Lake in Glacier National Park, Montana, shot on Kodachrome. This image not only shows radial flare streaks, but also a polygon flare spread, the shapes of which are caused by the shape of the aperture blades.

Today, there are two competing mini-industries: one dedicated to overcoming flare, the other striving to introduce more of it. In fact, a huge amount of effort goes into simulating various kinds of flare for movies; I've had a copy of Knoll Light Factory ever since I photographed John Knoll, the chief creative officer at Industrial Light & Magic, the mother of special effects companies.

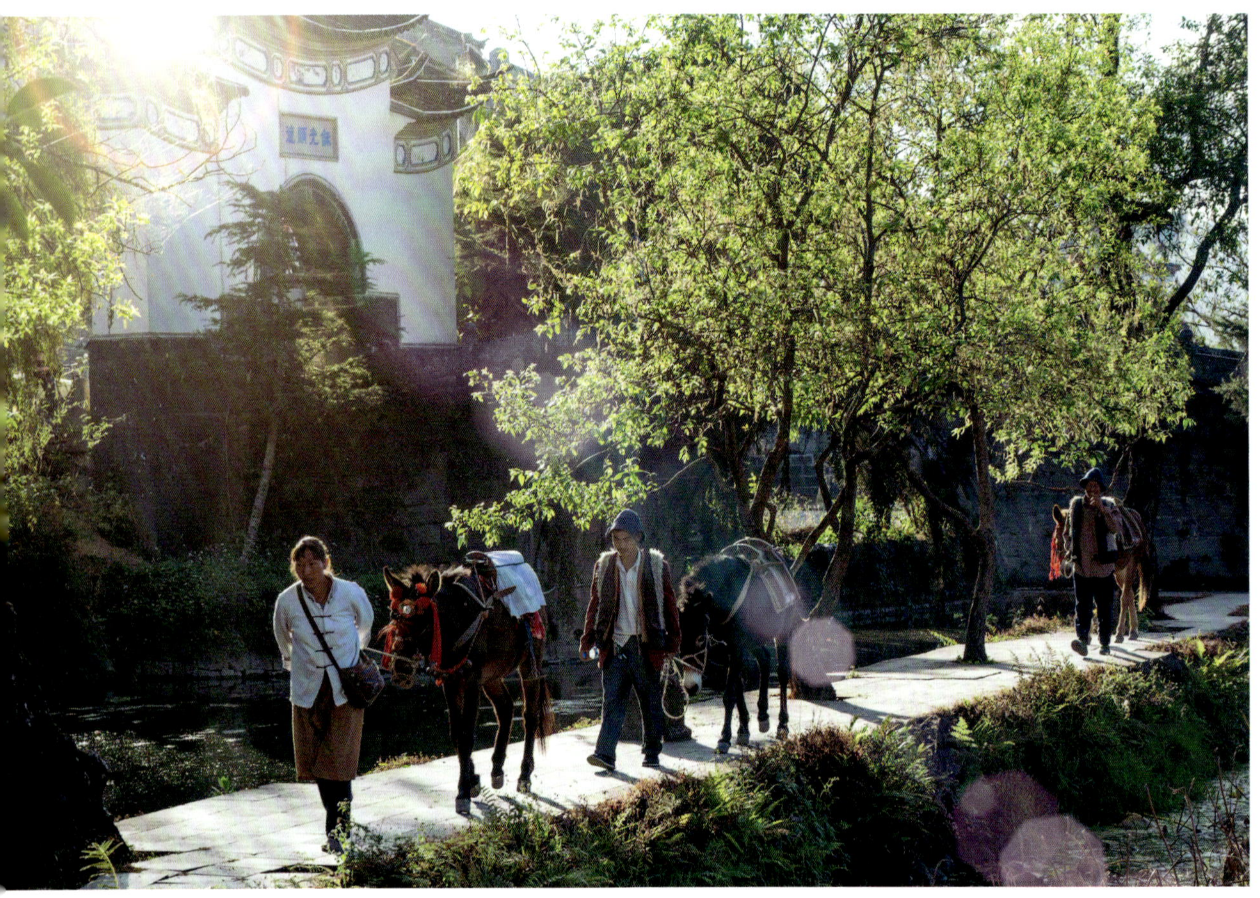

The definition of flare is non-image-forming light in the picture, and most of it comes from stray light reflecting from glass surfaces in the lens and filters. It ranges from generalized – an overall fog that weakens shadows – to streaks, glowballs and polygon spreads, some of which you can see being used here. 'Used' may mean a happy unexpected discovery when going through the edit, or a calculated creation by using a particular lens aimed at a certain angle towards a light.

What all flare has in common is that it adds to the exposure, which is why it belongs in this chapter. More than that, however, for its aficionados it adds a mixture of interesting graphics, a sense of glow and the elusive sense of actually being present at the time of shooting – you can feel as if you are there, with perhaps not enough time to make the shot perfect. As a form of subjective camera, it is often used in this way in cinematography.

Artificial flare superimposed on a digital image of a tea caravan in southwest China. The flare was added using the Knoll Light Factory app, which allows a variety of flare artefacts to be used.

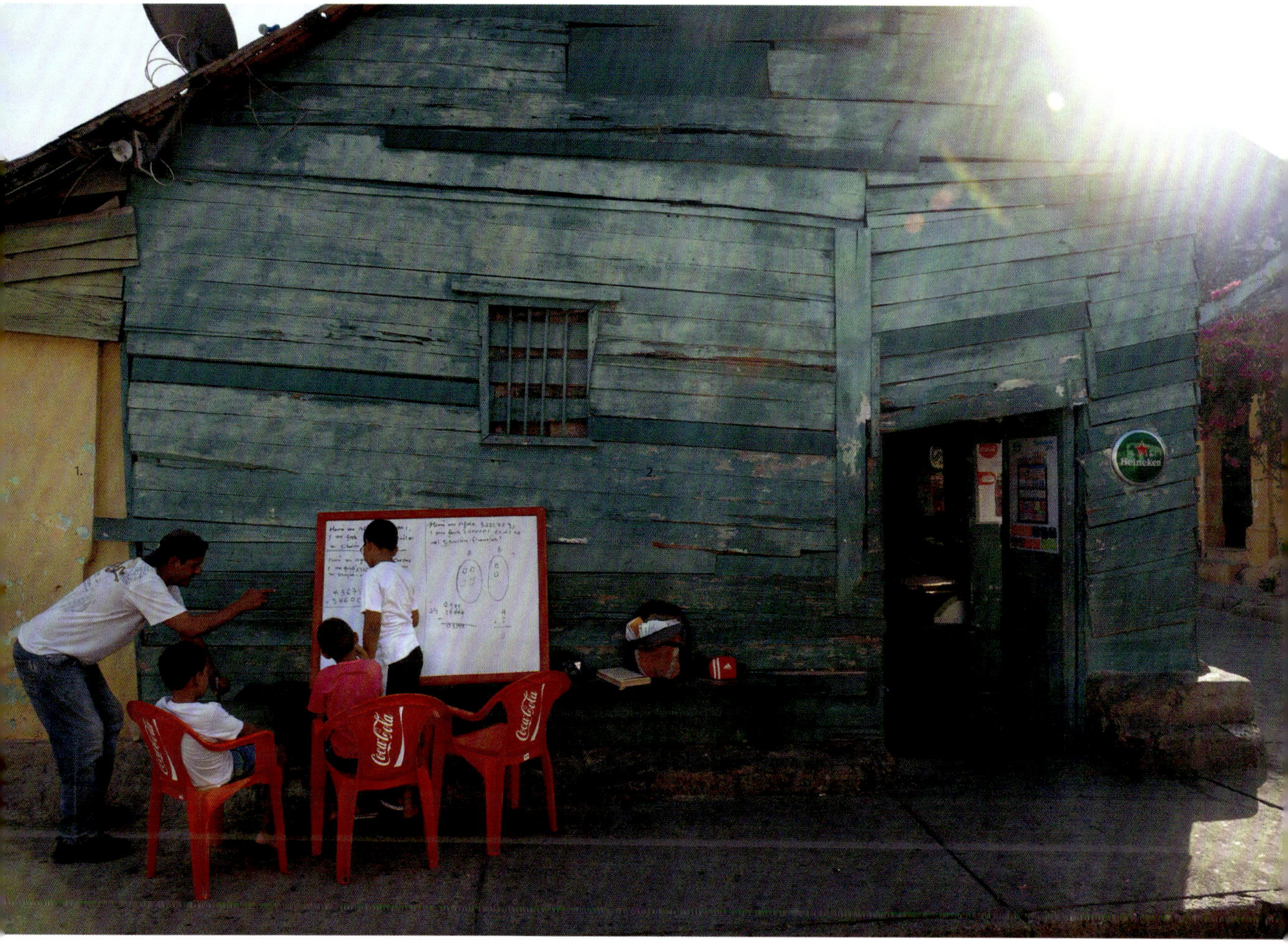

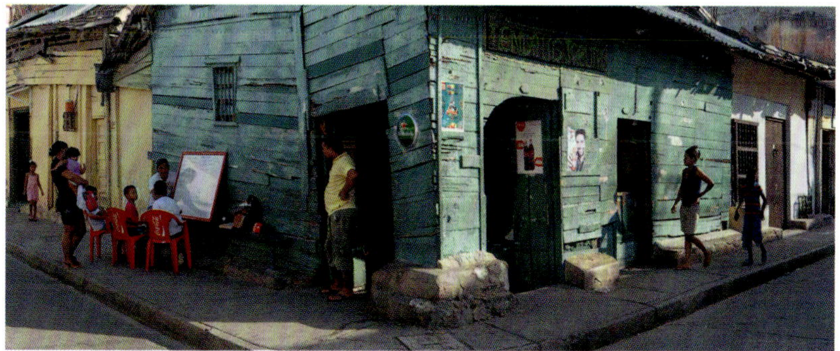

Digital flare added to a scene in Cartagena, Colombia. The reverse scene (left) reveals how the camera position was deliberately chosen to make use of the flare. The main problem was highlight clipping, which took some processing effort to counter.

6

HIGH & LOW CONTRAST

Contrast seems an obvious quality of photographs. We all know instinctively what a high-contrast picture looks like, and also a flat, low-contrast picture. It starts with the lighting and the subject. A light-toned, brightly lit subject against a dark background (say, a pale face in a shaft of sunlight with deep shadows behind) is a recipe for high contrast. On the opposite side, morning mist over a landscape limits the range, with no obvious blacks or whites. Both can be creatively effective, even when taken to the opposite extremes of stark, over-range images in just two tones – black and white – and pictures in which it's hard to make out any detail.

In practice, contrast in photography is not so simple. It operates
on different scales. There's the at-a-glance impression of contrast
that depends on large 'blocks' of light and shadow. Then there's
the smaller scale of how smaller subjects and elements contrast
with their immediate surroundings. At the extreme end of small
scale there's mid-tone micro-contrast, which is the crisp, slightly
unnatural look you get from what some people call HDR, and from
over-using textural sliders (such as Clarity) in Lightroom.

This is all very much the province of processing. In contrast to the
lowering or raising of overall tones to make darker and brighter
images, as we saw in the last two chapters, managing contrast is
more complicated and involves much more processing work. It
is also unavoidable, as the whole idea of choosing exposure in a
thoughtful, creative way necessarily includes processing the image
with subtlety and nuance. It's an integral part of working towards a
finished picture in which all the tonal values are just right for what
each of us wants each of our pictures to say.

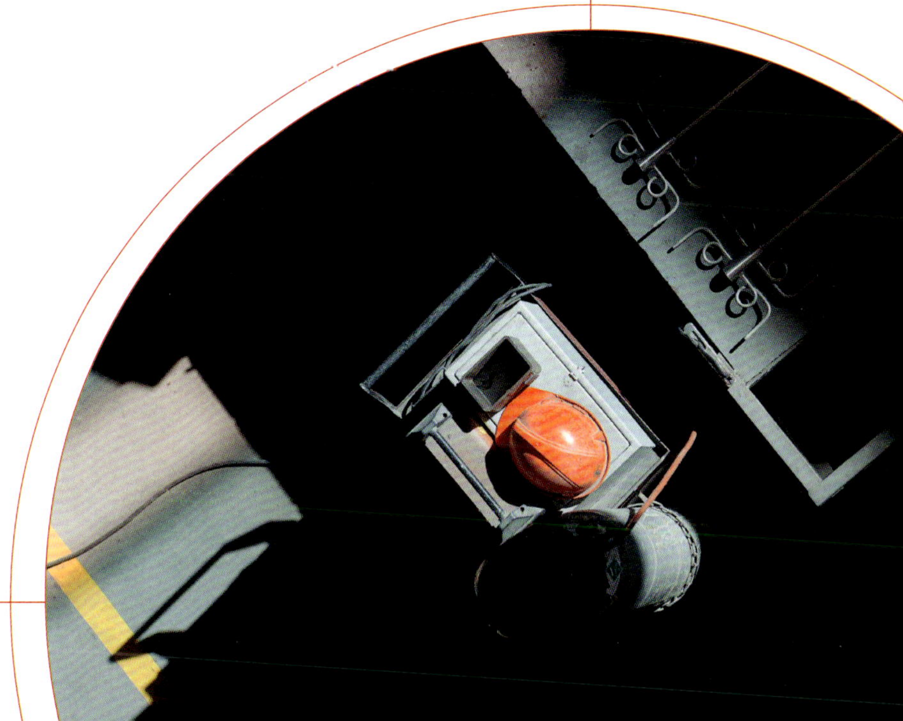

SLIVERS OF LIGHT

This is an exposure situation that comes from different lighting scenarios, but with a common result that always calls for close attention. As the title suggests, the striking feature is a thin strip of light that is much brighter than the rest of the scene.

The appeal of this type of scene stems from it being uncommon in its pure form. This means it offers a surprising choice in exposure, which creates totally different images – and that is why I have it in this chapter. What the examples shown here have in common is that the main subject is at least partly outlined, but where they diverge is that the sliver of light can either help to define the figure or face, or stand alone as a thin graphic shape in its own right. There are other ways of creating a sliver of light, including cracks that shape and hold back sunlight; using an attachment (called a gobo) in front of a light in the studio to achieve a similar effect; and, more unusually, employing a light source that itself is pencil-thin, such as a laser.

Exposure is the critical control, not only because it changes what happens to the light sliver itself – from holding all the tones inside it to a bright, featureless glow with soft edges – but because it controls whether the sliver is part of a fuller, opened-up scene, or is an isolated, enigmatic shape. Traditionally, there are two ways of handling this, but modern Raw processing engines and computational photography open up a full range of choice, and this makes it all the more important to decide whether scenes like these are simply a problem to be solved or an occasion to create something special.

The traditional choice, which is still perfectly valid and may be the best option, is between exposing down in order to hold detail and tone in the light sliver, and opening up so that it glows against a fully revealed shadow area. If you use film, there's the added likelihood of halation, which adds something akin to glow and a reddish edge. I mention this now because while technically it's a fault, most people nowadays find it attractive.

An elderly Burmese man in a cafe in Yangon. All the lighting action is along the lit edge and its transition to darkness, but fortunately there was just enough of a thin, dim edge at the back of his head to define its outline. The exposure is perfect for the effect I wanted.

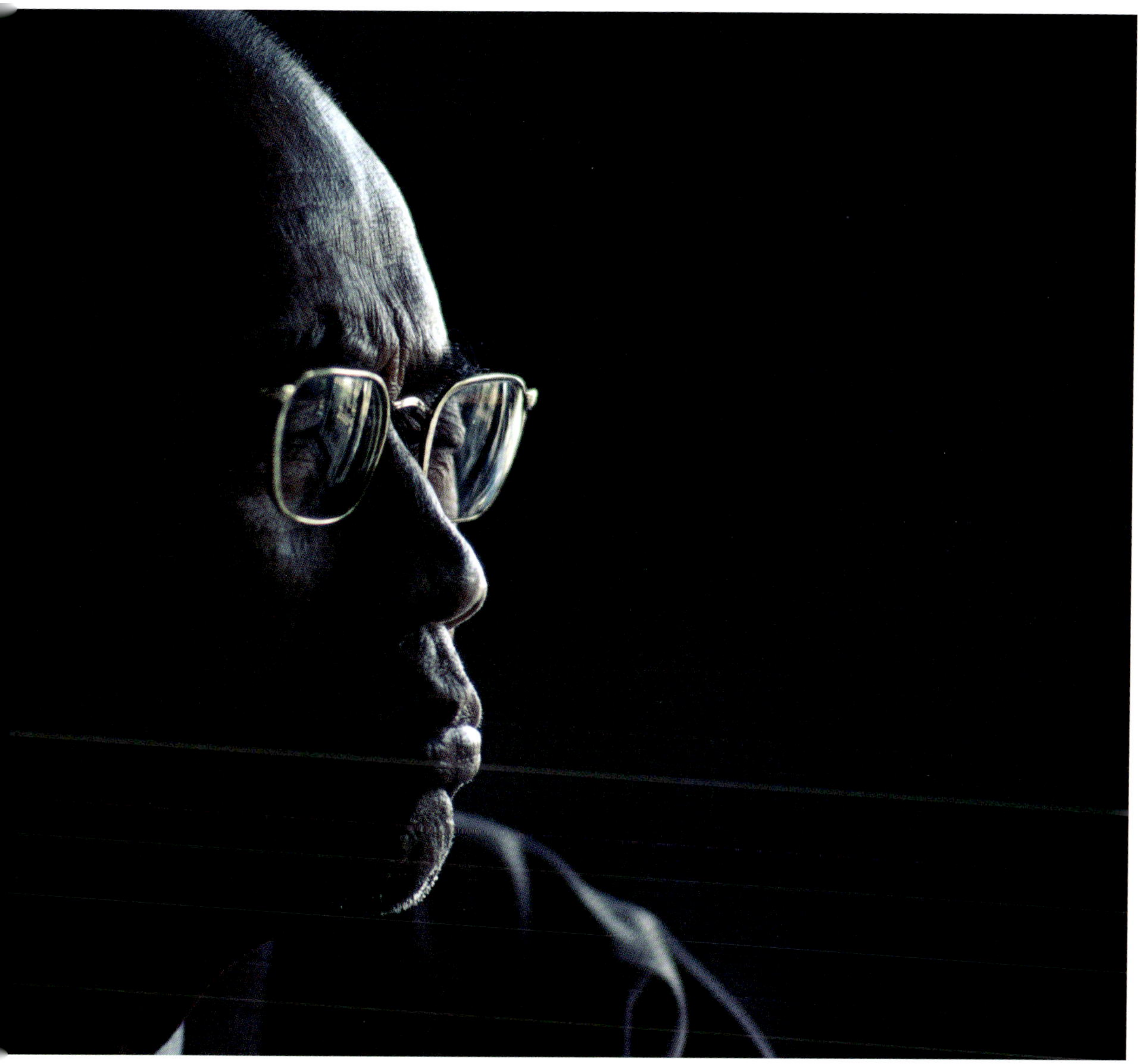

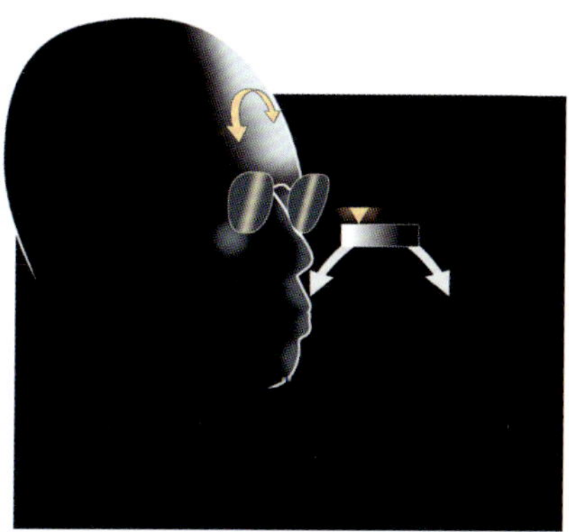

In this schematic, the upper arrow marks the 'terminator' – the transition from light to shadow. The edge light is naturally determined by the exposure, and here is at the point marked by the small yellow triangle.

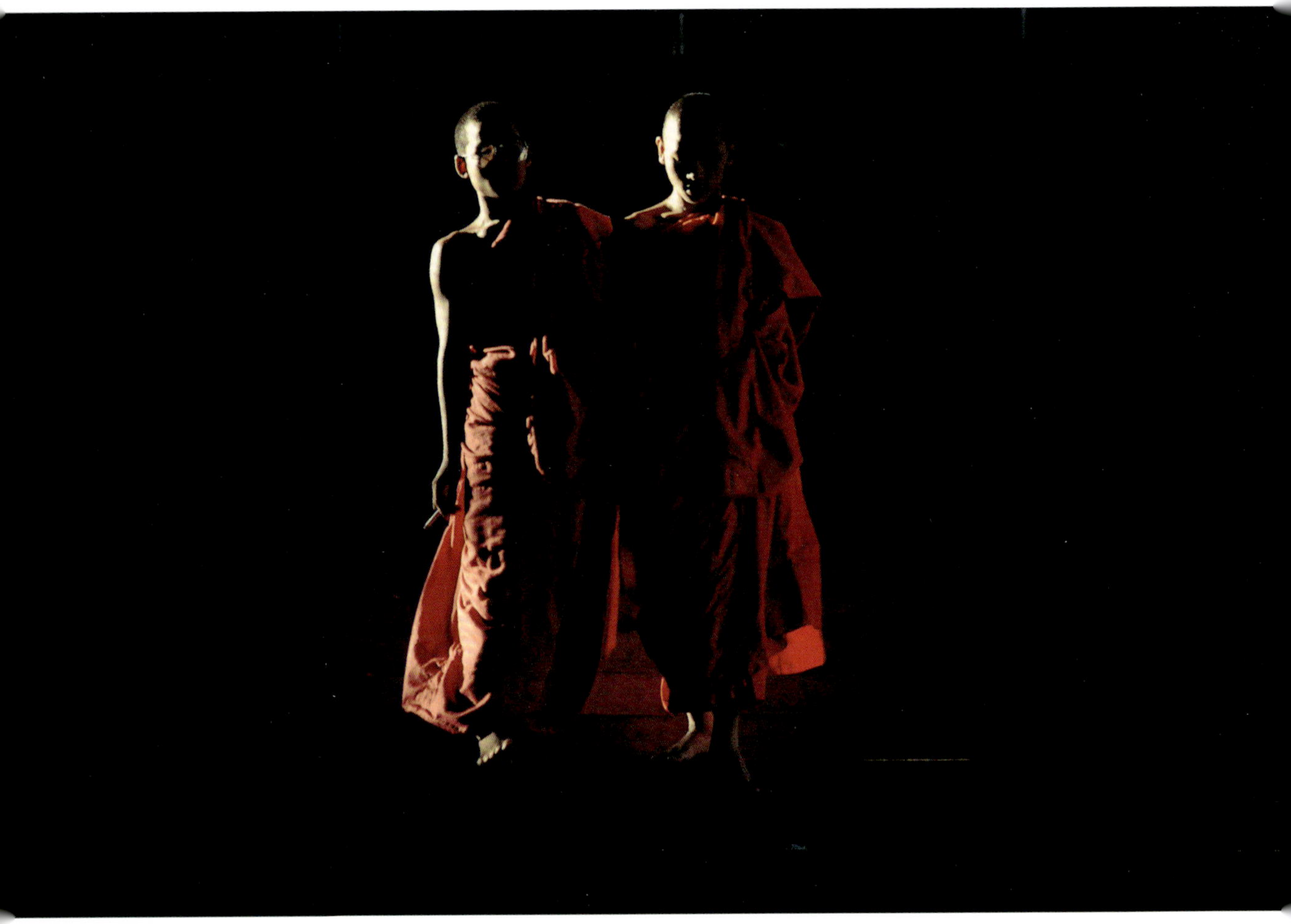

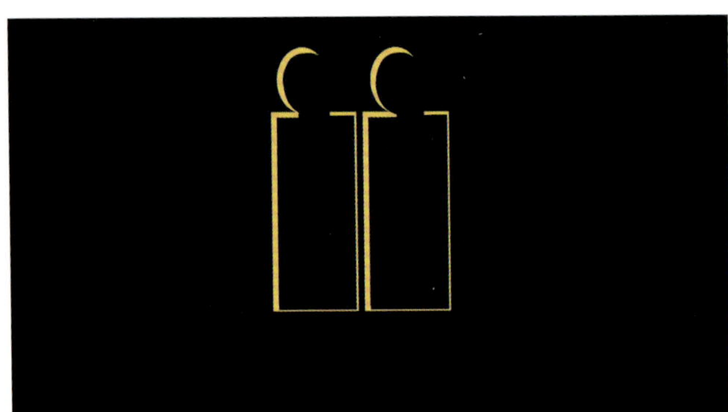

Underexposing this scene by two stops threw the surrounding details into darkness, while the two monks are illuminated with luminous edge lighting.

Getting the exposure right for the effect you want is tricky, because this lighting
scenario is difficult to meter – impossibly so in fast-moving street scenes. Worse
still, with film there's no way to check. Ultimately, practice and experience are
the only guides. With the picture of the two Burmese monks opposite, I saw the
possibility of making something unusual as people climbed up and down the
covered broad steps leading to the Shwedagon Pagoda in Yangon. A gap in the roof
allowed a thin band of afternoon sunlight to strike this spot, so any figures were
illuminated briefly.

I shot from this position for quite some time as different figures and groups
passed through, and what I wanted was the slight ambiguity of oddly lit figures
against a background so dark that it put them out of context. To achieve this, I
simply underexposed by two stops from the in-camera reading – rough and ready,
but I did this a lot in my film-only days, and it works for me.

By contrast, see what happened when I followed the meter reading without any
adjustment in the picture of the two men seated in a Mandalay temple (below),
again in Myanmar and also on unforgiving Kodachrome. For this scene, I wanted
the opposite effect from the Shwedagon steps shot. I wanted the shadows to
reveal everything, and an into-the-light glow that would surround the men and also,
importantly, catch the smoke rising from the cheroot (the moment was timed for
this). In fact, the smoke was the only significant movement, so there was much
more time to think than with the Shwedagon steps.

Two Burmese men sitting in
Mahamuni Temple, Mandalay,
with the sun backlighting the
smoke from a cheroot.

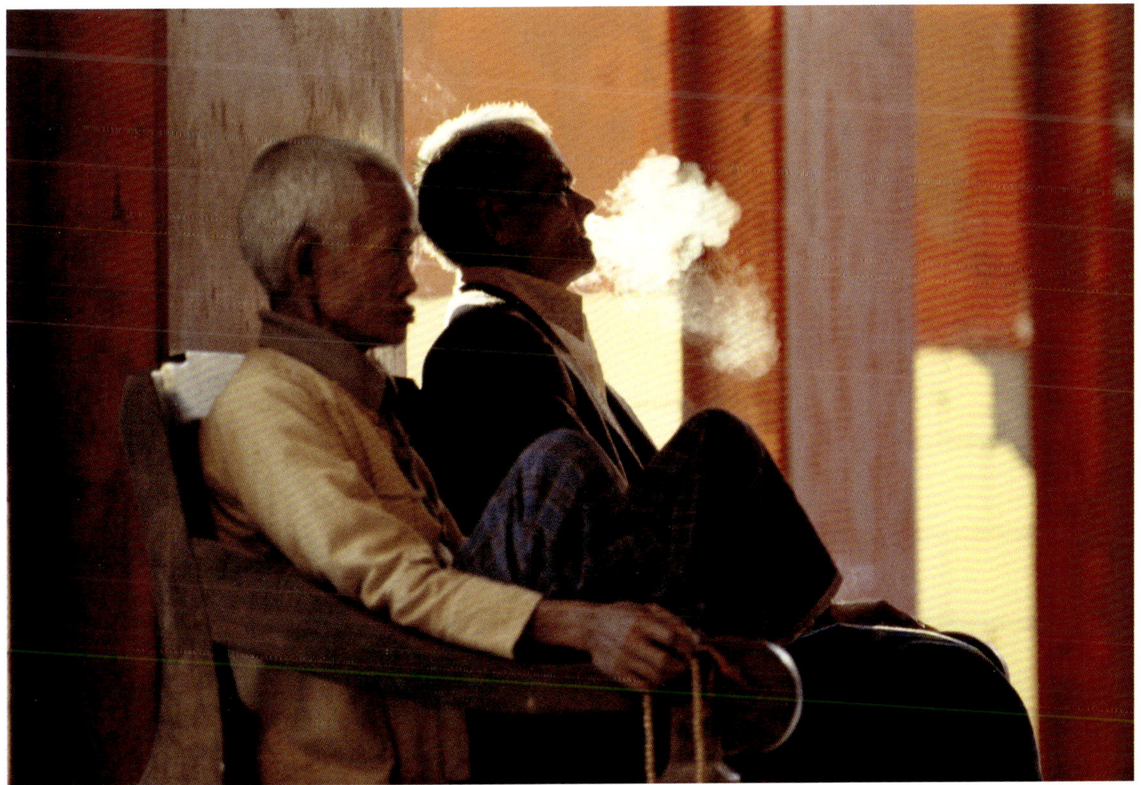

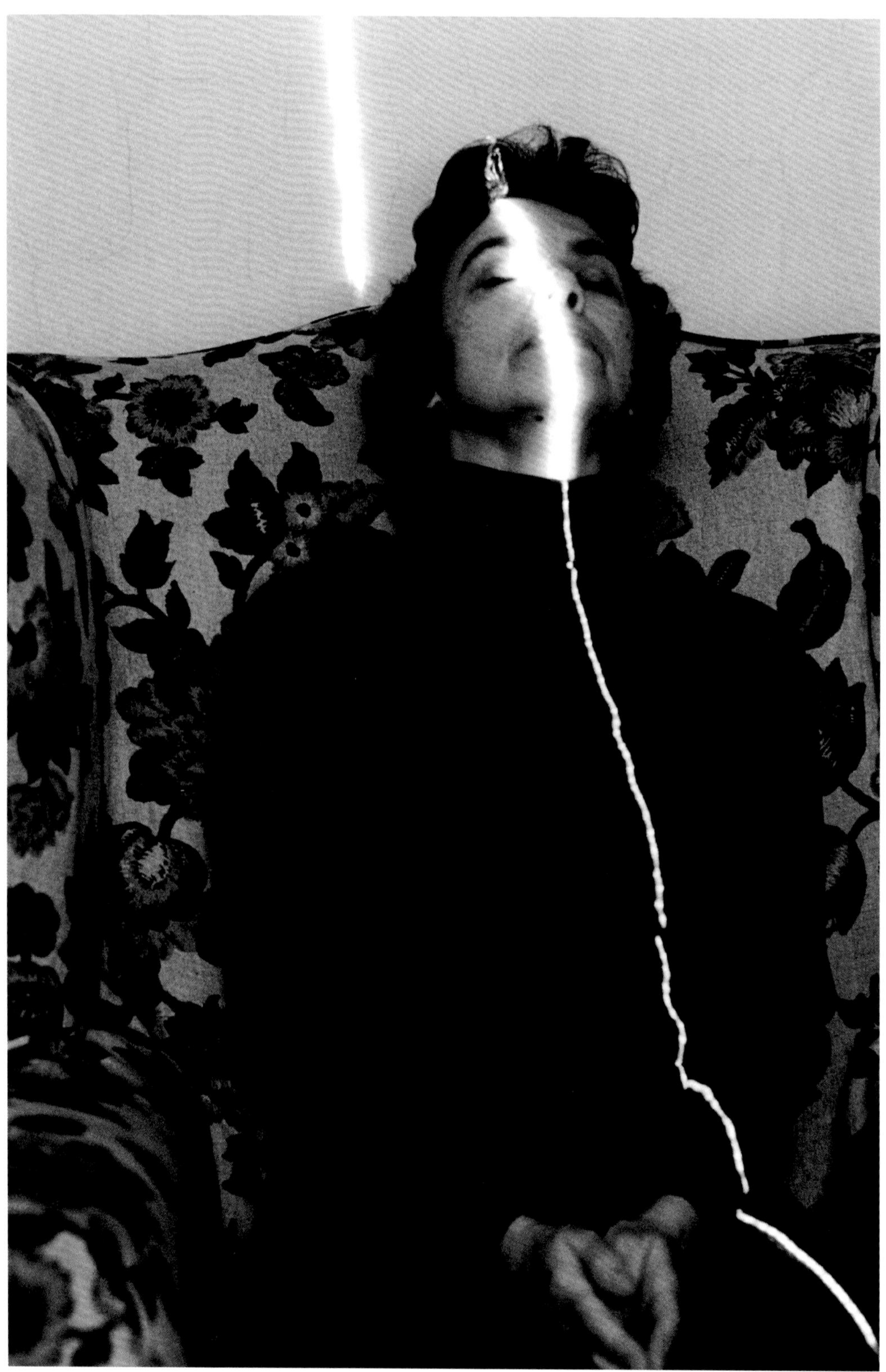

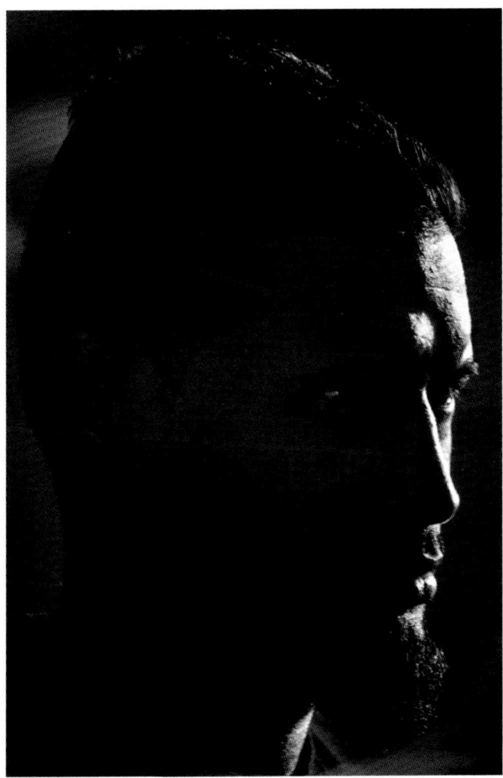

1.

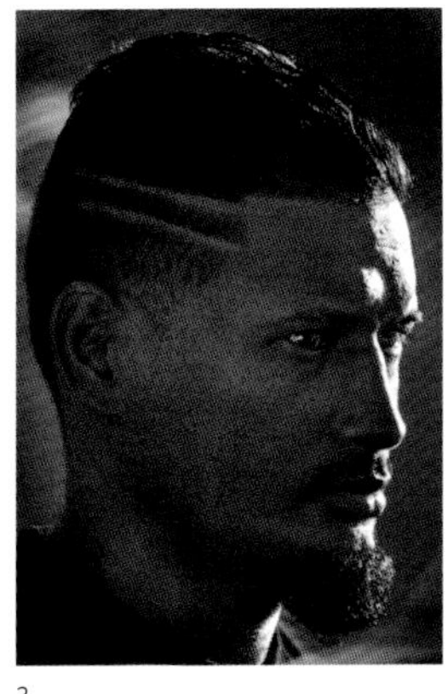

2.

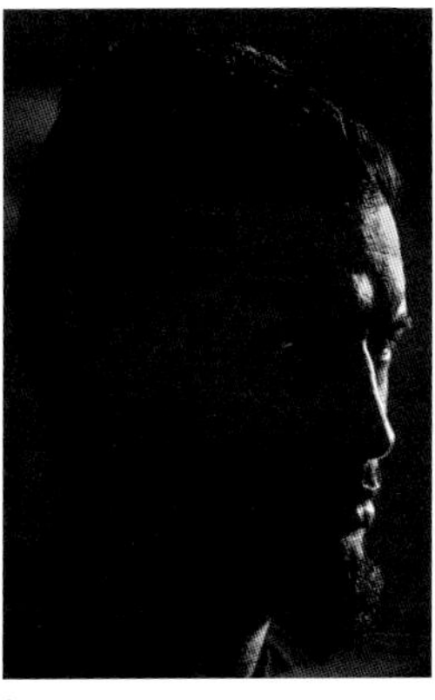

3.

1. My preferred version of the Réunion street portrait referred to in the text favours the edge light, while retaining hints of detail in the shadowed area of the face.

2. Here, the shadows have been opened up fully.

3. Edge light only, with no detail visible in the shadows.

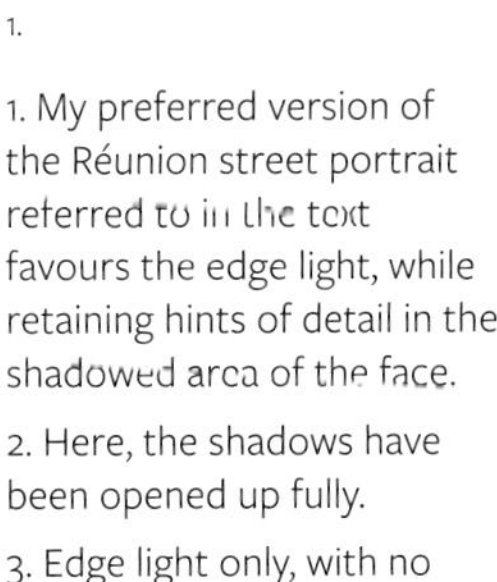

New York City, USA, 1977

One of a series of experiments in 1977 by Magnum photographer Erich Hartmann in which he used a laser light in a darkened room to add an unexpected sliver of light to a portrait – making it the most prominent feature.

Raw processing and computational photography have changed the game across all high-contrast scenarios, especially here and in the spotlight style of lighting on page 102. It's a rule of thumb that with a high dynamic range scene, a good sensor should give around two stops extra at both the shadow end and the highlight end – a very useful total of four stops that you can do a lot with in a Raw file. Of course, getting the full value depends on an accurate exposure every bit as much as it does with film; if the exposure is too high, there will be very little extra captured in the highlights, while the extra shadow detail won't be any more than two stops.

Let's work through the possibilities with the street portrait taken on Réunion Island. The third is darkened to hold all detail in the edge-lit skin. The main shot here is my preferred version, which makes the edge light the main actor, but with a sense of a dark glow (if that makes sense as a description) in the shadowed area of the cheek, and the catchlight in the eye opened up. Some of this can be handled by global image controls, but I prefer to rely more on local adjustment, which most closely mimics old-fashioned dodging and burning in the darkroom. The second version is what most software would do automatically; opening up the shadows for a completely different sense to the image, which for me is boring.

In other words, there's much more choice in how to render the scene than with film, but this isn't necessarily a good thing. There's a tendency I see across the board to let processing algorithms do their thing, which is always to reveal; to save detail and open up deep shadows. Computational photography does this automatically, according to the camera manufacturer's own policy on look, but you can tame this if you shoot Raw to gain access to all the data captured. Quite often, *reducing* visibility can make pictures more interesting.

ACTION IN SHADE

More than anything, this is a scenario typical of commercial assignments, in which there is some choice in setting up the shoot. There may be some limitations in terms of what locations are available and the light. As I mentioned in Sultry Light (see page 104) there are different levels of commitment and effort, so it depends on how much you're prepared to put into getting the conditions to be just so.

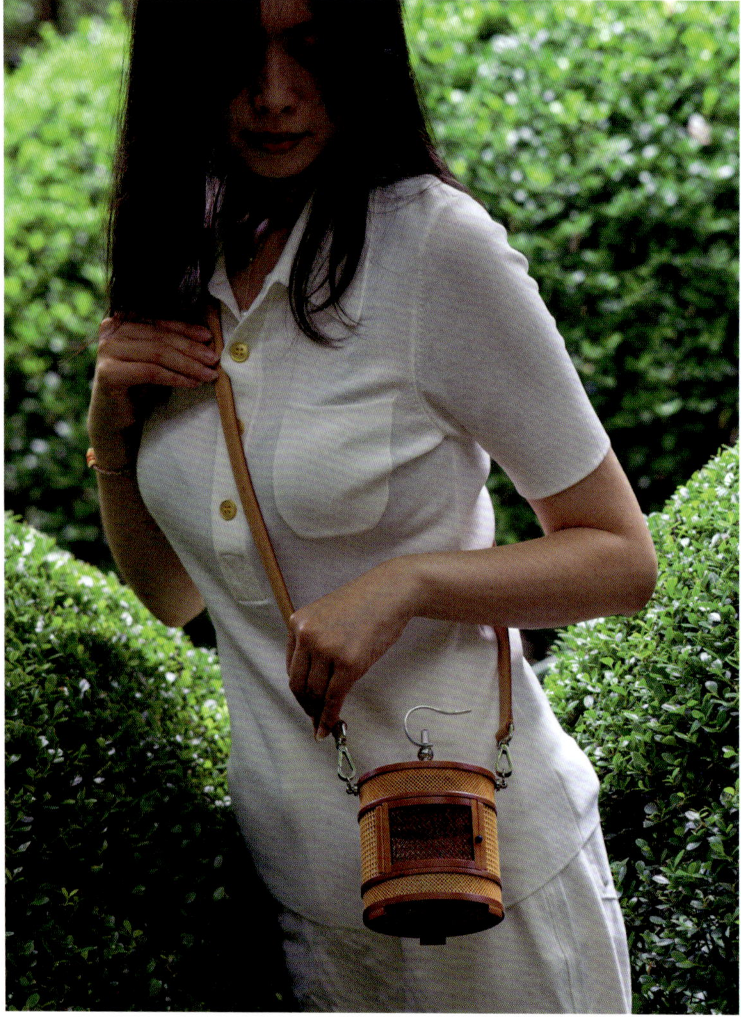

The final processed image strikes a tonal balance between the lit bushes behind (in hazy sunlight) and the shaded figure in the foreground, with the cricket cage – a modern fashion accessory – prominent.

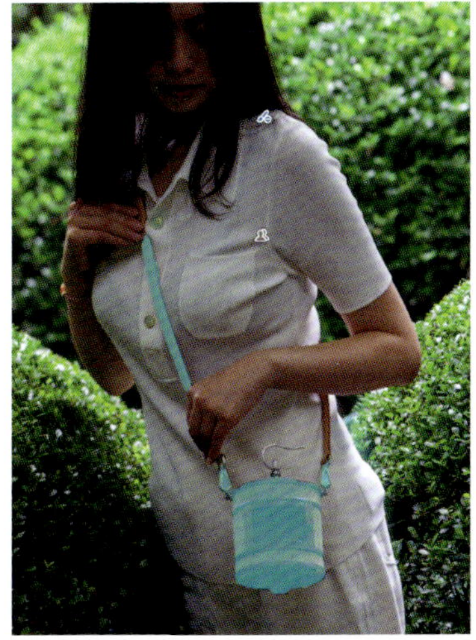 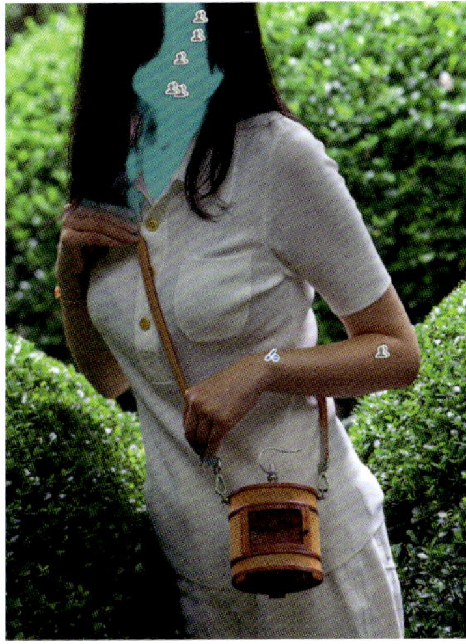 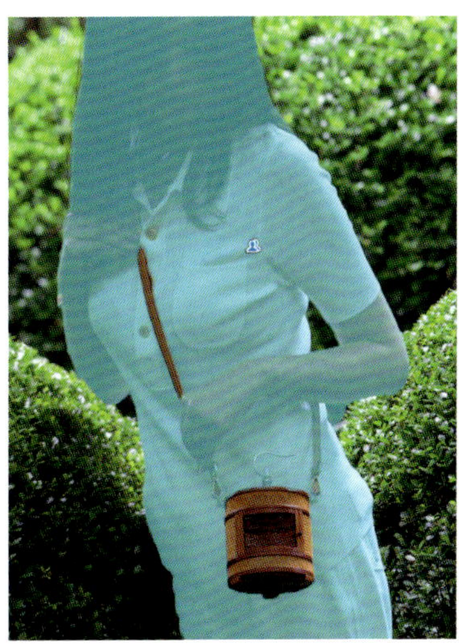

The masking needed, from left to right: the product (cricket cage), facial and neck skin, and the entire figure minus the cricket cage.

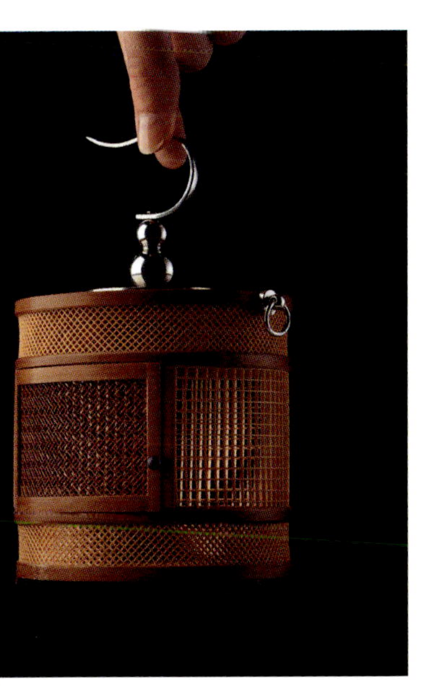

Typically, as here, for a fashion product shoot, the models and props are booked for a particular day, so you adapt to the conditions of the day. Every kind of light has its uses, and there's no point trying to claim that one is superior to another, but as one example, keeping the subject and action in shade rather than in direct light allows for considerable tonal control – as long as the exposure is right. Here, in a park in Shanghai, open shade on a bright but slightly hazy day kept the lighting even and did away with hard local shadows. This was fairly important, given that the subject was a newly designed fashion item – in the style of a cricket cage, which has a very specific cultural value in China and nowhere else. The assignment called for a shot of the cage being worn with its shoulder strap, and a close-up. In both cases, the essential quality was the exceptionally fine traditional workmanship in wood and bamboo, so this needed even, diffuse light with no local shadows to complicate the already intricate details.

To offset the lower-than-average contrast within the shaded area – essentially, the whole of the model and the cricket cage she's wearing – it's normal to photograph with a lit background in order to give the entire image more life and interest, and this is where exposure and processing become critical. In effect, this is the opposite to the way normal product light goes, which is to concentrate the illumination on the subject of interest, and it runs the risk of losing the viewer's attention from where it should go – the cricket cage in this instance – and the brighter and more colourful areas where it naturally tends to go. Nevertheless, almost filling the frame with the model, centering her, and cropping down on her head, all worked to counter this and to keep the focus compositionally on the cage. A passive reflector just out of frame on the right caught some of the background light to lighten the cage, and this was taken further in processing by making a selection of the cage only and raising the white point and increasing the exposure by a stop.

LOOKING OUT

To show how many different ways there are of photographing towards the light, each with different needs and moods, here is an architectural lighting scenario that's common with balconies, verandas and terraces – basically any building design that seeks to link interior and exterior.

The view out is an obvious treatment, but what's not quite so clear-cut is how to expose for it. Assuming that there's no other lighting involved, just natural daylight, the range is always high, typically five or six f/stops difference. Put another way, in the image opposite, the outside five times brighter than the foreground, where the camera is. If I were shooting digitally, and with a tripod, there would be a completely full choice of tonality, not only because of the dynamic range of modern sensors, but because an HDR sequence of frames from a few stops under to a few stops over could increase this dynamic range to whatever I wanted.

However, I wasn't shooting digitally in either of these cases; it was more than 20 years ago and I was using 4x5in Ektachrome transparency film. As I've already mentioned, film is generally a little more forgiving in the way that nothing ever actually clips – it rolls smoothly to white at one end and black at the other – but exposing for transparency film offers little room for mistakes. This means less freedom to interpret a scene, but by no means did it make life difficult – you simply have to work within the film's parameters. You could substitute Ektachrome with any other brand name, such as Kodachrome or Velvia, but they all had more in common than they had differences.

What I'm slowly getting round to here is that when it comes to the tonal 'character' of a photograph and the exposure needed to get to it, there is no best answer; there are different styles, and you can choose whichever pleases you. If you also want to please the majority of other people, that's going to place some constraints to do with popular taste, but otherwise it's quite an open playing field.

The Shaker village at Canterbury, Massachusetts. A rocking chair stands by an open door looking out onto autumnal colours. The exposure is slightly high for the exterior, but works perfectly well overall.

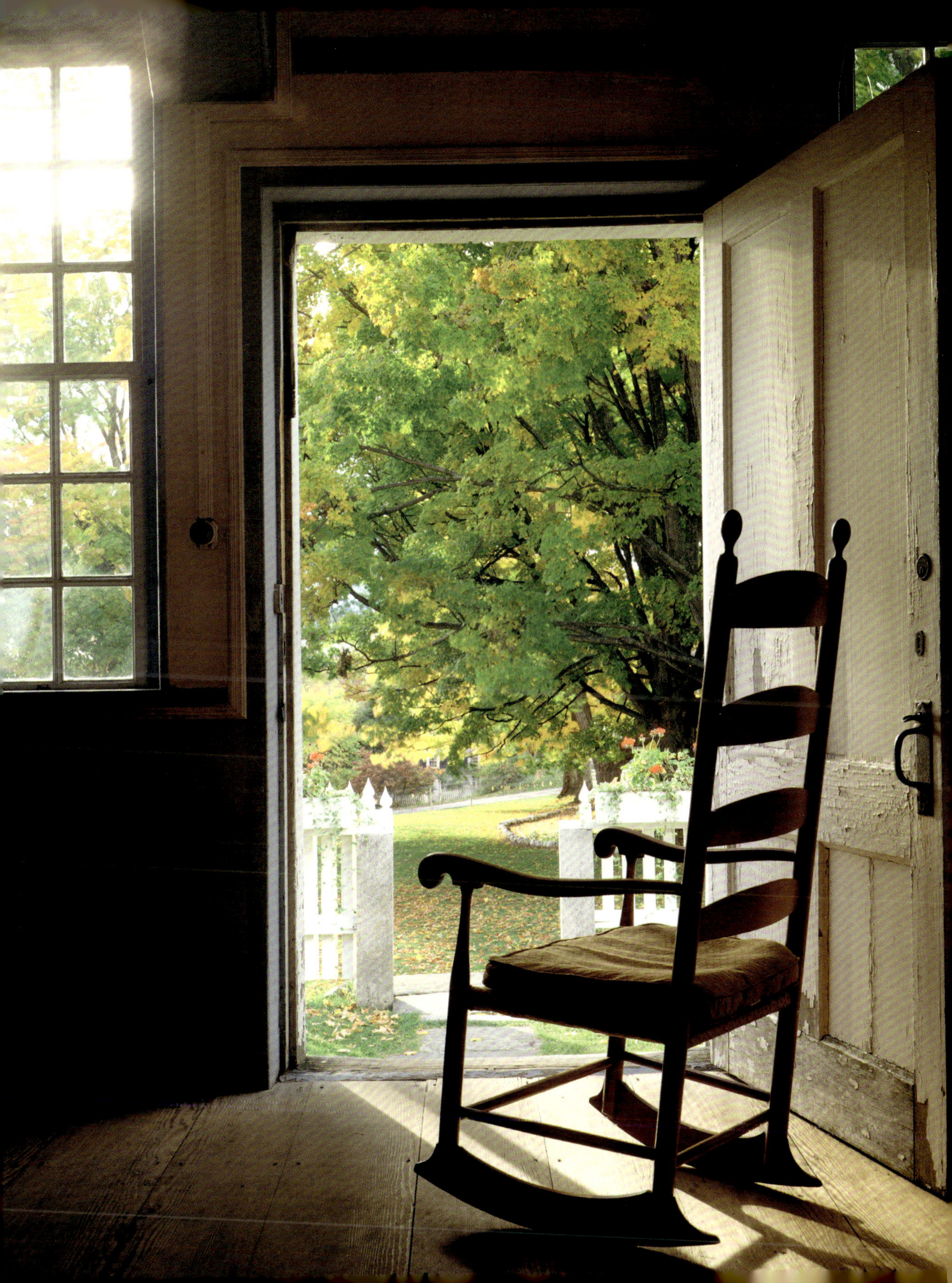

There's a reason for my using film examples here, which is to show that not only do you not need the total control that a high-bit-depth sensor and the possibility of shooting HDR sequences would give you, but that it might actually hold you back from making a more personal, creative exposure. In both of these images (below and opposite), I wanted to make a frame out of the shadowed foreground, and this is a very particular kind of composition. A frame needs to be very dark, possibly with a hint of detail in the shadows, but definitely not opened up.

As for exposing for the scene outside that's within this frame, that too has interesting possibilities. You could treat it as a self-contained scene within the image and give it a carefully average exposure. Alternatively, as in the photograph of a rocking chair on the previous page, you could go up to a stop lighter and it would still work, just in a different way. We then have two areas in the picture: the outside lighter than you'd expect and the shaded foreground darker than you'd expect. That forces them to work together for a combined sensory effect on the viewer. To my mind, it delivers a stronger sense of being inside a veranda looking out onto a bright and already hot morning in the tropics. Would I have done it differently if I were shooting it today with a medium-format digital back? No, definitely not.

One of Bangkok's royal palaces, Vimanmaek Mansion, photographed from a smaller teak structure across the lake. Thailand's tropical climate made open verandahs a practical necessity, and they are ideal for creating frames within the frame.

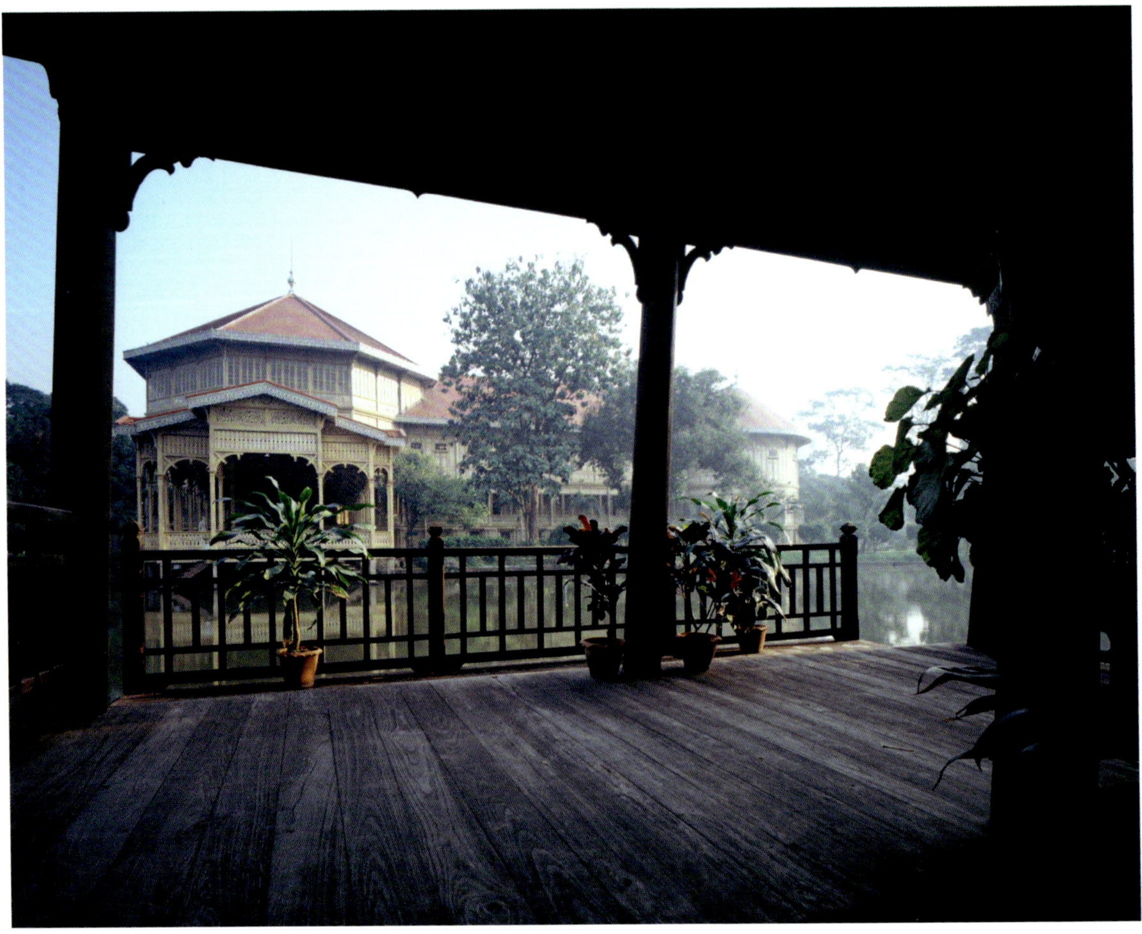

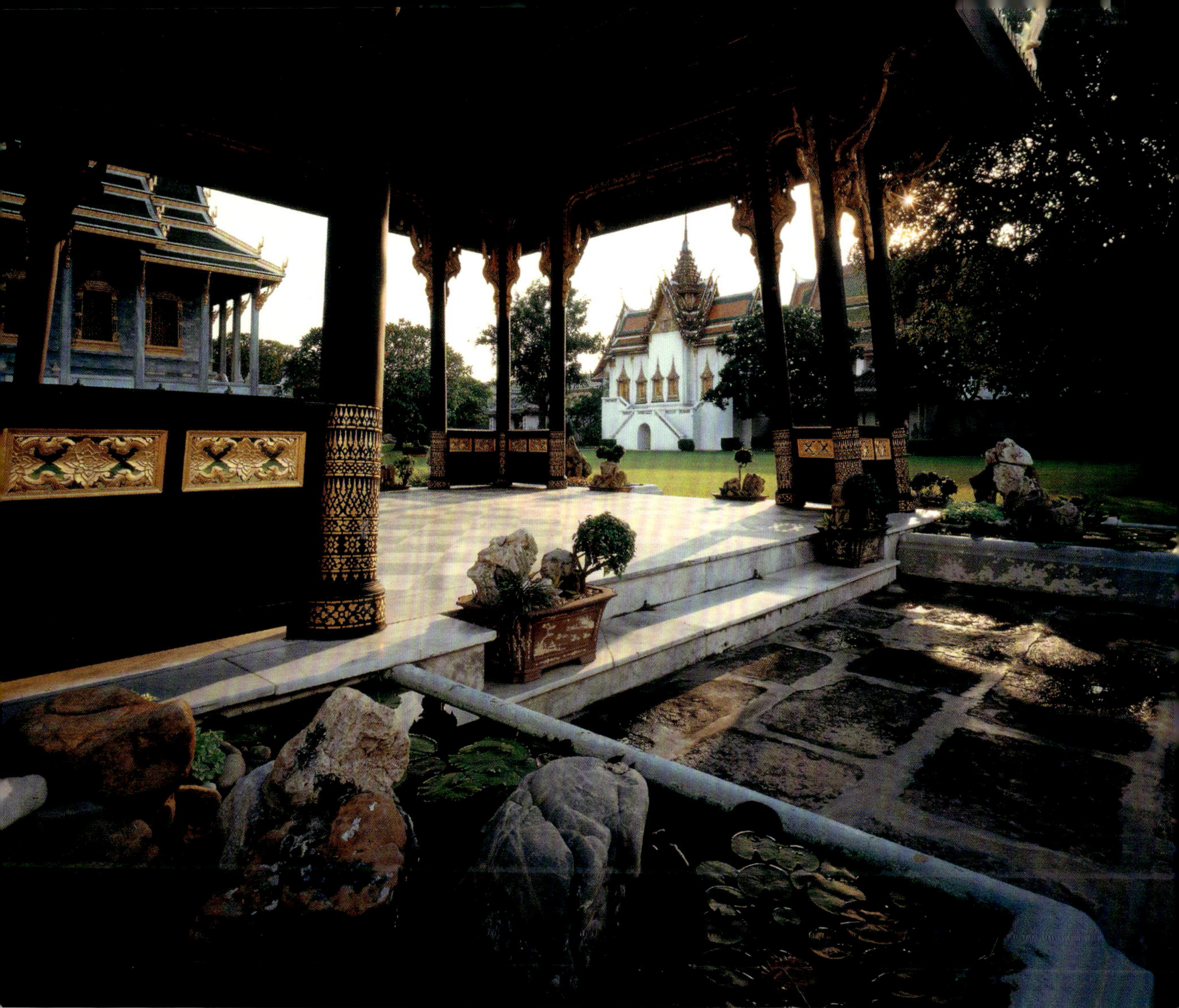

From the same project on Thai royal palaces, this late-afternoon scene is from the inner area of the Grand Palace. This small pavilion with inward-sloping pillars (those are not converging verticals) serves as a frame for the gardens and small palaces beyond.

SUN & SHADE TOGETHER

Depending on how you're accustomed to shooting, there are lighting scenarios where you have little room to manoeuvre because the subject and action come first, and you're compelled to follow them even into really unattractive conditions.

One of the most common of these conditions is a high dynamic range from a combination of hard, high sunlight and shade, together within the frame. Of course, 'unattractive' is certainly a point of view, but it's shared by most photographers, and most of us tend to avoid it if we can. We either don't bother with the scene in front of us or return when the light is more interesting and amenable. At the start of this book, I explained why the decline in editorial assignments has shifted exposure choices away from the 'everything-visible' standard to more personal interpretations, but documentary shooting itself continues in the guise of personal projects. Shooting that's driven entirely by subjects in action still needs a decision on the look, and therefore on the exposure that will deliver it. Contrasty, hard-light scenarios make this difficult to maintain, because the action might move between light and shade, or even straddle them, as is the case with the example here.

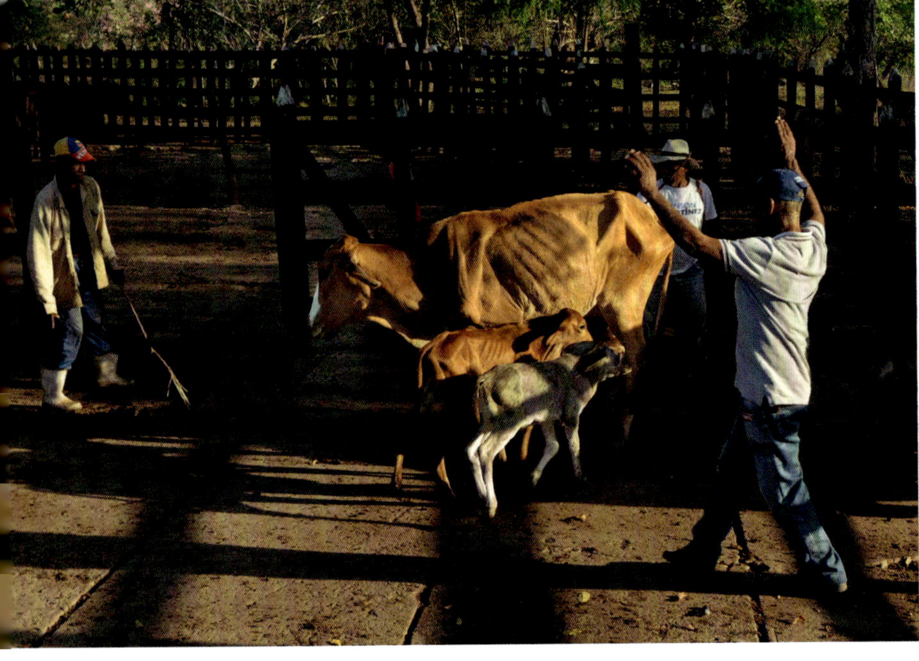

Taken earlier in the day, the lighting from a low sun is interesting enough and with good contrast for photographing in colour. But I knew this was not going to last. Here, the cattle are being herded into a holding area before they are loaded onto the trucks.

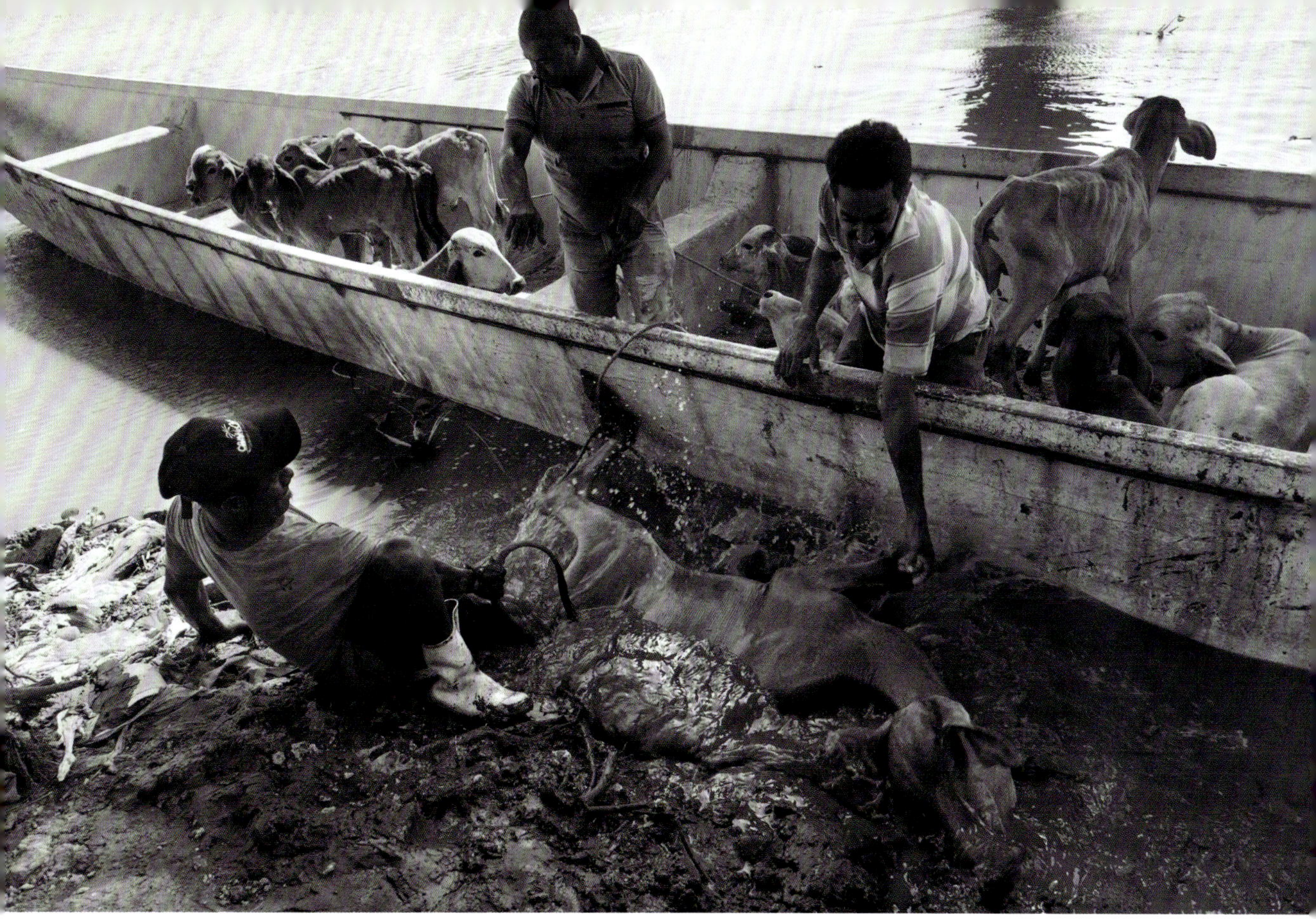

The day's shoot was a short story about moving cattle in rural Colombia downriver and across to the summer pastures on an island. The day started well before sunrise, but from experience I knew that by the time we'd picked up the *vaqueros* (cowboys), the cattle had been rounded up, the trucks had arrived and the cows and calves loaded, it would be closing in on midday by the time we got to the river crossing. This is the tropics, so by late morning the sun is very high.

I wanted the pictures covering the whole process to work together and make up a series, so there were basic exposure decisions to be made before shooting. As the colour picture opposite shows, the first hour or two of the day had good side-lighting and a decent colour palette of browns against cooler shade, but it wasn't going to last. The location, too, would change from the ranch with its trees to the flatter, almost featureless waterscape of the river, and who knows what else. As it turned out, there was a lighting surprise in store for me, in the form of a new bridge arching over the river at the point where two dozen calves were going to be transferred from the trucks to a long boat. Obviously, as this was the middle of a tropical day in a season with cloudless skies, the *vaqueros* chose to do the tough work as much as possible in the shade, so the boat would be partly in sunlight and mainly in shade, and any overall view would have to include both.

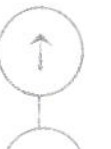

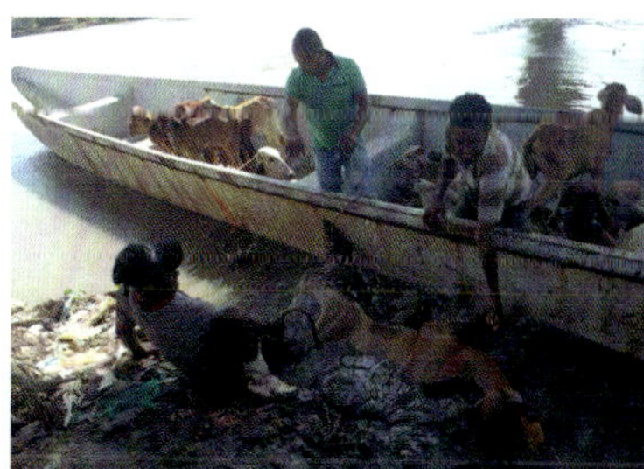

With the action taking place in the shade of a bridge, and a bright tropical day beyond, this shot of calves being manhandled into a boat was demanding to process, as the original unprocessed colour file reveals.

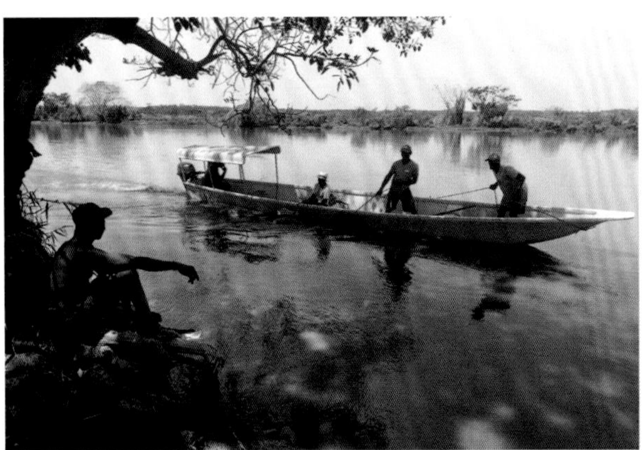

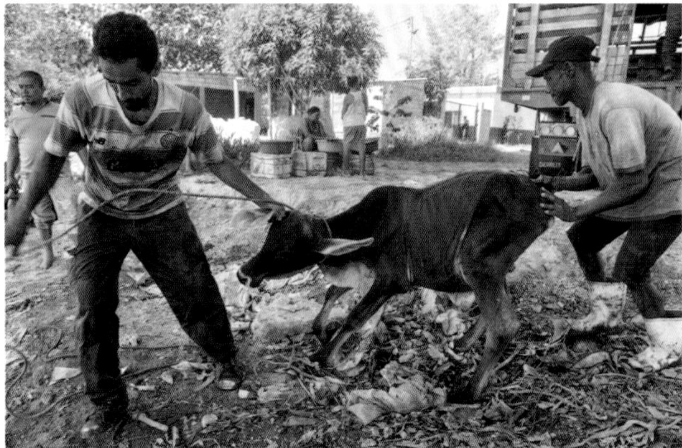

Returning to the initial decision on the look that should carry through the entire day, it would have been good to continue in a similar style to the colour shot on page 146. However, this wasn't going to be possible throughout the day, as under a high sun – which would light most of the day's story – the rich colour saturation was likely to disappear. Moreover, I was doing this story in the first place because of the action, which is interesting and a little unusual, involving adult cattle swimming and calves on the boat, and I was fascinated by the skills needed to move cattle in this way. These were experienced *vaqueros* who spend their lives doing this, and there would be many moments difficult for me to anticipate but good to capture.

Therefore, the first decision was to shoot in black and white, which always demands a mental shift towards discounting the colour, elevating the tonal subtleties and shapes, and switching to 'seeing' in monochrome. A huge practical advantage, which also pushed me away from colour, is that black-and-white processing allows more extreme shifts in brightness, especially locally, without straining any credibility.

Because micro-second details of action were going to be at the core of the story, I wanted these to stand out clearly, with healthy contrast and good tonal separation, and I guessed that this was going to be more in shade than in sunlight. In this case, there were going to be very bright, contrasting backgrounds or distance, probably with some flare, and I simply needed these not to be too distracting. In any case, flare in black and white can be useful for softening contrast in unimportant backgrounds. All of this meant there would be a lot of local adjustment in the processing. My exposure strategy was to go for average on the main action, framing as tightly as possible to keep the sunlit, overexposed areas to a minimum. My usual method is smart metering (I'm attuned to my camera's 'idiosyncrasies' in making adjustments), aperture priority and working the exposure compensation dial to go lighter or darker.

The main picture on page 147 shows the exposure issues for the dynamics of the scene, and what they need in local adjustment. It's also a good example of my view that exposure extends right through to processing (this is, after all, why Adobe use the word 'Exposure' for the first slider in ACR). There was a lot of shooting from roughly this viewpoint, and you might wonder why not shoot with the exposure set manually for shade? The reason was that I also had to turn around and change

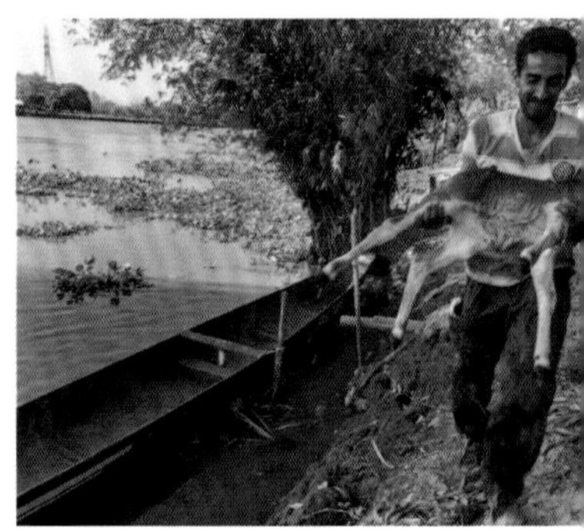

Three of the other images that made up the story, each of which was taken when the sun was high, and in a mixture of shade and sunlight. Black and white gives continuity, despite the individual lighting conditions.

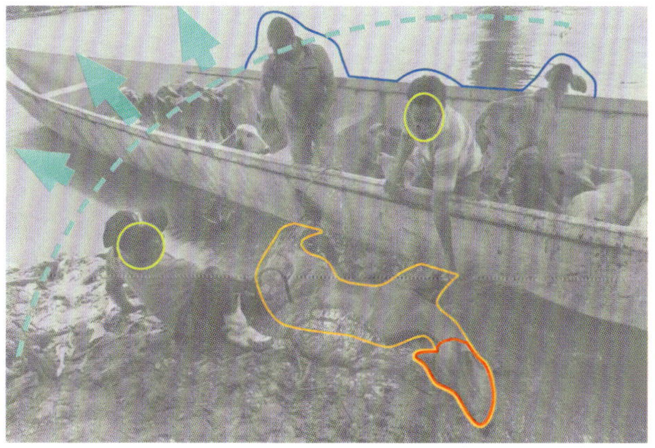

position as the calves were being manhandled out of the truck, and for other opportunistic scenes like the man carrying the small calf in his arms. Changing the exposure manually takes slightly longer than Auto, and it wasn't worth the risk of losing a shot.

This image captures the moment as one of the larger calves slips and a *vaquero* goes down with it into the water, but it's important that we can see all the detail. The unprocessed colour image (see page 147) looks terrible, but as I always shoot Raw plus JPEG, I knew it had all the data I need. You can also see how pointless colour is to this particular image, and how the green shirt in particular distracts from what is going on.

I started my processing with global adjustments that are aimed at the shadows in general: raising the Exposure by ½ stop, increasing Whites and lowering Blacks. Then I take down the overexposed areas of the water and the prow of the boat. Next is the calf, which needs to be fully textured and visible, as it's the focus of the action, and this includes extra exposure for the head, as there's a slight danger of the animal not reading clearly. The faces of the two men involved with the calf also need to read clearly, and their skin is dark, so the tones need to be lifted with radial filters. Flare around the head and shoulders of the man at the left and the calf looking out from the boat – inevitable with the strong sunlight from above the frame – needs correcting by raising the contrast.

The processing plan for the main image. On top of the global settings described in the text, all above the cyan dotted curve was brought back from overexposure with a reduction of one stop, Highlights and Whites lowered, and Contrast raised. The fallen calf (orange outline) had Whites raised, and its head (red outline) increased by ⅔ stop with Contrast and Whites also raised. The area outlined in blue, which was flaring against the bright water, had Contrast strongly raised, and the faces of the three men had their range stretched by raising Whites and lowering Blacks strongly.

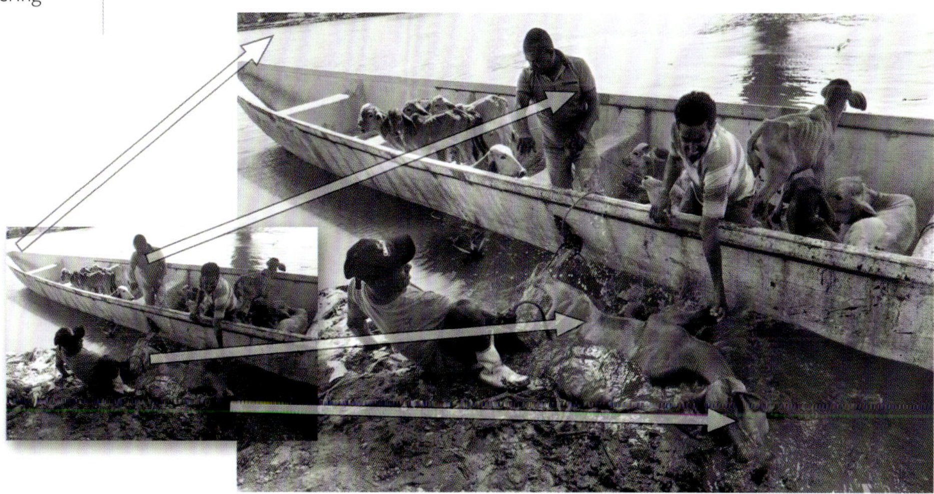

WIDE PANORAMA EXPOSURE

Post-production software makes it easy to assemble panoramas that are stitched together from sequential overlapping frames, and I for one like doing this when it's appropriate. At the least, it means that we can decide on an angle of view as wide as we like while using whatever lens we have at hand.

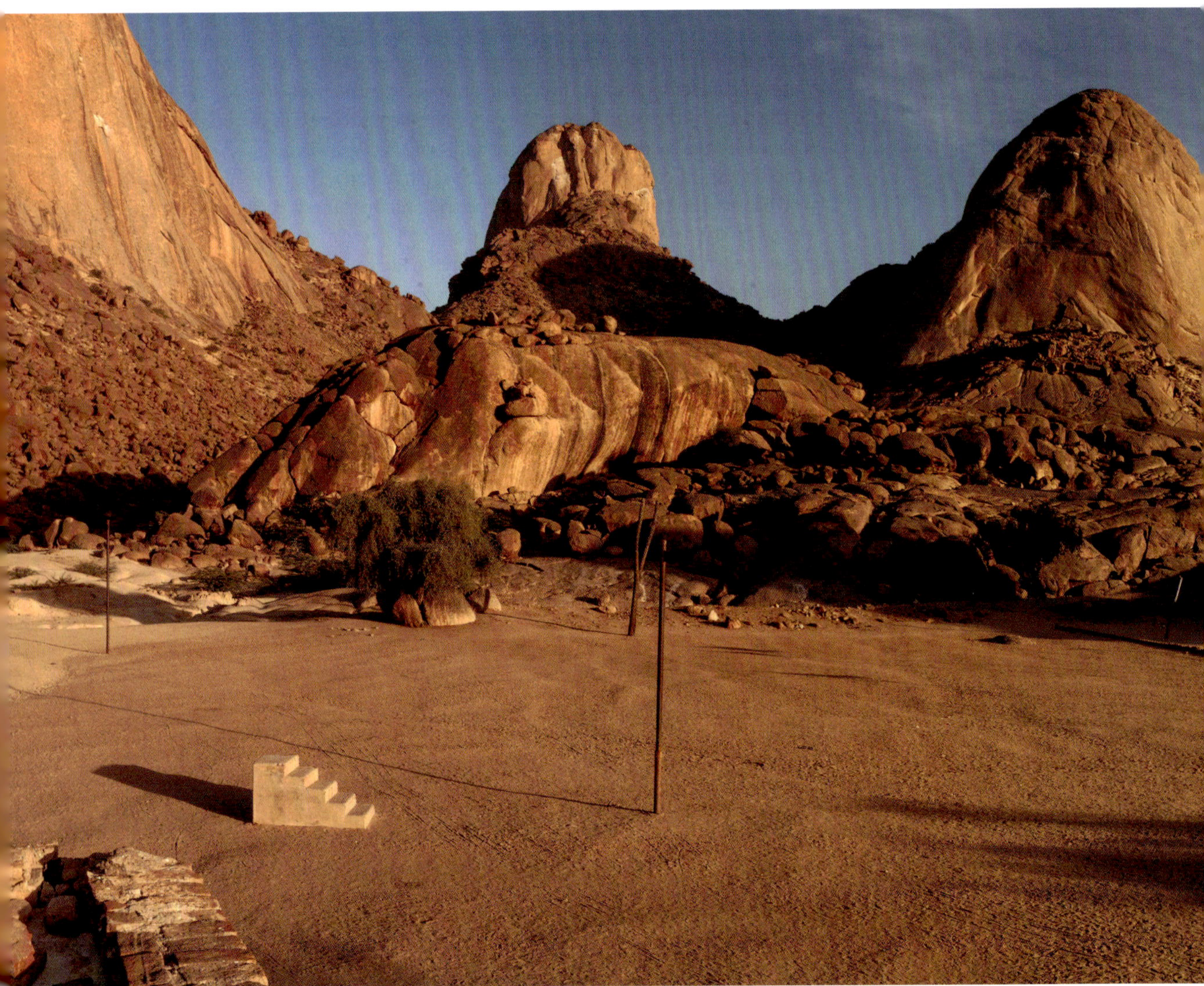

It needs no more than turning the camera about half a frame's width, pressing the shutter and keeping on going – normally sideways, but there are also occasions for going up and down to create a long vertical image in the manner of a Chinese mountain-water painting. I'll admit to the temptation to keeping on going too far, but the results are too thin and diminish the view, so this freedom to choose our frame shape needs to take into account the way we look at finished images. Even for a landscape panorama, there's an optimum width, though there's no formula. One of the few useful compositional suggestions is to have a form of 'stop' at each end so that the panorama looks naturally satisfying.

The Khatmiyah Mosque at the base of the mountains in Kassala, eastern Sudan. This pan-and-stitch panorama covers approximately 90 degrees horizontally.

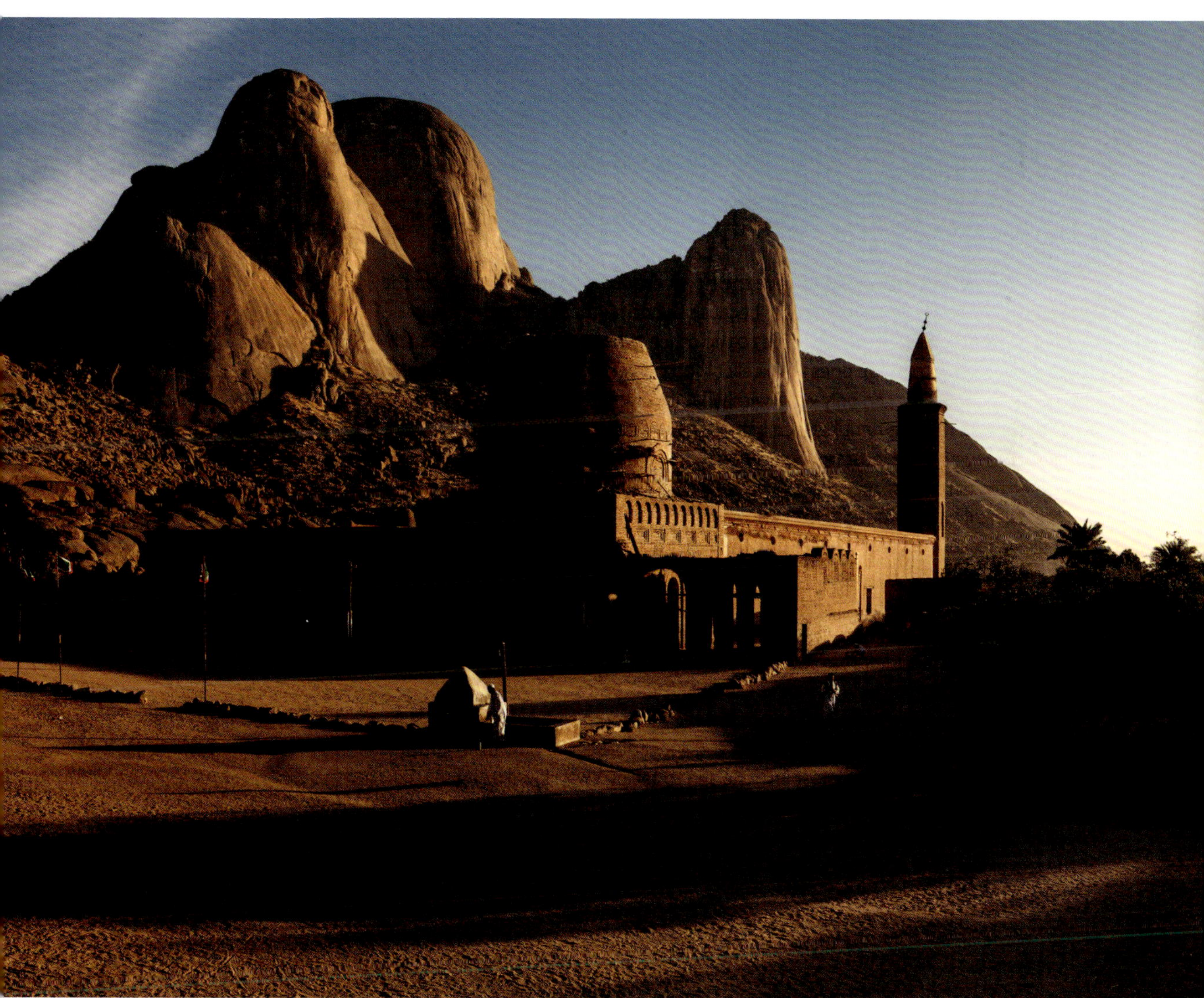

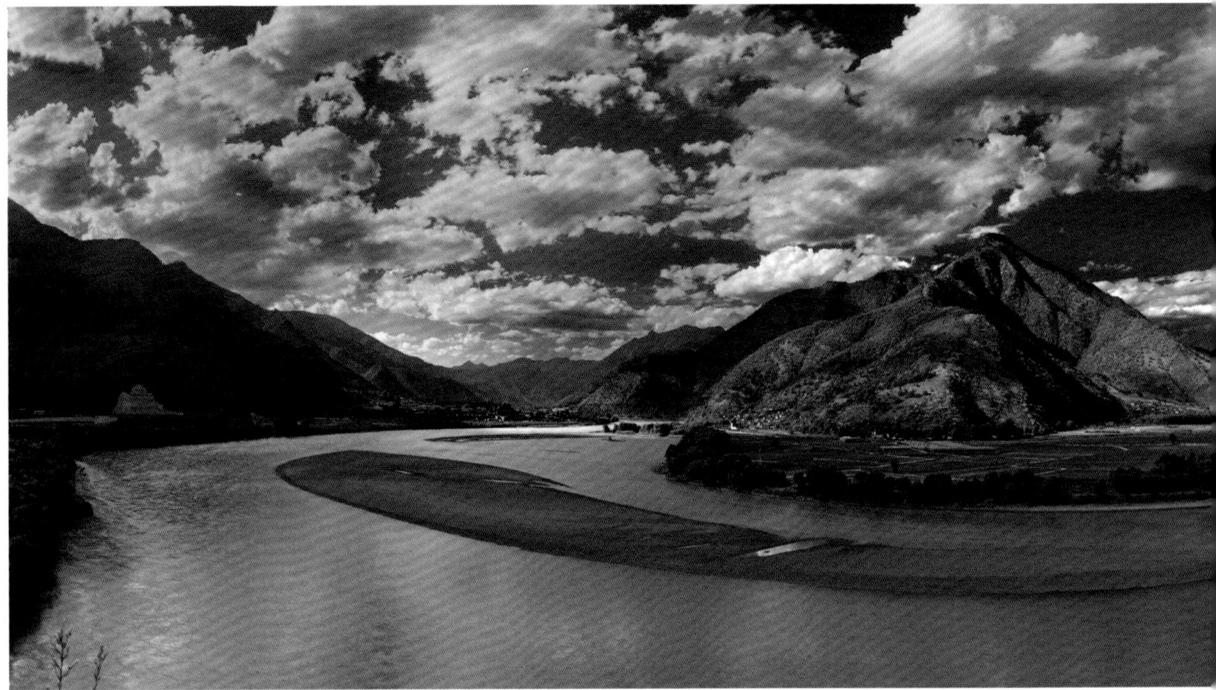

That apart, wide panoramas also have their own exposure needs, especially in the early morning or late afternoon, simply because the camera's angle to the sun is likely to be very different from one side to the other. While stitching software such as Photoshop's PhotoMerge does an excellent job of blending frames to even out exposure differences, it can only work with what it's got in the original exposure, so it's important to find the right balance between setting the ideal exposure for each frame and keeping the exposures close enough together for the software to handle. The wider the panorama, meaning the wider the total field of view, the more likely it is that there'll be a serious difference in the brightest from one end to the other. The panorama shown here, for example, has a wide range because the left side is almost facing into the sun.

The subject here is the First Bend of the Yangtze River at Shigu in Yunnan, which demands a big, wide treatment. I'm a geographer by education, and for me this is one of the world's most impressive phenomena. Within less than 10 kilometres (6 miles), the upper Yangtze – known as the Jinsha, or 'Golden Sands' – does a complete 180-degree turn, changing from flowing due south to flowing north. This is the only viewpoint that makes any sense, and it's a 100-degree view from left to right, which means shooting almost into the sun to facing away. I was using my old Hasselblad SWC, and the combination of its 38mm lens and 44x33mm sensor meant I needed seven overlapping frames when used in vertical format, as the illustration at the top of the page opposite shows.

A seven-frame stitch of the First Bend of the Yangtze River in Yunnan was needed to encompass the view of the river flowing towards the camera on the left and away on the right.

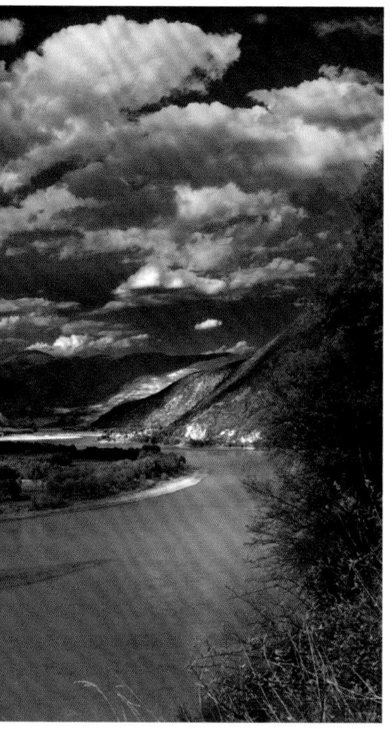

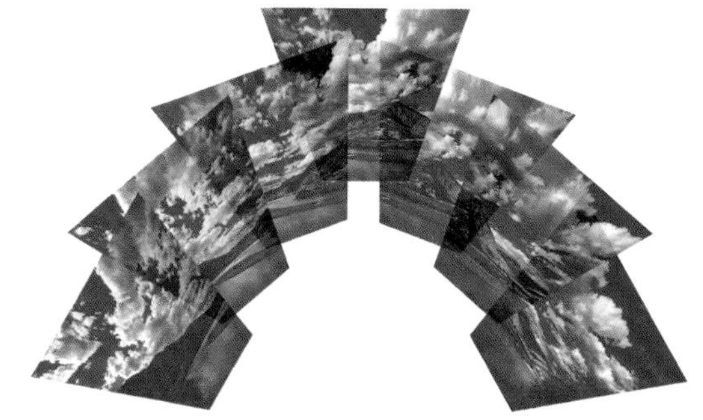

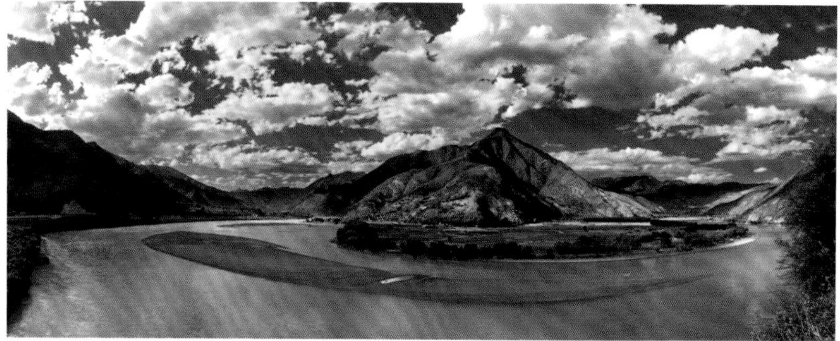

The seven frames needed (in vertical orientation) for the main image. Below these is an early version of the panorama, which was less than successful at handling the whites of the cumulus clouds. They aren't clipped, but they also lack the full range of tones.

Stitching the images together is a simple matter, but adjusting the exposure between the frames so they would roughly match meant a little calculation: the frames at the left needed a little over a stop less exposure than those at the right, with processing taking up the fine adjustment. Fortunately, the Biogon lens on the Hasselblad SWC doesn't exhibit any vignetting, so matching the tones from frame to frame was not a problem.

From the outset, I wanted as much drama and contrast as reasonably possible, so a black-and-white conversion was in order, as it meant I could use the channels to darken the blue of the sky. Of course, this increased the contrast from the darkest sky to brightest cloud tips, and the whites of the clouds are the key to the whole appearance of the picture. Simply avoiding highlight clipping in the clouds doesn't do full justice to a scene like this – they need careful adjustment during processing to reveal their subtleties. Clipping would be a disaster in such a scene, so it was important to keep the exposure down. Although the Hasselblad's sensor has a good dynamic range, relying on that alone was not enough – clouds like these need to show their volume, and that depends heavily on holding detail and good contrast in the brights and highlights. Doing this across a differently exposed stitched panorama only added to the complexity.

SKY DRAMA

Skies can be a world of their own, and if you frame so as to give them pride of place, they deserve exposure attention. The most dramatic are those with clearly structured clouds that are at least partly in sunlight, and the dynamic range can be spectacularly high.

As you just saw, panoramic images tend to take in a lot of sky, and when there are significant clouds, they demand exposure attention. If your composition gives them pride of place, they deserve both careful exposure and processing. Sky drama is the territory of clouds that have shape, and the larger the better. Thunderheads (cumulonimbus) and tornadoes in their different ways win on sheer drama, but for exposure and processing difficulty, fair-weather cumulus clouds take some beating, as on the previous page.

The principle for dramatizing skies believably is threefold. Firstly, you need to hold the highlights down a little more than you might expect, in order to retain the cloud texture fully. Secondly, contrast should be raised around lit areas using a broad, soft mask (radial masks are the most generally useful). Thirdly, shadowed areas should be taken down while still hinting at detail (setting the darkest parts just above clipping, while raising the white point often does a better job of increasing local shadow contrast than a contrast slider or curve). You can see all three of these at work in the image shown here, which was taken in early morning sunlight as it cut briefly through stormy clouds over Cadair Idris in Wales.

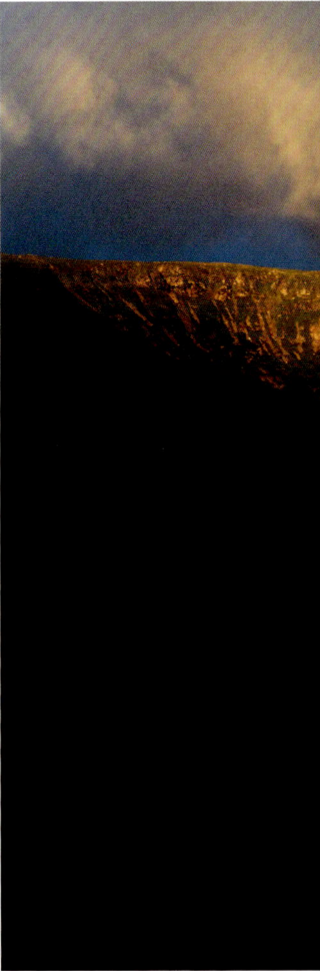

A stormy sunrise over Cadair Idris, a mountain in Wales. Below left is the JPEG that accompanied the Raw file. The processing of the Raw file was very much a matter of personal taste – I wanted to let the shadowed landscape below the mountain become almost featureless, and concentrate attention fully on the lit cliff face and cloud.

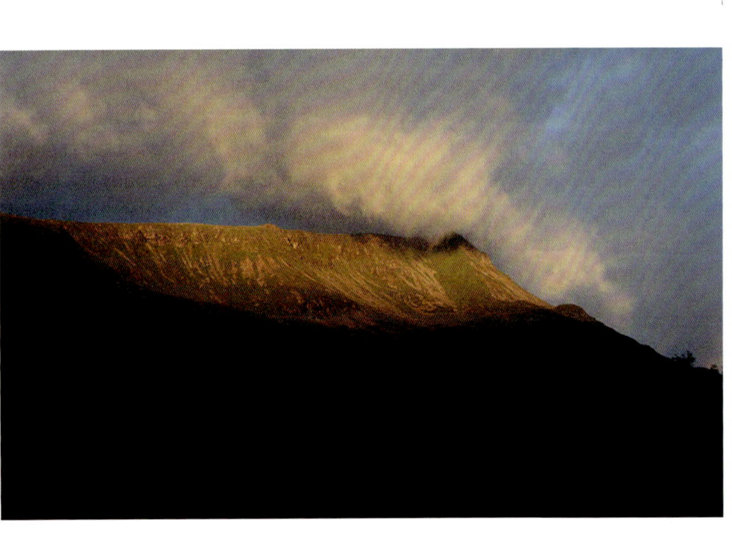

I would always suggest avoiding local tone-mapping operators, such as Clarity and Texture. Obviously, this is very much a personal opinion, but there's reason behind it. Skies are full of smooth gradations and don't have detailed texture, so compared with the land beneath, they're at a much lower frequency. If you want to stay faithful to that and keep them believable, the last thing you want is the kind of tone-mapping associated with HDR images.

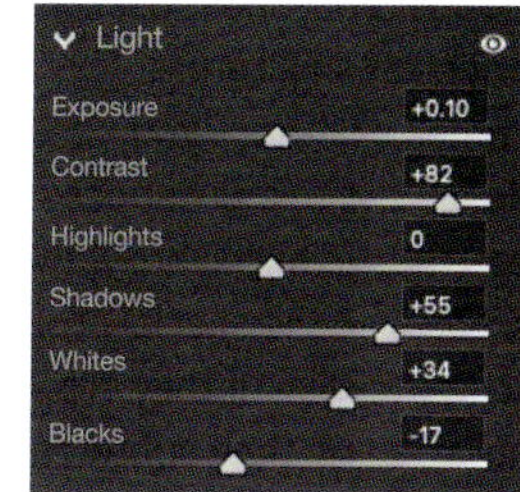

The Light settings in ACR relied primarily on raising Contrast and lowering the Blacks significantly.

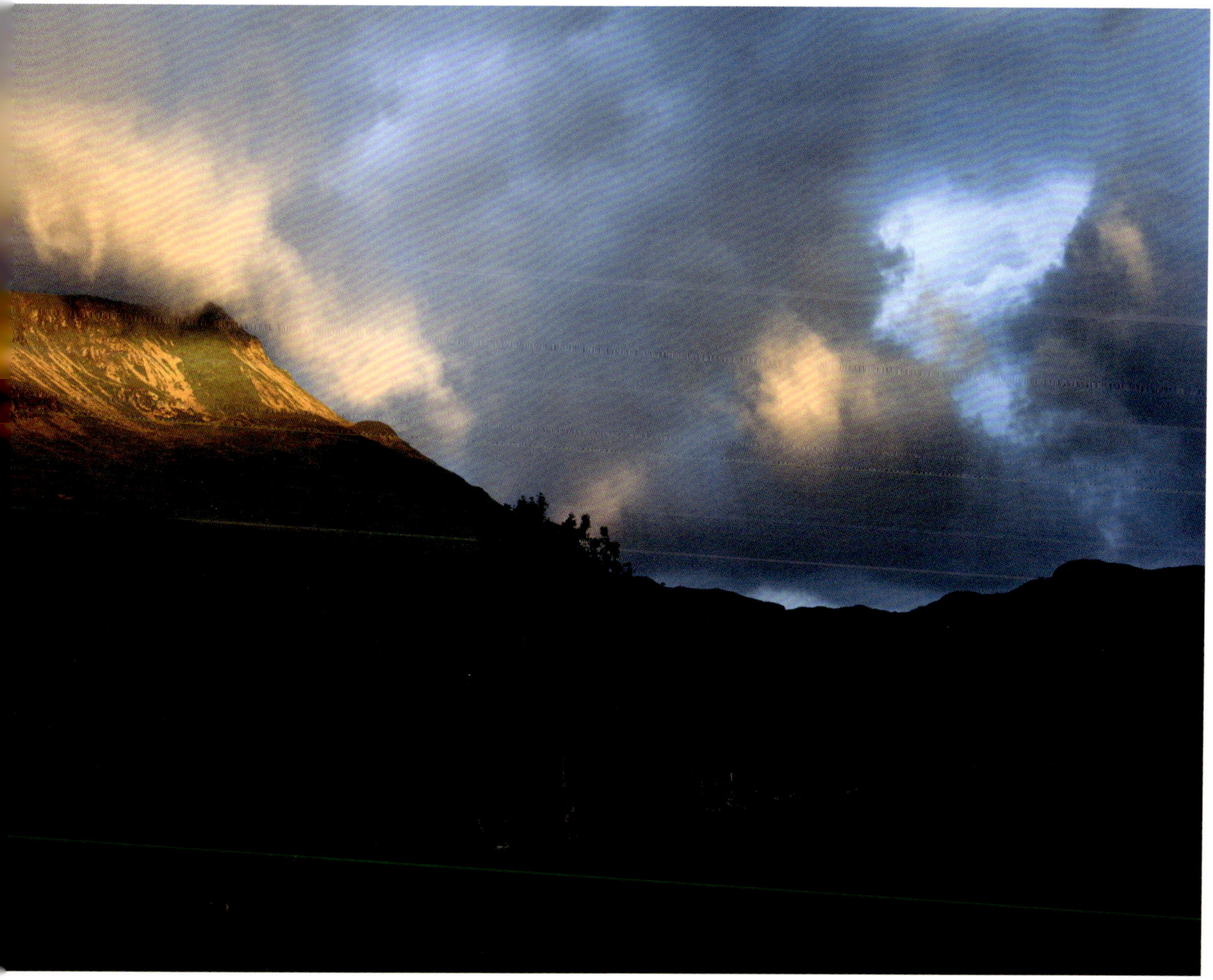

That said, you may need an HDR sequence if you are photographing tall, brightly lit cumulus clouds, especially in the thinner air at altitude, as in this picture of a building storm over grasslands in western China. The full dynamic range of these clouds is beyond most sensors – and by full I mean holding textural detail in the brightest small areas. This is at its most challenging with this thick variety of cumulus because you need to show the complex texture in the sunlit parts in all its detail, and this all happens in the brightest 20 percent of the tones. It's extremely easy to clip highlights without noticing while concentrating on the rest of the scene, and the special problem with cloud highlights is that they draw attention to themselves. If they clip, the sense of texture is lost, and cloudscapes depend above all on their subtle range of texture. This image, and details from the exposure sequence I shot (below left), ought to make this clear.

The exposures needed for the HDR sequences for this panorama were taken at increments of 1½ stops.

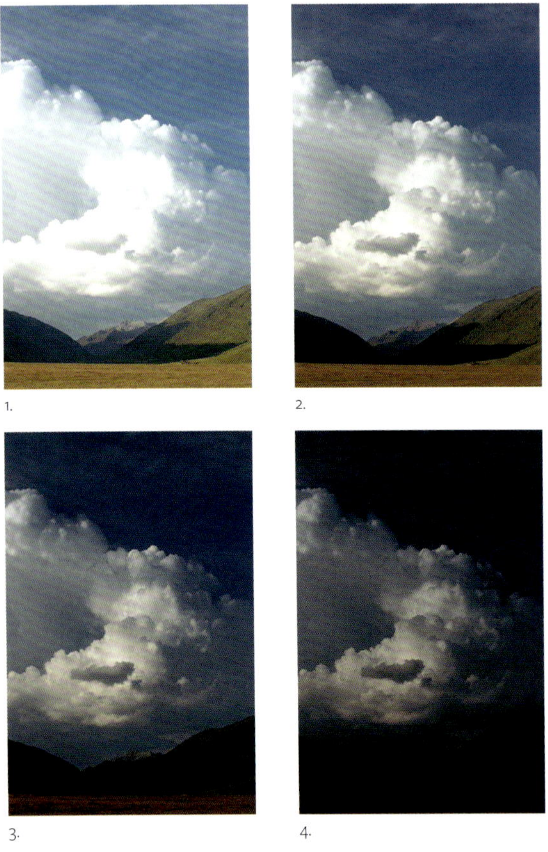

1.

2.

3.

4.

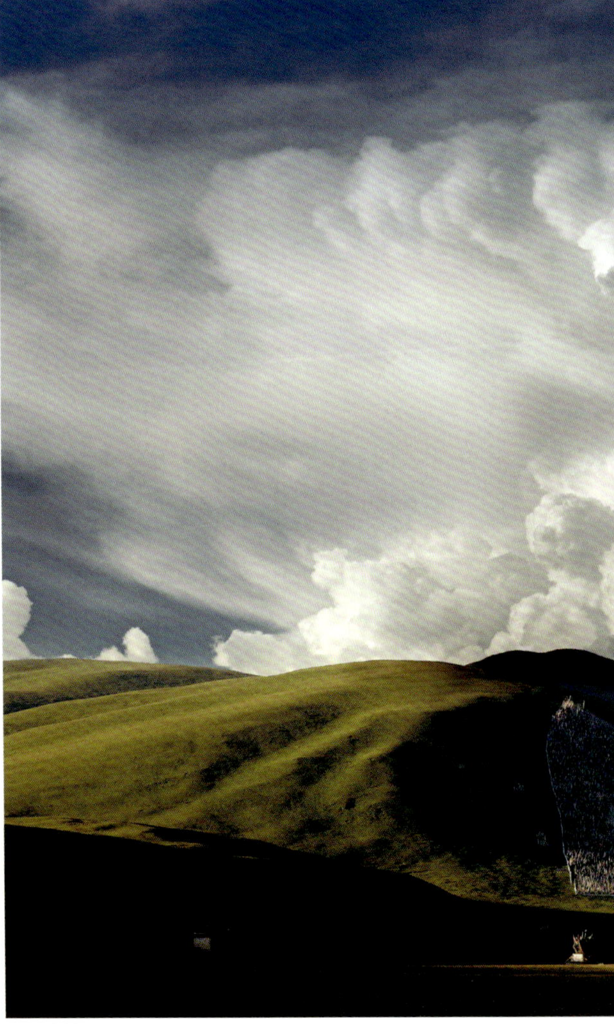

Another specific issue to consider when shooting is movement in the clouds, which may require the exposure sequence to be shot quickly. Some cameras have a dedicated mode that will help with this, but everyone has their own techniques. Mine is to shoot a first frame at the camera's metered exposure at aperture priority, then use the Nikon's exposure compensation dial to shoot a sequence of frames getting darker by 1½ stops until the brightest highlights are a mid-tone, then shoot a sequence getting brighter until the darkest shadows are a mid-tone.

A late afternoon storm shrouds the northern Daxue Range. Partly in shadow, a huge field of Buddhist flags covers a hillside by the Xianshui River, south of Daofu, Sichuan, China. This was a pan-and-stitch panorama, which complicated the HDR shooting, and I had to work fast, as cloud systems like this have vertical movement.

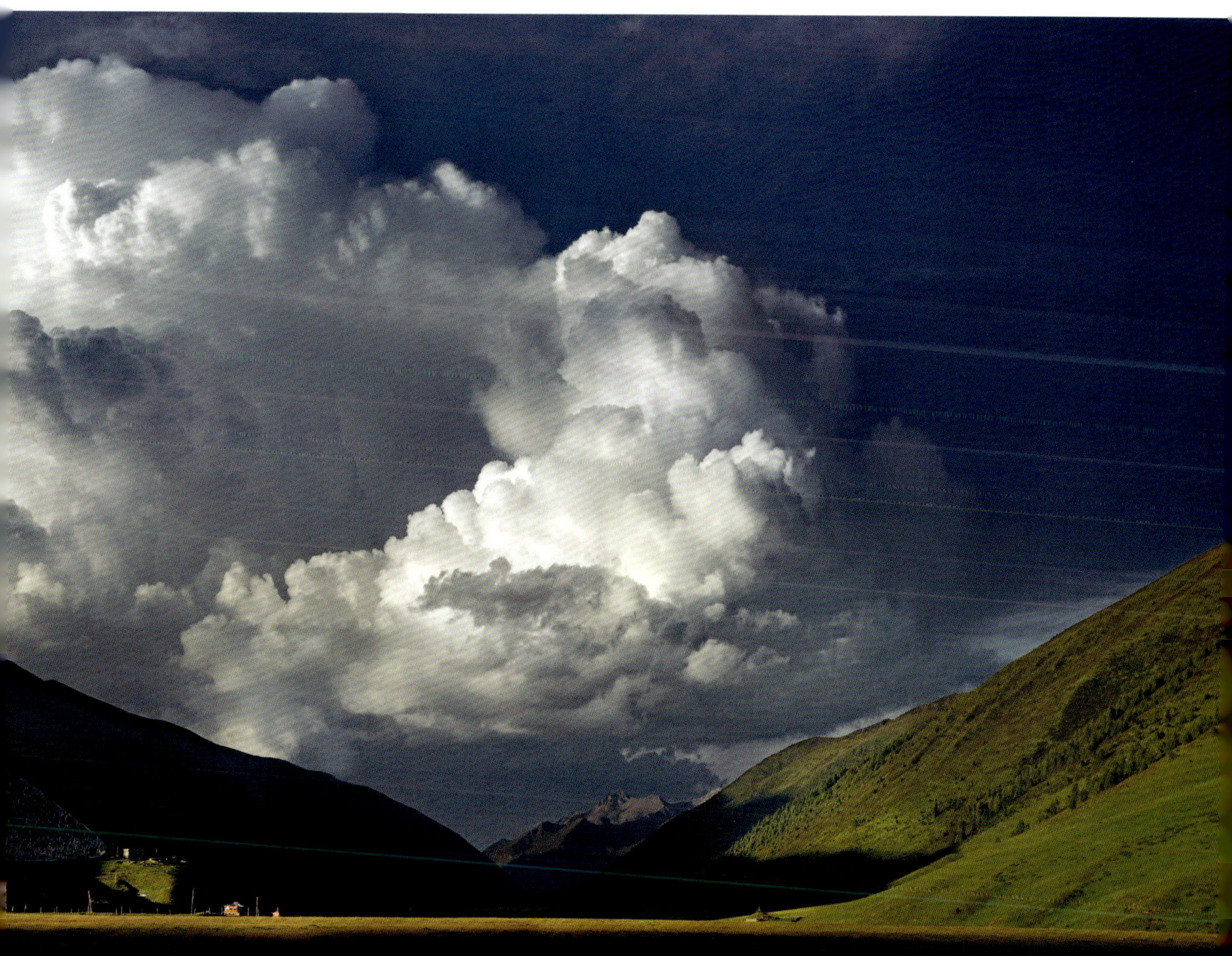

HDR

HDR in photography has come a long way since its beginnings, and I have a particular opinion about this because I made the mistake of writing a book about it back then. Two mistakes, in fact. The first was writing it too soon, when the available software was new and a bit primitive (I had early adopter syndrome). The second was that I imagined that everyone would, like me, want to use it to make high-range scenes look better and more realistic.

The interior of Khampun House, Ubon Ratchathani, Thailand, is built in a traditional style. Shot at midday without any photographic lights, the dynamic range is high.

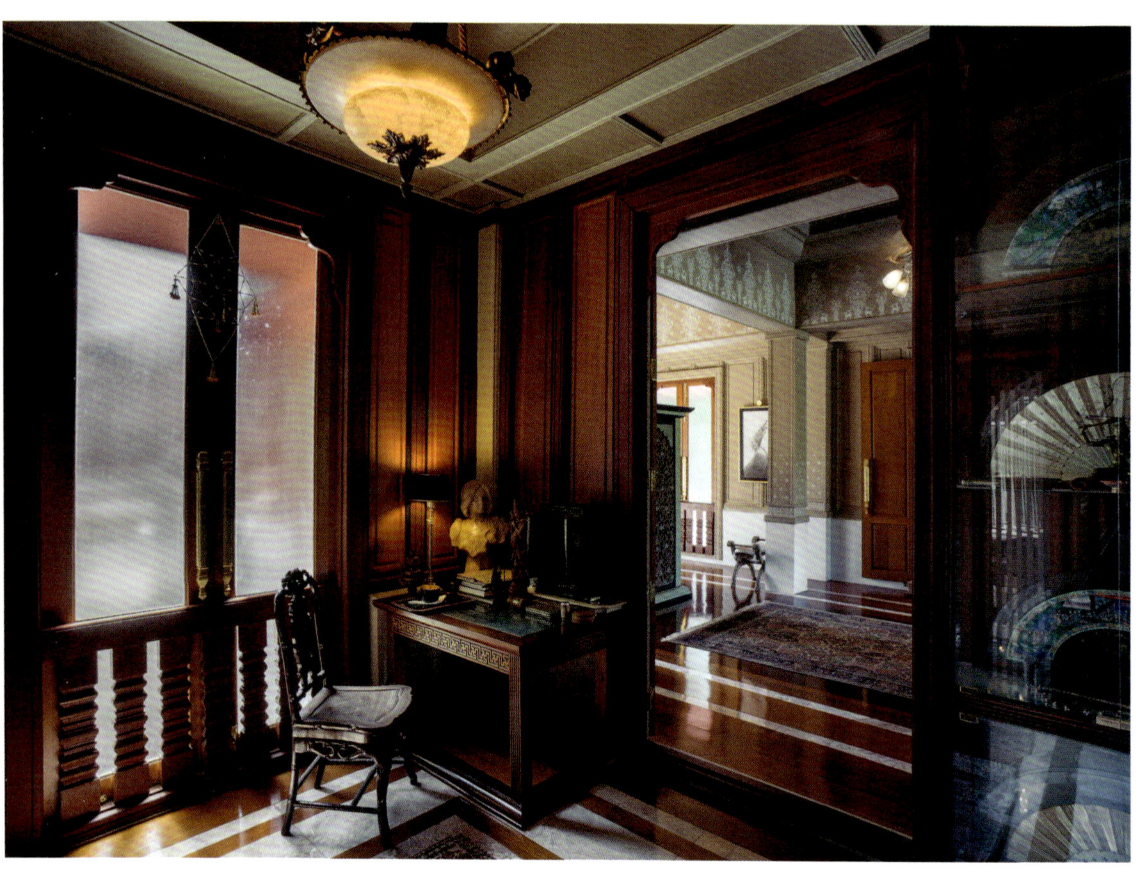

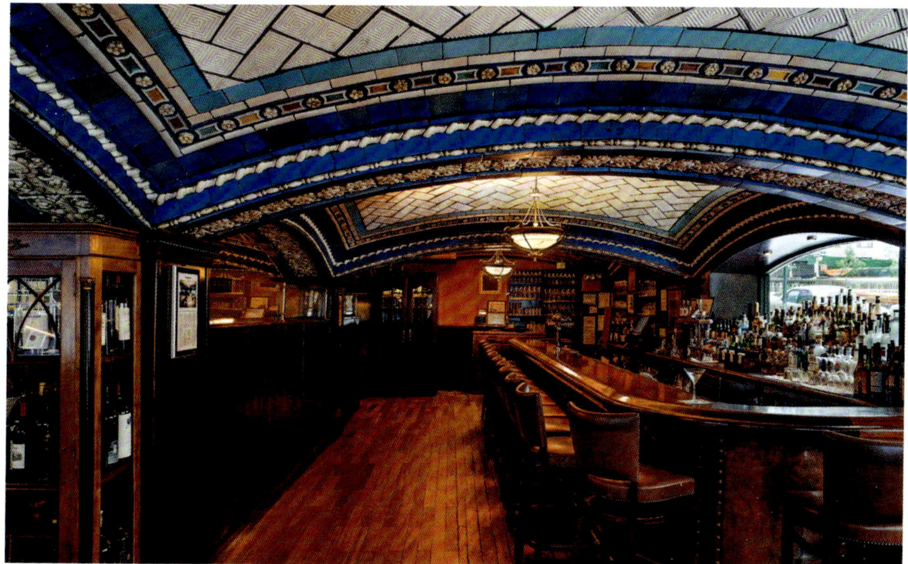

As it turned out, most people who ended up sharing their efforts online actually liked the way that HDR – when taken to extremes – made pictures look weirdly unphotographic. Although HDR tools have improved over the years, the core problem was not in making the file – that was solved ages ago – but in rendering it.

You could say that the problem is the paper in front of you: it has a very low dynamic range, so there are lots of compromises needed when you try and cram a high dynamic range image into it. Even the latest OLED screens don't have the range. For a print, or a page in a book like this, it isn't a technical problem, because you could never make a combination of paper and ink (or silver) that had a high range. Rather, it's a perceptual problem and a perceptual solution, which means it really does come down to judgment and taste. You have to decide how far you can go in preserving all those details in the shadows and highlights before the result looks artificial – and you can define 'artificial' in any way you like.

Personally, I prefer a result that looks like a traditional photograph, so the effort goes into concealing the HDR-ness so that it doesn't look in any way special. This actually takes more effort. I'm not in the business of recommending one product over another, but my process is to make a 32-bit floating-point TIFF in Photoshop, open it in ACR and then use local adjustment masks (typically radial ones) to finesse the image. Basically, I treat it as an updated version of printing a black-and-white negative in the darkroom – old-fashioned in principle, but with all the fine control that modern digital processing has to offer.

The Della Robbia Room at the former Vanderbilt Hotel in New York has exquisite Guastavino tile vaulting. Again, this was photographed without any photographic lights, instead relying on the technique described.

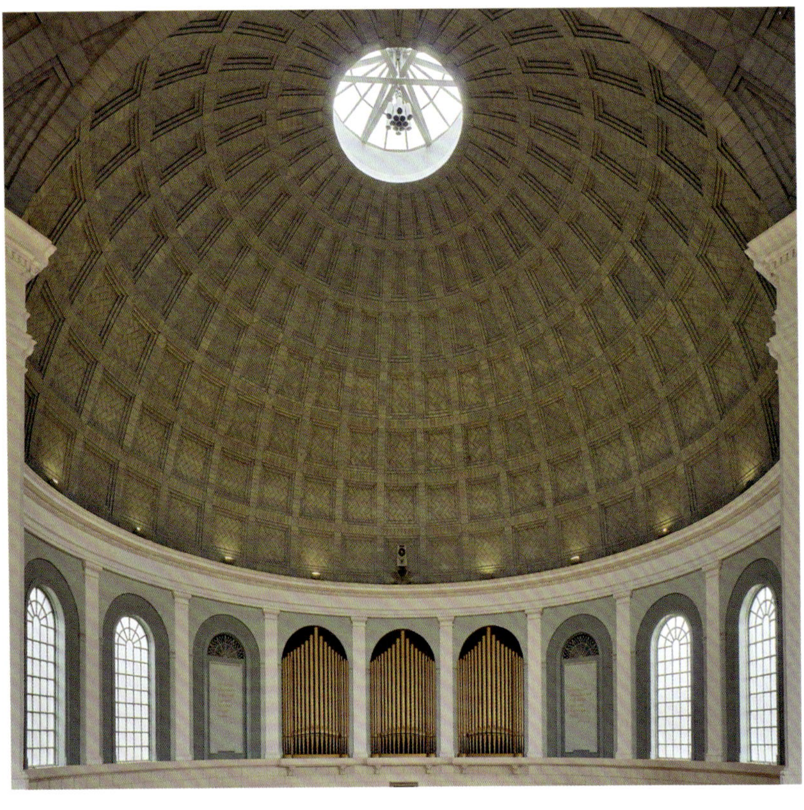

The Guastavino tile vaulting of the First Church of Christ, Scientist, in Cambridge, Massachussetts. Any scene that includes the light sources (windows on a cloudy day in this case) will almost inevitably be out of the range of a normal sensor.

Vaulting over the nave of the Riverside Church, New York. The colour version below was originally prepared for the 2010 book, *Guastavino Vaulting: The Art of Structural Tile*. Since then, I've turned against any hint of mid-tone micro-contrast, which this has, and have reprocessed the files for a more realistic version in black and white (right). This also removes the unnecessary distractions of colour.

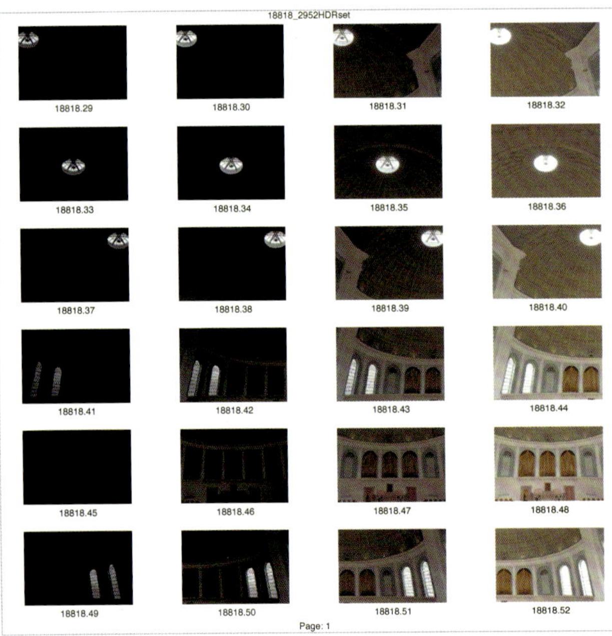

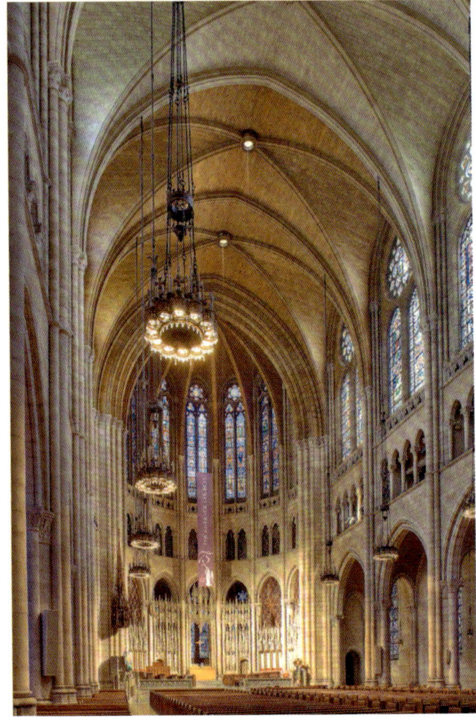

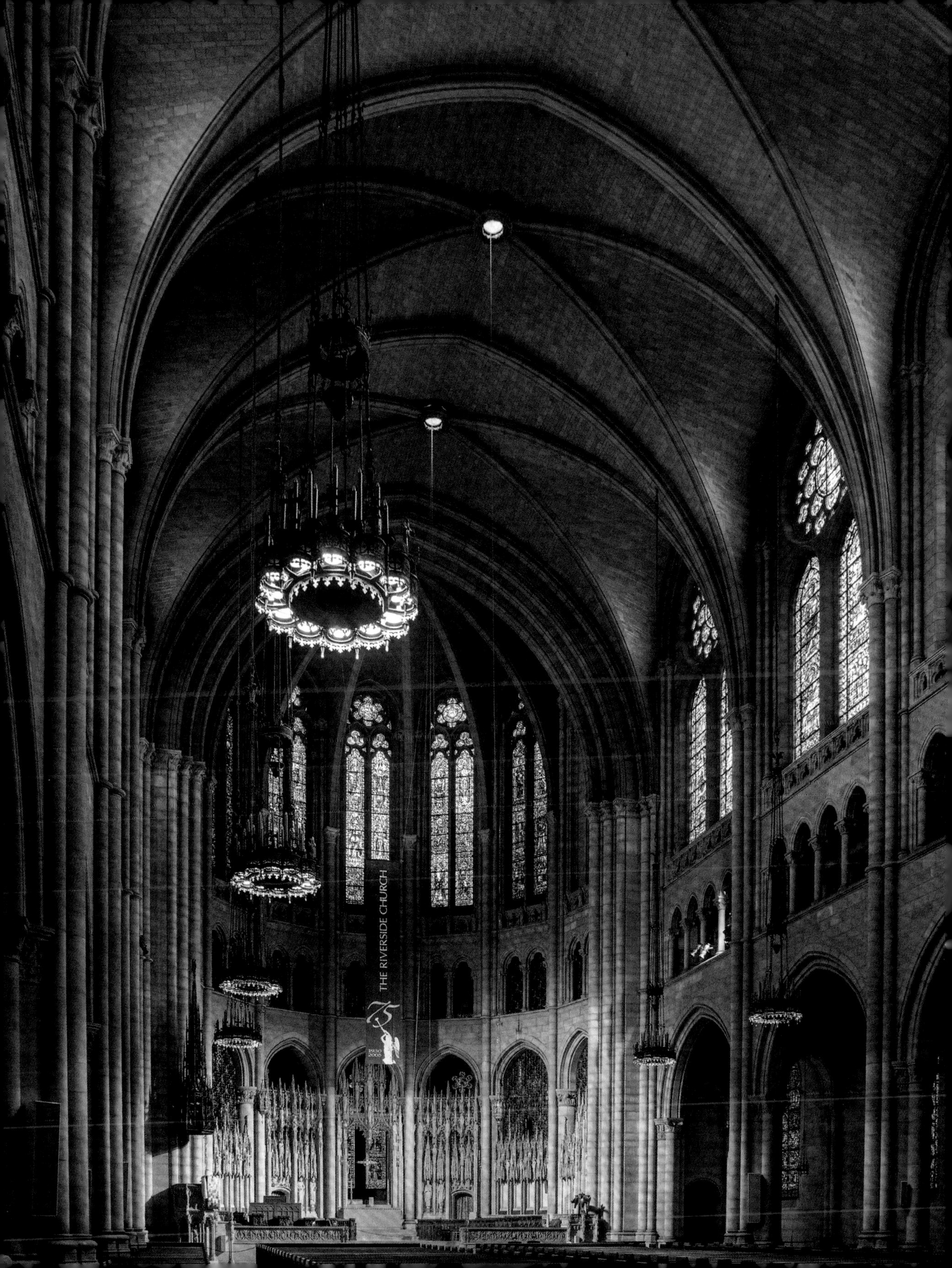

THE RIVERSIDE CHURCH
75
1930
2005

SOFT & FLAT

I f there's any distinct trend that's contemporary in processing – at least on social media – then it's surely towards increasing contrast and saturation. In the way we see and judge images, the two are closely related, because when you increase contrast, colours seem more intense to most people.

Presets, apps and processing courses always advertise in this way, simply assuming that improvement calls for more punch, more visual impact. Largely it's true – an average taste in imagery tends towards impact rather than subtlety, all the more so if the person behind the camera (which is usually a phone) is offered the choice. This is reinforced in a natural way by social media platforms because most pictures are presented first as thumbnails that are viewed on phone screens, and tiny images work in a different way to their larger counterparts. Put simply, pictures with strong contrast, distinct colour and quite simple graphics stand out better.

All of this works against quiet images on social media, but out of that competitive context, it's also an opportunity, perhaps counterintuitively, to be quietly distinct. The choice of framing and viewpoint apart, the prerequisites for a softer, flatter approach to exposure and rendering lie in lighting and atmosphere. As the examples

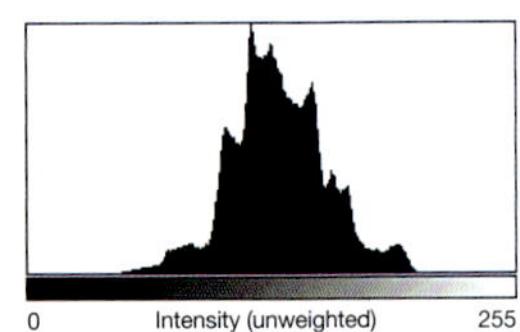

Mist in the hills of northern Thailand, in a village of the Akha ethnic minority.

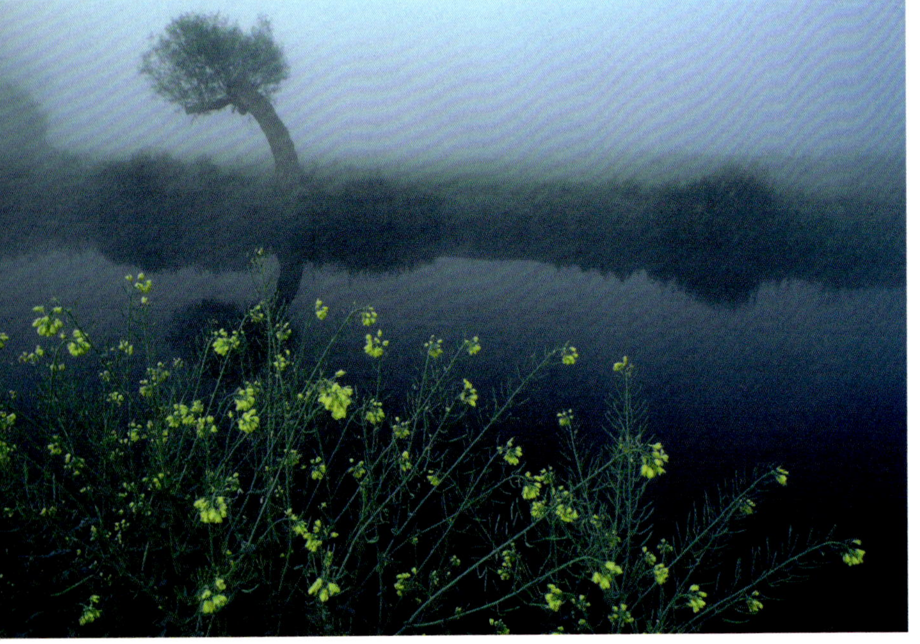

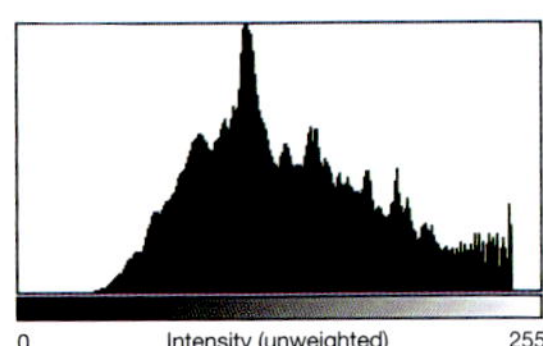

The yellow flowers of wild turnip and a pollarded willow in early morning mist on the banks of the River Stour. The river runs through Dedham Vale, on the borders of Essex and Suffolk.

here show, mist and haze are both perfect and typical. If you look at the histograms
that accompany each image, there is plenty of headroom at the left and right. These
are low dynamic range images, and like all flat imagery, they offer scope for varying
both brightness and contrast. In both exposure and processing, it's important to
decide whether the overall effect should be bright, dark or somewhere in between,
and that's entirely a personal choice. I'd suggest not increasing contrast during
processing, but that's just my view and assumes the goal is to be soft.

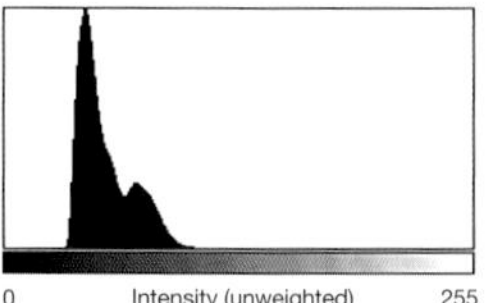

An old sycamore in London's
Hyde Park, shot in two
different ways from almost
the same viewpoint. The
smaller version (opposite)
is conventional, while the
larger (below) allows flare
from the sun to degrade
detail and contribute to a
more atmospheric rendering.

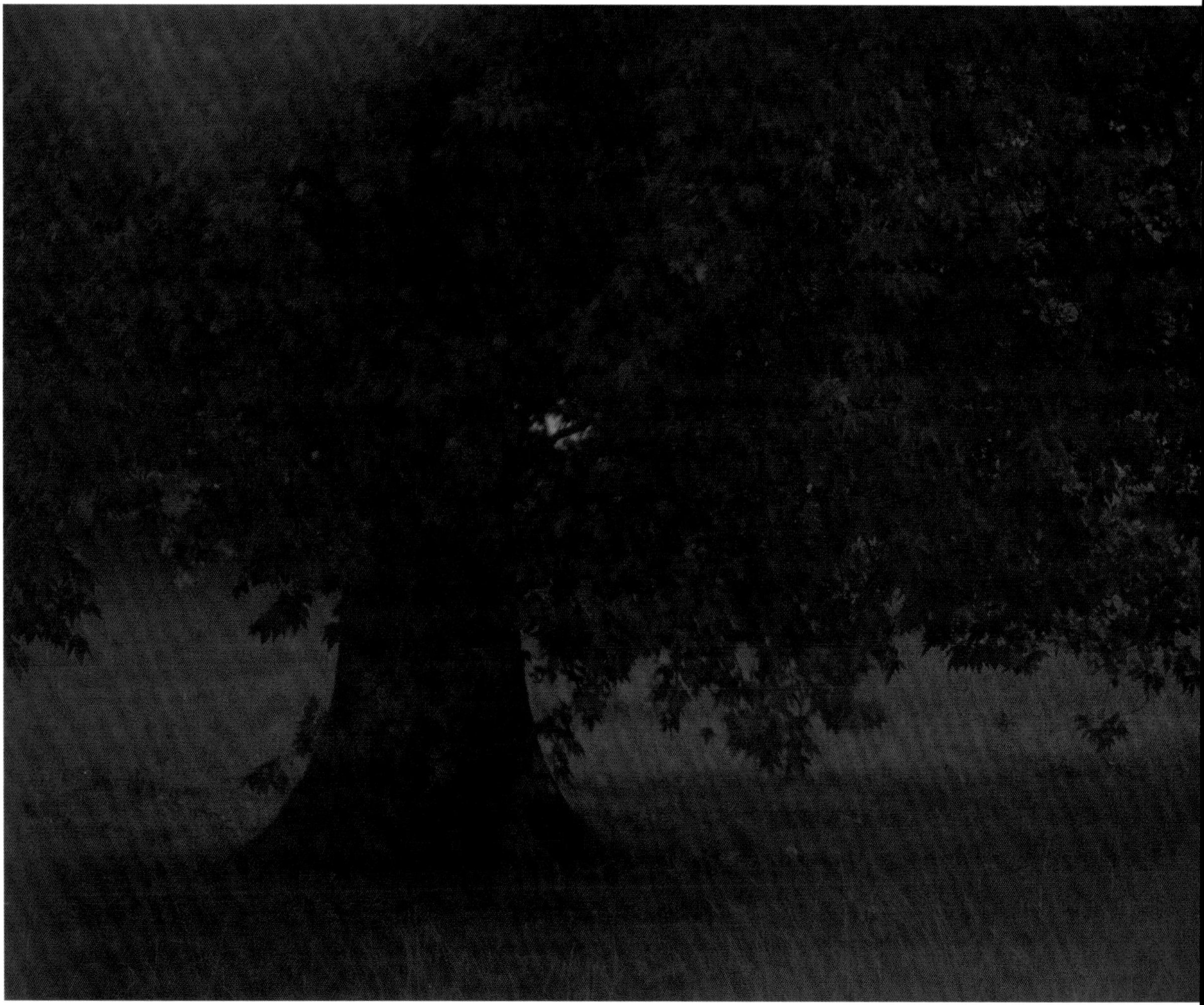

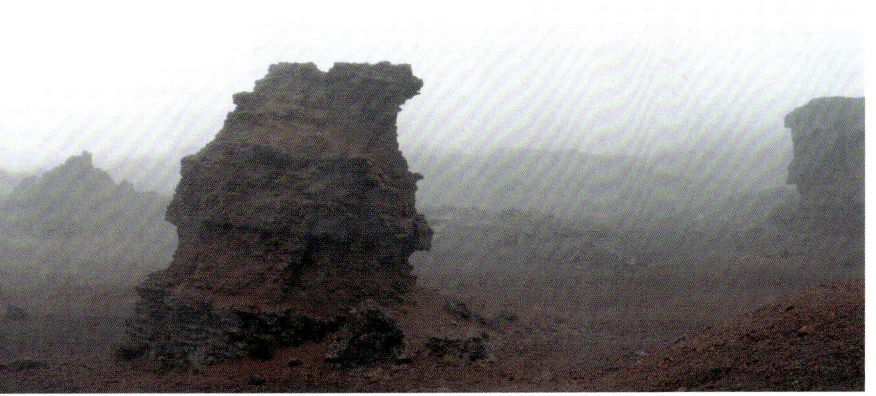

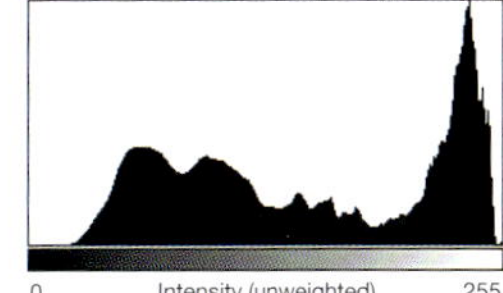

Low cloud shrouds La Plaine des Sables, a volcanic plateau that is part of the Piton de la Fournaise massif, Réunion.

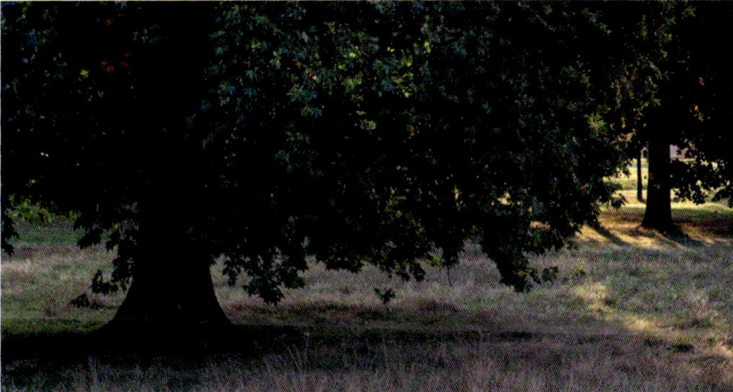

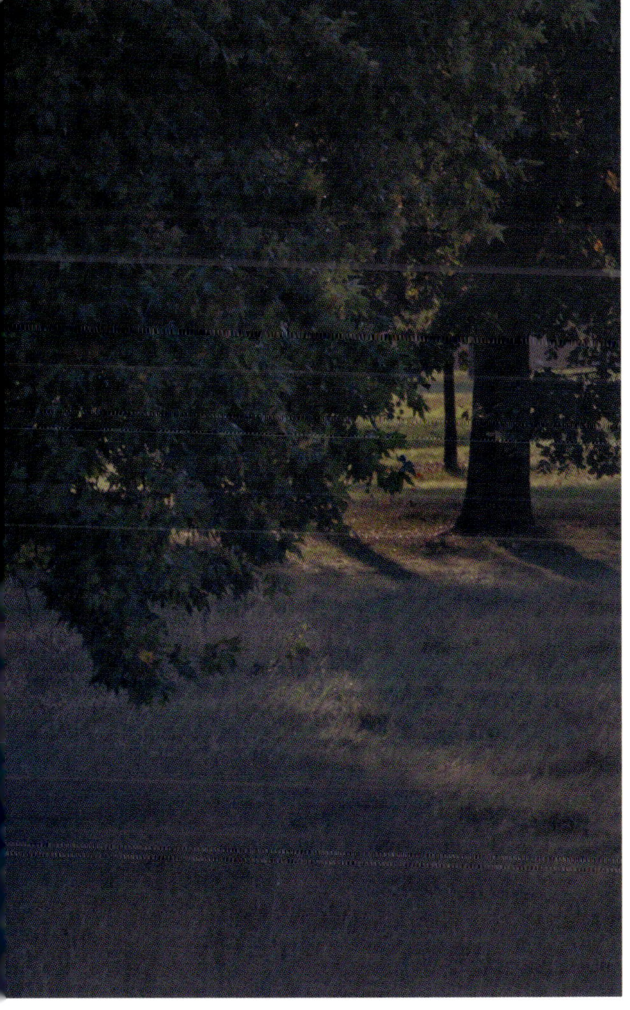

LOCAL NUANCE

W hile strong and distinctive exposure styles tend to get the most attention, nuance and attention to detail are the hallmark of professionalism. At the risk of being repetitive, processing is an integral part of creative exposure, and supporting the original idea of the photograph is usually the main part of the job. Most of the detailed work is local adjustment, and the point is very much *not* to draw attention to itself. These final pages are about just such a workmanlike approach; nothing flashy, just thinking clearly about what needs to stand out, what needs to fall back and how to balance the tones across the picture.

A Bhil schoolgirl drinking water during a morning break. This is the final version of the image and in addition to the key processing steps outlined in the text, the exposure has been lowered overall, the contrast slightly increased and the saturation of the girl's face, scarf and pullover increased slightly.

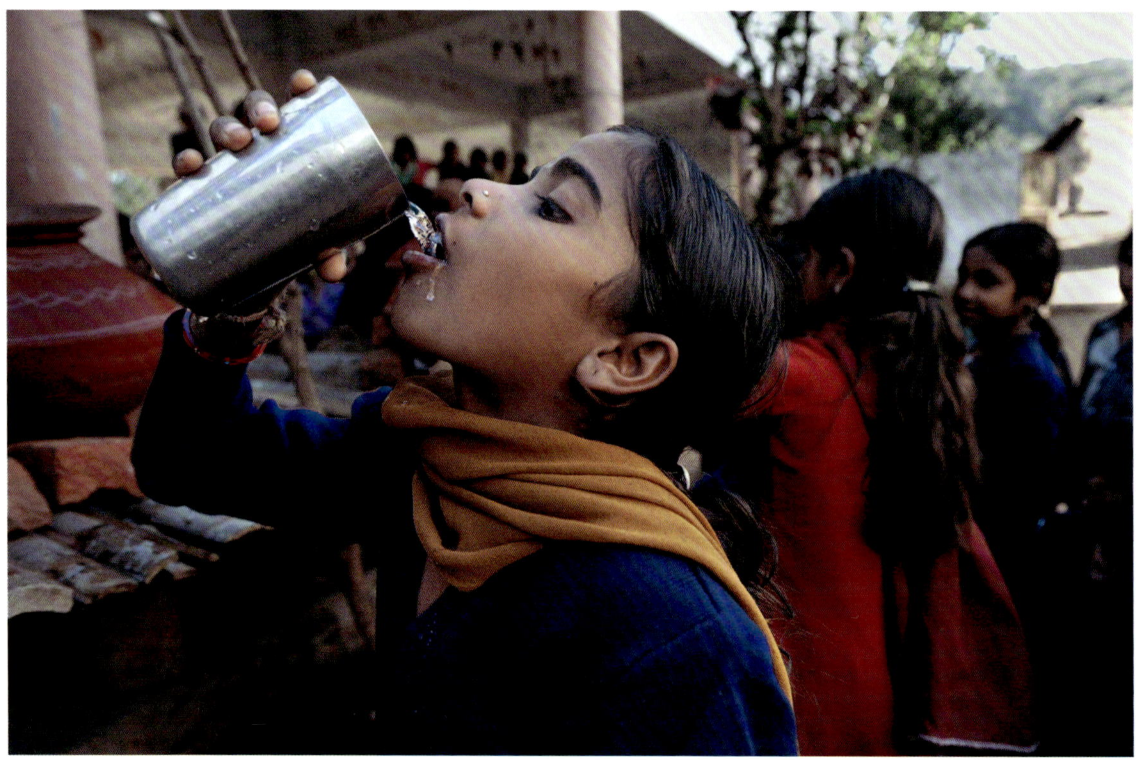

This shot was taken at a charitable school for children of an ethnic minority in the Indian state of Gujarat, at a break between lessons. It was late in the morning and the sun was high, so even partly in shade there's a lot more lighting contrast across the scene than I'd have preferred. While shooting, I already had in mind the processing that would be needed to knock back the sunlit areas in the background and focus attention on the girl.

There was an interesting cultural action in play. The drinking water is stored in earthen jars to keep cool, but the metal cup is shared by everyone. Nobody touches the cup with their lips, and the only way to ensure this is to hold it a little higher and pour the water into the mouth. This might sound like labouring an obvious point – and the subject is of course, a young girl drinking – but it sets the goal for processing. The focus of attention is not just the girl's face tilted back and her expression, but ultimately the glittering stream of clear water.

There are three steps involved. The first is to reduce the brightness and contrast of the sunlit background at the upper right. The second is to make the face more prominent by selecting the head of the girl and her arm holding the cup, inverting the selection and darkening the background. Finally, the short stream of water needs to sparkle, as it is the ultimate focus of attention in the picture. To do this, I select it with a feathered brush and make small adjustments to Contrast and Clarity.

The original unprocessed image file and the key areas for adjustment. The girl needs to be masked and inverted to darken the upper background (orange), then the upper-right background darkened and flattened even more (red), while her pullover needs to be brightened (aqua). On top of that, the stream of water and surrounds have to be lifted and a little increase in saturation.

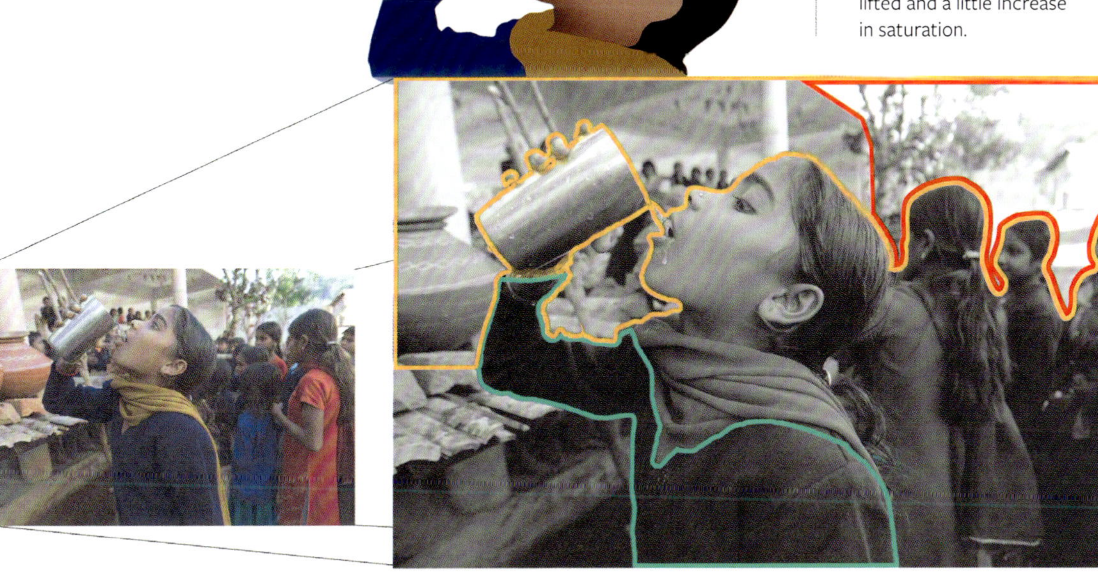

With the scene shown here, I was on assignment for a book that would eventually be published as *The Life of Tea*. The image shows the sorting of the new season's tea leaves near Suzhou, China, but it had a special problem right from the start – the colour. Everything else was good: the light from the open door, the intense concentration, and I had time to move about and to wait. This lady was the most absorbed of anyone in her work, and this was exactly the right moment to take a shot, as she was carefully picking up the classic 'bud and two leaves'. But the colours! The pink pullover, while not exactly the complementary of the green leaves, was right across the colour wheel and the two made an inconveniently striking pair that simply took all the attention away from what was actually happening.

The picture really needed to be in black and white, and if you think it might have been a pity not to see the green of the leaves in a book about tea, consider that in a 300-page book, you can easily have too much green. We used to make a joke about the Chinese expression for wok-firing the leaves, which they call 'killing green', and that became one of the tasks for the book: to 'kill the green' that kept popping up in front of the camera constantly. This was just such an occasion.

The ultimate focus of attention is, or should be, the tiny bud in her fingers, and careful processing can do much to help this, even after the main culprits for distracting – the pink and green – have been quashed. A simple radial brightening centred on the leaf with accompanying darkening of the surrounds would be, well, too simple. Certainly, the foreground and background, which together surround about three-quarters of the frame edges, can be relieved of detail and darkened, but there are other more interesting things going on in the picture, particularly in her face, including the thick lenses of her spectacles, which at this angle to the light are refracting beautifully.

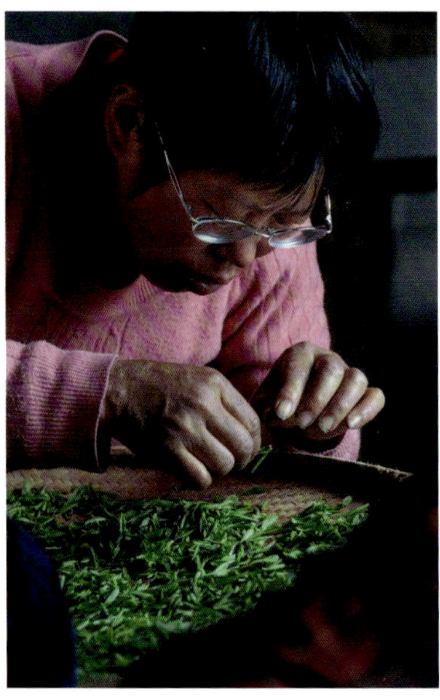

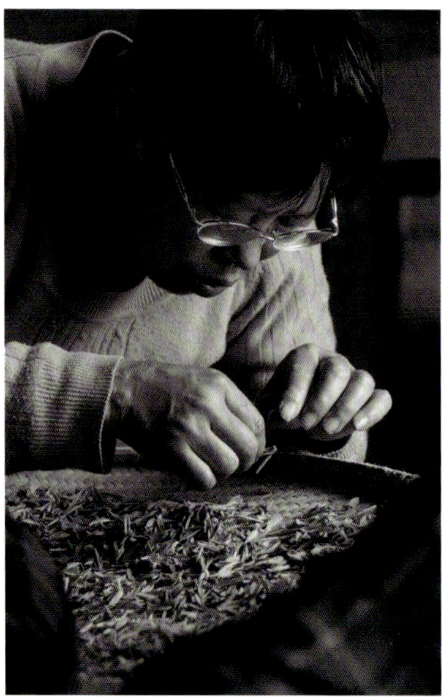

At the far left is the processed colour image, which serves as the starting point for the black-and-white conversion. To the left, a 'straight' (that is, default) black-and-white conversion from the colour image, created using ACR.

Below is the annotated processing plan that explains the many decisions I made. Of course, this is just one person's way of doing it – mine – and there are always many interpretations possible. However, reassessing a colour image for processing in black and white calls for some thought in how the natural attention is redistributed. An example of this is the fingers. Regardless of skin tone, the highlights on fingers in almost any picture where hands are prominent appear brighter in black and white than they do in colour. The skin colour here is certainly more muted than the pink and green, but in black and white the highlights on each finger jumped out too strongly, and needed local adjustment to push them back so they didn't compete with the tiny leaf.

The finished image aims to focus attention on the tiny leaf in the picker's hands. The steps that were needed to achieve this are shown in the schematic on the left.

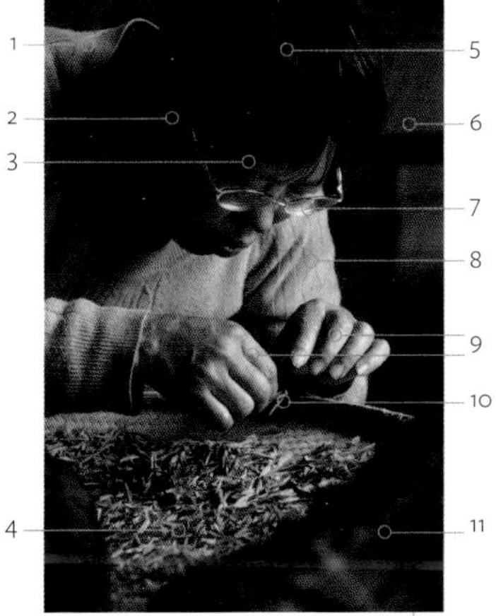

1. Darken neck of pullover

2. Brighten side of face

3. Lighten forehead to contrast with hair

4. Darken leaves radially outward from centre

5. Increase contrast to show hair highlights

6. Darken background

7. Increase contrast within spectacles

8. Darken the pullover

9. Lower highlights on fingers

10. Increase contrast and brighten single leaf

11. Deepen foreground to featureless black

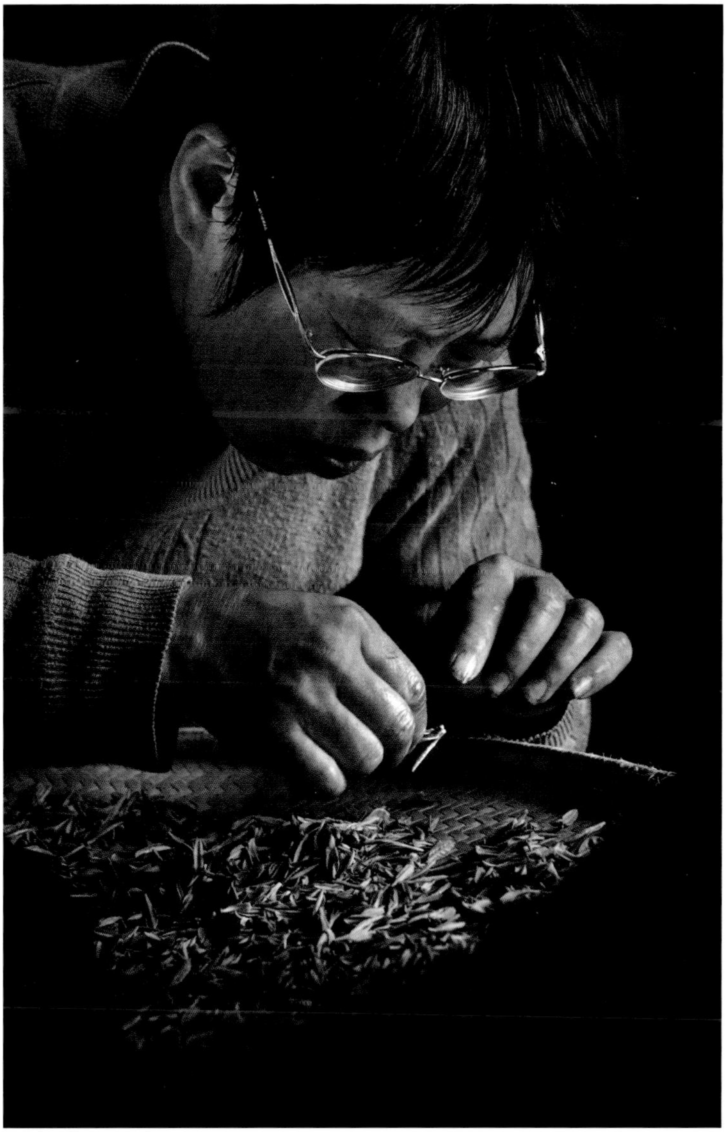

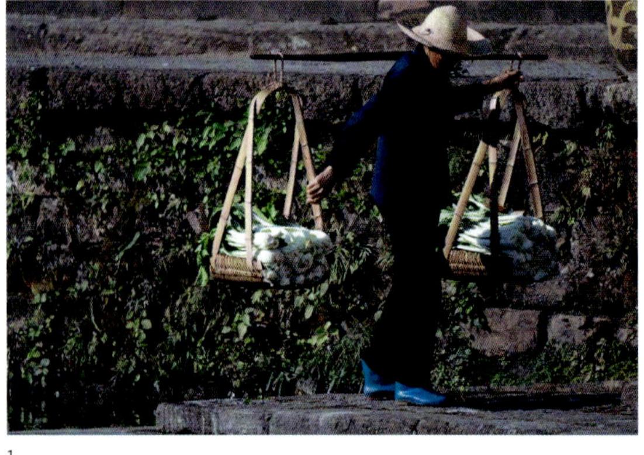

1.

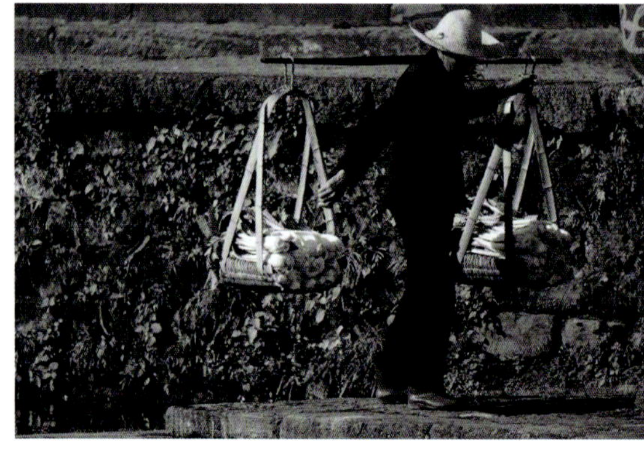

2.

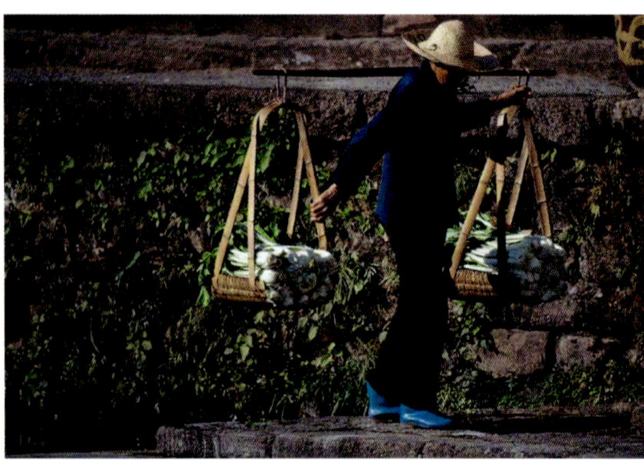

3.

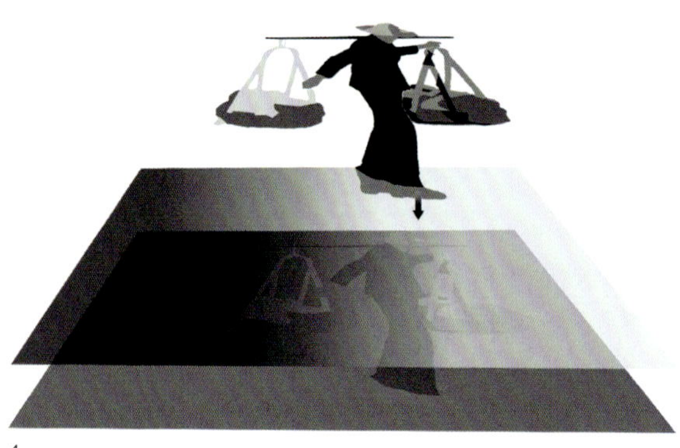

4.

This is another example where the role of the processing is to clarify the scene. The subject, framing and moment are all straightforward and documentary; in other words, content rules in this picture, not graphics.

First is the matter of colour or black and white, and the main driving force these days is personal preference. I personally have no formula, but if the colours (or the colourfulness) are neither striking nor contribute to the image, I tend towards black and white for its cleaner focus on tonality, shape and lines. In this case, though, it came down to nothing deeper than the blue boots, which were just too distracting for me. To show what I mean, I made a basic optimized version from the original Raw file – there's nothing obviously wrong with it, but the colours definitely distract.

It's a simple image, but there are problems in making the figure of the man, who's carrying an old-style pannier with the vegetables he's just been washing in the pond, stand out against the stone wall. He's dark, but the vegetables in the two baskets are bright, and they're all against a single wall that ought to provide contrast, but of course can't contrast adequately for bright and dark at the same time. The late afternoon sun is just grazing the stonework, which gives it a good texture, but the ideal would have been for the left side to have just fallen into shadow.

1. The unprocessed colour original

2. The unprocessed original in black-and-white

3. Optimized colour version

4. The basic shading gradient on the wall; darker at left

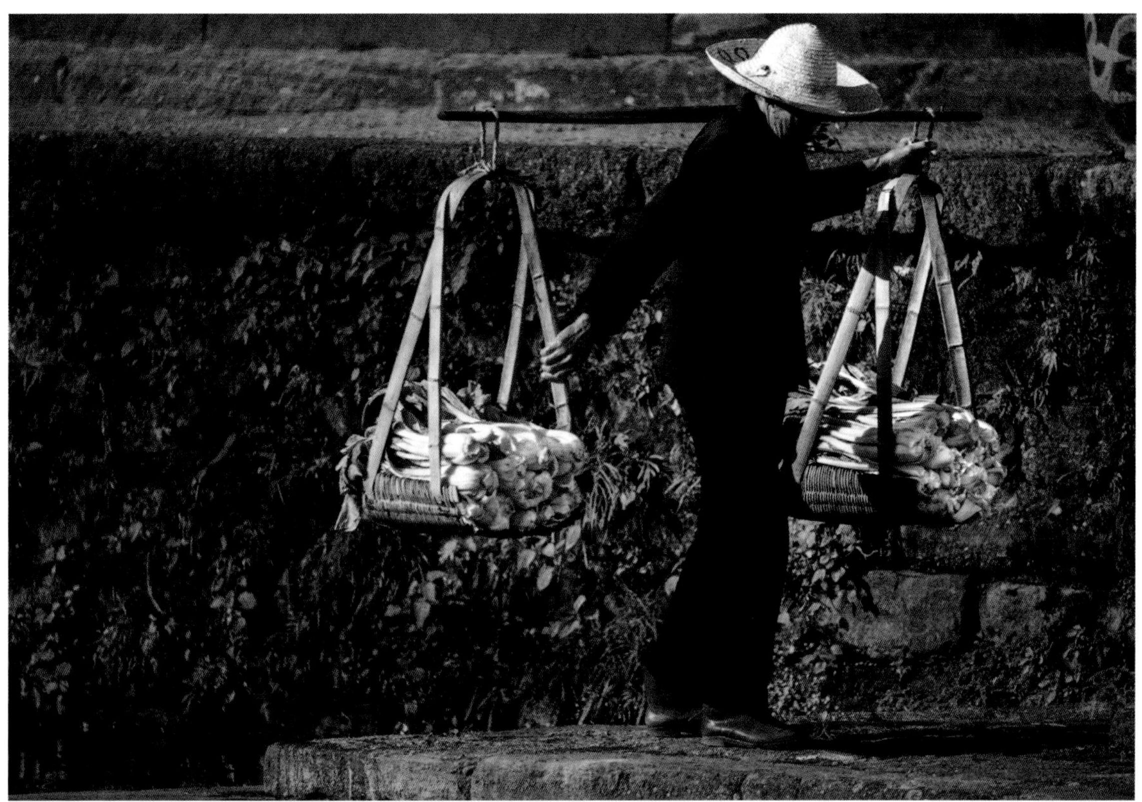

The final image has a carefully shaded wall that is designed to help both the bright panniers and the dark clothes of the man stand out.

However, we can simulate that in the processing, from left to right, stopping just short of the man. Content-aware masking helps, as it means we can select the man and his panniers, reverse the mask, then softly fade out the right half of the background and darken. As this is black and white, we can then select the man's clothing and take it down to black to increase his contrast with the wall. Finally, the right-hand pannier isn't quite as brightly lit as the left, so we can take that up to almost white. There's a little more detailed work to do to make the entire figure stand out, including using the channels to darken the green on the wall, lighten it on the vegetables and darken the stone at the very top and bottom.

This may sound like a lot of work for an undramatic result, but this degree of effort and attention to detail is standard in the professional world. There is also always a plan because – as I've probably said too many times by now – processing should be treated as a part of the entire lighting and exposure process.

INDEX

PICTURE CREDITS

60, 61, 64 Ernst Haas/Getty Images

63 Courtesy of and copyright The Gordon Parks Foundation

65 © Harry Gruyaert/Magnum Photos

71 Ernst Haas/Getty Images; 117 Gainew Gallery/Alamy Stock Photo; 118 Artokolor/
Penta Springs Ltd/Alamy Stock Photo

138 © Erich Hartmann/Magnum Photos